D1617259

media, news and reality programming, investigative and image work results in an insightful, timely and comprehensive study that genuinely succeeds in moving knowledge forwards. An impressive feat of scholarly work, and an important contribution to the literature.'

Chris Greer, Professor of Sociology,
City University London, UK.

POLICING AND MEDIA

This book examines the relationship between police, media and the public and analyses the shifting techniques and technologies through which they communicate. In a critical discussion of contemporary and emerging modes of mediatized police work, Lee and McGovern demonstrate how the police engage with the public through a fluid and quickly expanding assemblage of communications and information technologies.

Policing and Media explores the rationalities that are driving police–media relations and ask how these relationships differ (or not) from the ways they have operated historically; what new technologies are influencing and being deployed by policing organizations and police public relations professionals and why; how operational policing is shaping and being shaped by new technologies of communication; and what forms of resistance are evident in the manufacture of preferred images of police? The authors suggest that new forms of simulated and hyperreal policing using platforms such as social media and reality television are increasingly positioning police organizations as media organizations, and in some cases enabling police to bypass the traditional media altogether. The book is informed by empirical research spanning ten years in this field and includes chapters on journalism and the police, policing and social media, policing and reality television and policing resistances.

It will be of interest to those researching and teaching in the fields of Criminology, Policing and Media as well as police and media professionals.

Murray Lee is an Associate Professor in Criminology at the University of Sydney Faculty of Law. He is the author of *Inventing Fear of Crime* and co-author of *Fear of Crime: Critical Voices in an Age of Anxiety*, both published by Routledge.

Alyce McGovern is a Senior Lecturer in Criminology at the University of New South Wales.

New directions in critical criminology
Edited by Walter S. DeKeseredy,
University of Ontario Institute of Technology

This series presents new cutting-edge critical criminological empirical, theoretical, and policy work on a broad range of social problems, including drug policy, rural crime and social control, policing and the media, ecoside, intersectionality, and the gendered nature of crime. It aims to highlight the most up-to-date authoritative essays written by new and established scholars in the field. Rather than offering a survey of the literature, each book takes a strong position on topics of major concern to those interested in seeking new ways of thinking critically about crime.

POLICING AND MEDIA

Public relations, simulations and communications

Murray Lee and Alyce McGovern

Routledge
Taylor & Francis Group

LONDON AND NEW YORK

First published 2014
by Routledge
2 Park Square, Milton Park, Abingdon, Oxon, OX14 4RN

and by Routledge
711 Third Avenue, New York, NY 10017

Routledge is an imprint of the Taylor & Francis Group, an informa business

© 2014 Murray Lee and Alyce McGovern

British Library Cataloguing in Publication Data
A catalogue record for this book is available from the British Library

Library of Congress Cataloging-in-Publication Data
A catalog record has been requested for this book

ISBN: 978-0-415-63212-6 (hbk)
ISBN: 978-0-415-63213-3 (pbk)
ISBN: 978-0-203-09599-7 (ebk)

Typeset in Bembo and ITC Stone Sans
by Deer Park Productions

Printed and bound in the United States of America by Publishers Graphics,
LLC on sustainably sourced paper.

CONTENTS

SECTION I
Police and media: setting the scene

SECTION III
Policing the police

ACKNOWLEDGEMENTS

First and foremost we would like to thank the participants in our project: the various state police organizations and their corporate communications and media departments who were kind enough to share their valuable time and thoughts with us. In particular, we would like to thank the ongoing support of the NSW Police Force in being open enough to engage in critical research such as this.

We would also like to thank the University of Sydney Faculty of Law, the University of NSW School of Social Sciences, the University of Western Sydney and Charles Sturt University for valuable research support for the projects that make up this book.

To Dr Kelly Richards, Garner Clancey, Carolyn McKay and Simone Eisenhauer, all of whom were employed as research assistants on the projects discussed in the book: thank you for all the valuable insights and intellectual contributions to the final work. The book would not exist without them.

We would also like to send a special thanks to the students in SLSP3002 Social Policy Research Project at the University of NSW in 2011, who provided significant assistance and input into the carrying out of the police observational documentary study. Without their involvement the research data would not be as rich as it is. Thank you to Hadeel Al-Alosi, Tracey Barnett, Lucy Burke, Hitoishi Chakma, Susanne Ech, Francesca Ferguson-Cross, Tannory Islam, Wener Li, Xicong (Sunny) Ma, Conor McKeown, Kathleen Morris, Yves-Christopher Pincemin, Kemal Salic, Ananya Srivastava, Zhi

Tian and Ammar Topolovic. Thanks also go to University of Sydney Masters research student Rodger Watson, whose analysis of data helped inform elements of the observational documentary study.

Appreciation also goes to the many colleagues who have helped shape this book. Dr Rob Mawby has been most generous with the collegial support and feedback on our ideas over a long period of time. His work and ideas have been very influential in the shaping of this book. Associate Professor Russell Hogg also provided valuable feedback on chapters of the book. And to Elaine Fishwick and Dr Bree Carlton, thank you for your valuable intellectual input.

Murray would like to thank Wendy, Manon and Tate Lee, Beth and Brian Lee, all of whom endured and supported the writing of this book. Special thanks also go to his colleagues at the University of Sydney for their sage advice, particularly Associate Professor Thomas Crofts and Associate Professor Gail Mason.

Alyce would like to dedicate this book to the memory of her father, Robert McGovern. She would also like to thank Roslyn, Christopher, Kimberley, Raquel and Skylar McGovern for their support. Special thanks also go to her colleagues at the University of NSW, particularly Dr Sanja Milivojevic and Professor Marc Williams, for their advice and guidance during the process.

Some of the themes in this book have been drawn from the following publications and are reproduced with permission:

Lee, M. and McGovern, A. (2013) 'Procedural justice and simulated policing: the medium and the message', *Journal of Policing, Intelligence and Counter Terrorism, Special Issue: Organisational and Procedural Justice: Applying Theory to Police Practice,* vol. 8, iss. 2, pp. 166–183.

Lee, M. and McGovern, A. (2012) 'Image Work(s): "Simulated Policing" and the New Police (Popularity) Culture', in K. Carrington, M. Ball, E. O'Brien and J. Tauri (eds), *Crime, Justice and Social Democracy: International Perspectives*, edn. 1st, Palgrave Macmillan, Hampshire, UK, pp. 120–132.

McGovern, A. and Lee, M. (2012) 'Police Communications in the Social Media Age', in P. Keyzer, J. Johnston and M. Pearson (eds), *The Courts and the Media: Challenges in The Era of Digital and Social Media*, edn. 1st, Halstead Press, Ultimo, pp. 162–176.

Lee, M. and McGovern, A. (2012) 'Force to Sell: Policing the Image and Manufacturing Public Confidence', *Policing and Society: An International Journal of Research and Policy*, vol. 22, pp. 1–22.

ABBREVIATIONS

ABC	Australian Broadcasting Corporation
CAD	computer-aided dispatch
DPA	Director of Public Affairs
FLEPIOA	Florida Law Enforcement Public Information Officer Association
KPI	key performance indicator
LAC	local area command
LSA	local service area
MDT	mobile digital terminal
NSW	New South Wales
PEATS	Police External Agencies Transfer System
PIO	public information officer
PMO	police media officer
PMU	police media unit
QPS	Queensland Police Service
SA	South Australia
SAPOL	South Australian Police
SMILE	Social Media, the Internet and Law Enforcement Conference
SOP	standard operating procedures
TC	tropical cyclone
WA	Western Australia

INTRODUCTION

When Kym Charlton, Director of Police Media for the Queensland Police Service (QPS), a police organization with jurisdiction over one of Australia's largest states, recently left her position she published her farewells to the police and public on social media. It was a fitting farewell given the changes she had overseen in her role:

> Tomorrow, I leave Queensland Police Media and Public Affairs after five wonderful years […].
>
> It was with considerable trepidation that I pressed 'publish' on the QPS Facebook Page in 2010 – I had heard all the horror stories about social media – but I had faith that the service needed to be in social media, so we could talk directly with you. Thanks to your support, the page has gone from strength to strength, and remains a safe place to get and share public safety information. We presently have nearly 363,500 'likes' and last week we reached 1.15 million people on here.
>
> Robert Peel, when he spoke of the Principles of Policing in 1829, could have had little idea how the principle of 'the police are the public, and the public are the police' would be brought to life through social media. Thank you for embracing

our efforts in social media, and making our social media channels world leaders in law enforcement and emergency services.

On here, you've helped us solve crime, find missing people,
and keep each other safe. We've laughed and cried, and
proven that social media is a place where great good can
happen. We even saved a cow or two […]. I hope we have
given you the chance to get to know the service, and our
officers, in a way you may not have previously, and gain a
little insight into the challenges our officers face every day […]
Kym. *(QPS Facebook 2013)*

The text of Charlton's message is instructive on a number of levels.
Firstly, one of her key achievements during her five years in the
position was obviously the move of QPS into the realm of social
media, a move admittedly achieved despite some 'trepidation'. One
can almost feel the anxiety as she, having presumably sold the idea of
using social media to a police service historically known for its conservative disposition, presses 'publish' and a new era of police public
relationship for that service is born.

Secondly, she clearly articulates the capacity of this platform to
speak directly to the public. The public, she suggested, got to 'know
the service' in a 'way you may not have'. This new power, to speak
directly to the public, brought to life the early principles of Peel's
police. Peelian or not, as we will illustrate in this book, social media
has significantly reshaped police/public communications.

Thirdly, the platform has operated as more than just an opportunity for the police to disseminate information. Rather, Charlton
reflects that the public have 'helped us solve crime' and 'share public
safety information'. In this sense, social media is constructed as not
just empowering the police, but the public too.

Finally, Charlton's statement demonstrates the pace of change in
police/public relations. In five years we have moved from pressing
'publish' for the first time on a Facebook posting, to reaching
'363,500 likes' for the page and '1.15 million people on here'. In five
years the shape of police/public relations has changed irrevocably.

Charlton's post on the QPS Facebook site seems like the obvious introduction to our book. Her farewell sums up much of what

this book is about: the rapid changes to the ways in which police organizations are engaging with the media and ultimately with the public. While the book is not exclusively about social media, but rather the plethora of ways in which media and public relations are becoming increasingly central to operational policing, social media is a significant element of these developments.

Despite the importance of police, media and public relationships, this field remains little studied by academics in general and criminologists more specifically. In the past 15 years only a few key publications have addressed this field. These include Rob Mawby's *Policing Images: Policing Communication and Legitimacy* (2002a), Leishman and Mason's *Policing and the Media: Facts, Fictions and Factions* (2003), and less specifically the bodies of work from Robert Reiner (e.g. 2010) and Peter K. Manning (e.g. 2003). What many of these publications have overlooked though – more due to timing than any explicit omissions of the authors – is the emergence of new technologies and social media into the police/public relations realm. This book addresses the knowledge gap.

Addressing this knowledge gap has also taken on increased urgency in light of the recent media scandals in the United Kingdom and the subsequent Leveson Inquiry (2012) into the *Culture, Practice and Ethics of the Press*, which investigated, among other things, relationships between journalists and the police. As that Inquiry made clear, journalists and the police have important but separate roles in a liberal democracy, roles that require ongoing scrutiny:

> In our mature democracy, policing must be with the consent of the public not least because it has to involve the public in the reporting and detection of crime. The public must be kept aware of policing concerns and must engage in the debate. Therefore the press also has a vital role: it must encourage the public to engage in the criminal justice system by coming forward with evidence; it must facilitate that assistance and it must applaud when criminals are brought to justice as a result. The press must also hold the police to account, acting as the eyes and ears of the public. It is not, therefore, surprising that these different roles and responsibilities that the police and the press

have are capable of pulling in opposite directions: there needs to be a constructive tension and absolutely not a self-serving cosiness.

(Leveson 2012: 20)

Beyond these issues of scandal and police media symbiosis, we suggest contemporary police media and public relations is an important field of study for a number of other pressing reasons. Policing has always been about image and communications; however, in the late twentieth and early twenty-first centuries image, communication and information have become central to the production and reproduction of our cultures. If social relations are indeed a result of the forms of communication a society uses, as Marshall McLuhan (1964) suggests, the ways in which policing organizations communicate with the public will likely have very real effects on the way in which the public conceives of crime, justice, law enforcement and even itself in relation to these. Baudrillard (1994) has famously suggested we live at the end of history in a hyperreality where we only have simulations or simulacra of reality, where all is composed of references but with no referents. In an era where reality television feeds us our most immediate images of policing, where policing is recorded in real time by operational police and by public onlookers seduced by the action of policing, and where these images are immediately loaded onto social media sites such as YouTube, Baudrillard's ideas appear prophetic. Ironically, at a time when, following the ideas of Wilson and Kelling (1982), policing was to return to the beat, perhaps it is more accurate to suggest it has hit the highway – the information superhighway, that is. One of the key arguments we advance in this book is that we have seen the emergence of what we call simulated policing (O'Malley 2010), and it is from this hyperreality, this new realm where policing is becoming pure representation, that such a capacity has emerged.

But this book offers much more than a theoretical exploration. It is also the culmination of over a decade's worth of empirical research into the ways in which police, media and public relationships operate. Indeed, a number of separate research projects make up the empirical data on which our discussions, arguments and conclusions rest. These projects have included interviews with journalists, interviews with police media officers, interviews with directors of police-public affairs departments, interviews with Assistant Commissioners, documentary analysis of police historical data, surveys of public viewing habits of law enforcement reality television programmes and content analyses of law enforcement reality television programmes. On top of this, the research has entailed hundreds of hours of monitoring social media and traditional media. While we do not pretend to know all there is to know about this complex and dynamic relationship, we do believe this research allows us to offer important insights into this field.

The book is organized in three separate sections. Section I outlines the context and conceptual framework of the book and contains three chapters. Chapter 1 traces the development of professionalized police media departments in modern police organizations, and the scope and form these departments take. Chapter 2 outlines the key logics that we see as driving contemporary police engagement with the media. We make a case for the interrelated logics of image work, risk and responsibilization, and trust and legitimacy as being key logics of this engagement. Chapter 3 outlines the four key conceptual frames that inform our analysis: simulated policing (O'Malley 2010), cultures of control (Garland 2001), the viewer society (Mathiesen 1997) and tactics of resistance (de Certeau 1984).

In Section II we explore three separate domains of police media relations as examples of what we term simulated policing. Chapter 4 explores the ways in which police media releases are reproduced by news organizations and, in recent times, how police organizations are increasingly producing their own news – both textually and visually. We suggest that there has been a significant restructuring in the way crime and justice news is delivered. Chapter 5 discusses the emergence of social media and the ways in which this has been embraced by policing organizations, providing a communications avenue that allows police to bypass the traditional media altogether. This, we suggest, is increasingly rendering policing organizations news organizations in and of themselves. Chapter 6 explores the increasing police engagement with reality television and the implications of this to both policing cultures and the way the public consume information about crime. We suggest that this medium has opened up a range of new opportunities for police organizations to deliver preferred images to a public hungry for images of crime and justice.

In Section III we explore a variety of resistances to the dissemination of preferred police messages and how such resistances can take hold in the face of the ability of police organizations to structure crime news and information. Chapter 7 discusses the role of new technologies and social media in subverting attempts by police organizations to control information and its flow. It looks at tactics deployed by a range of groups and actors who aim to uncover and publicize police corruption, malpractice, excessive use of force and the like. Chapter 8 explores resistances in the realm of the more traditional media. Specifically, it looks at the ways in which journalists, and even the police themselves, circumvent police official protocols and practices in the search for a good story or for personal or political ends. It discusses the use of unofficial police contacts and leaks in the production of news stories and in investigative journalism more generally.

In the end, this book should be seen as a snapshot – a snapshot of a fluid and rapidly changing field of police, media and public relationships in the early part of the twenty-first century. As criminologists we ignore this field at our own peril, for in contemporary times it is through these relationships that the public receive the vast majority of their information about crime and justice. We suggest in this book that images of policing have become *policing*. The two are increasingly indistinguishable. Policing in the twenty-first century is nothing if not hyperreal.

SECTION I

Police and media: setting the scene

Section I of this book sets the scene contextually, historically and theoretically. Here we situate contemporary police media and public relationships, outline the logics that we believe drive police engagement with the media, and detail the theoretical frames we use in this book.

Chapter 1 explores the context of the relationship between police and the media. First we discuss the place of crime in the media, and the role of the police and the media in shaping, framing and influencing public understandings of law and order issues. Secondly, we look at the current academic literature on police media public relations. Thirdly, we explore the development of professionalized public relations and media departments in police organizations, focusing particularly on this development in the UK and the USA, but also introducing an Australian case study that contextualizes these international developments. Finally, this chapter explores who these police public relations people are by drawing on research undertaken in Australia, as well as examples from the international literature. In short, the chapter sets the scene for the remainder of the book by exploring the both the role of institutions and the backgrounds of individuals involved in the production and construction of news about policing and news about crime more generally.

Chapter 2 explores the logics that drive contemporary police engagement with the media. By logics we refer to the rationalities that underlie modes of media and public engagement. The chapter draws on empirical research from Australia and related literature and research from the UK and the USA in particular to illustrate these logics.

Chapter 3 details the theoretical frameworks we use to conceptualize contemporary police, media and public relationships. We argue that public relations and image work are now no longer bounded by the limits of the traditional mass media. Rather, contemporary information technologies and the emergence of social media have created a new landscape in which policing takes place, and opened up a range of possibilities for both 'image work' and operational policing. We explore this by proposing a framework that uses the concept of simulated policing in the context of the viewer society and increasing cultures of control. We conclude the chapter by exploring the converse of these new opportunities and cultures of control.

1

LOCATING POLICE MEDIA PUBLIC RELATIONS

Introduction

Since the advent of modern police services relationships between the police and the media have been complicated. Like lovers too blinded by their passion, each needs and is made stronger by the presence of the other. Yet there are the fights. Silent treatment. Cheating. The spreading of innuendo. They can't live together, yet they are compelled to speak daily. Yes, their tangled history is as complex as is their present.

This chapter explores the context of the relationship between the police and the media. First we discuss the place of crime in the media, and the role of the police and media in shaping, framing and influencing public understandings of law and order issues. Secondly, we look at the current academic literature on police media public relations. Thirdly, we explore the historical development of professionalized public relations and media departments in police organizations, focusing particularly on the UK and USA and a case study of more recent Australian developments. Finally, drawing on our own research as well as the international literature, this chapter explores who these police public relations people are. In short, the chapter sets the scene for the remainder of the book by exploring both the role of institutions and the backgrounds of individuals involved in the dissemination of news about policing and information about crime more generally.

Crime in the media

Media outlets allocate significant column space and airtime to stories about crime and criminality. Indeed, Stan Cohen (1972: 17) noted back in 1972 that the mass media devote a great deal of energy to 'deviance, sensational crimes, scandals, bizarre happenings and strange goings on', and if anything the coverage of the strange and grotesque has only increased since then with the proliferation of news magazine style infotainment and reality television style programming – to say nothing of emerging media sources like the Internet (Jewkes 2004). There can be little doubt media coverage plays an integral role in the ways in which the community frames and views issues of crime, law and order, and social control (Chibnall 1977; Hogg and Brown 1998; Lee 2007; Pearson 1983). As a plethora of academic research has indicated the community does not, for the most part, get its information about crime and crime control from personal experience but from their engagement with the mass media (Bloustien and Israel 2006). Moreover, the mass media outlets, and the agents of social control from whom they access the information for their reportage, will have their own ideological agendas (Hall et al. 1978) which can see the public 'manipulated into taking some things too seriously and other things not seriously enough' (Jewkes 2004: 85).

Media outlets and their staff are influenced in their publication choices by their real, and imagined, audiences. They also take an active role in the construction of crime stories, 'agenda setting' and reproducing the hegemonic ideologies of the primary definers – those with the power to speak authoritatively about crime – with which they communicate (Hall et al. 1978; Philo 1990; Surette 1998). In this way, as Bloustien and Israel (2006: 46) put it, news programming does not simply mirror crime and its control; '[j]ournalists actively construct their stories by choosing particular kinds of events and presenting them to their assumed audience in terms of what they think will make such events intelligible.' Nonetheless, sociologists, media theorists and criminologists have long understood that both the construction and public consumption of crime stories is complex, bi-directional and multidimensional (Mawby 2007; Reiner 2002). It involves lines of power (Jewkes 2004), but it also involves resistances, the mediation of the cultural and socio-political context of the receiver (Eco 1972), and sometimes an ironic play of meaning from consumers who do not 'read' the information in the anticipated way (Wood 2007). Nonetheless, individuals and institutions that are in a position to provide media organizations with information about crime, justice and social control are likely to have a significant influence on the construction of crime narratives within particular cultural milieus (Chibnall 1977; Cooke and Sturges 2009; Philo 1990). Policing organizations are unquestionably key primary providers and definers in the production of crime news.

In 1977 Steve Chibnall argued that crime reporting had been 'ignored by academic researchers or treated as essentially apolitical' (1977: 1). Since then, much has been written about the way in which crime is reported in the media, and the ways in which journalists and mass media organizations go about constructing or mediating news.[1] Indeed, the media has been seen as increasingly central to the growing public and political preoccupation with crime, and subsequently with concerns about fear of crime (Hall et al. 1978; Hogg and Brown 1998; Lee 2007; Pearson 1983). However, Chibnall's formulation of eight 'news values' have prevailed as a framework to explain the ways in which the media make decisions about which crime stories make the news.

Chibnall (1977) suggested crime stories are of value to media organizations where they include the elements of *immediacy, dramatization, personalization, simplification, titillation, conventionalism, structured access* and/or *novelty*. As these have been well discussed in related academic literature (Leishman and Mason 2003; Mawby 2002a; Reiner 2010; Jewkes 2004) we will just give a brief overview. *Immediacy* entails the need for the newest and freshest of stories. *Dramatization* simply implies that media outlets prefer the dramatic to the level-headed argument. *Personalization* asks is the criminal or the crime fighter and 'identity' or 'celebrity'? If the actors are special, or can be made special by media framing, the story is of more value. *Simplification* is where binary opposites, good versus evil, hero versus villain, are of greater currency than shades of grey. Who wants to be told that crime has complex social causes? *Titillation* is where the bizarre, the sexualized, the scandalous provide better value than the mundane everyday occurrence. *Conventionalism* is where crime stories are populated by familiar characters in well known scenarios. Here the stories make 'common sense' to the consumer. *Structured Access* is where preferred expert sources with cross-institutional legitimacy are the key sources and commentators of crime news. Police are one of the key organizations where structured access to crime news is concerned. *Novelty* is the need for a new angle on a story. New technologies or approaches in policing or new ways of committing crime provide a story with novelty.

Recently, both Jewkes (2011) and Mawby (2010b) have added to Chibnall's news values categories to reflect the changed media world and greater audience sophistication that has developed since the 1970s. Jewkes' list, revised from Chibnall's original proposition, consisted of twelve core values[2] that she argues structure crime news. Many of Jewkes' values are similar in all or part to Chibnall's list, but with three fundamentally new additions: *risk*,[3] *proximity*[4] and *children*.[5] Furthermore, Jewkes argued that there are three overarching news values – crime, negativity and novelty – that underpin news values. Similarly, Mawby (2010b) has proposed twelve news values[6] for crime reporting, largely consistent with the work of Jewkes and Chibnall. He believes these are reinforced by two constants – timing and narrative. Importantly for the current book, Mawby's news values were articulated in the context of his work in explaining media engagement with police organizations and their increasingly strategic and better resourced public relations departments.

Audiences, however, cannot simply be seen as passive consumers of crime stories. As well as taking into consideration what we know from the media effects literature, which is often critical of the 'hypodermic syringe'[7] models of media consumption, audiences themselves are now increasingly choosing, or being asked to engage in, the news-making process. This can manifest in a number of ways, such as audiences being encouraged to send tip-offs, further information and images to news agencies.[8] Such exchanges have been primarily facilitated by new technological developments that increase the capacity of the general public to view, capture and disseminate events in real time. Indeed, a pluralist reading of the relationship between media and public would argue that changes to the media landscape not only allows for a more inclusive news construction process, but also provides for a greater capacity for counter-definers to find a voice in the media (Jewkes 2011). This is also demonstrated in the proliferation of media platforms and the growth of the Internet, if not always in the diversification of media outlets.[9]

With the topic of police and media it is vital to be cognizant of the processes of news construction, given:

- the privileged position that police organizations hold as primary providers and definers of crime news; and
- the key role of the media in disseminating crime news to the public.

It is clear that police media organizations are able to provide media outlets with stories that include many of the attributes of newsworthiness discussed above (Mason 2009; Mawby 2010b).

Policing and the media

As we have stated, the most influential source of information about crime, justice, and social order are policing organizations themselves. As the agencies responsible for the maintenance of order, and with a monopoly over the state-sanctioned use of force (Weber 1964), police are also in a privileged position when it comes to the ownership and dissemination of such information (Cooke and Sturges 2009). But there are also very good reasons as to why the public would want their policing organizations to be able to communicate with the media.

For the police organizations, communication with the media is vital for the dissemination of important information to the public.

Policing relies heavily on the cooperation of the public, and media involvement in the publication of information about crime and justice can, and does, lead to the apprehension of suspects, helps to communicate public risks and facilitates public assistance in policing matters. For the media, policing and crime news have long contributed vital material to the compilation of news reportage. As Jiggins (2004: 7) noted, '[t]he first edition of the Melbourne Age newspaper (No. I – Vol. 1, 17 October, 1854) devoted nearly half a page of its scant 8-page first edition to the proceedings of the Criminal Sessions, the City Court and the Police Court.' The proliferation of crime content in news reportage has only increased since then. Indeed, associations between policing organizations and the media can be traced throughout the history of police services, showing a 'long fascination of the modern media with all aspects of criminal justice' (Finnane 2002: 134; Kiel 1989: 254). While early understandings of the police and their role were primarily acquired through the print media of pamphlets, newspapers and memoirs, blurring the lines between fact and fiction (Mawby 2007: 147–50, 151–6), today the police play a much more active role in their portrayal, both fictional and factual (see also Schlesinger and Tumber 1993, 1994).

Freckelton (1988: 78) has highlighted the 'symbiotic' relationship that exists between police and media, a relationship that he suggests is not conducive to high-quality, critical, investigative journalism. He argues that there exists an unnecessary and improper reliance upon 'unnamed police sources' and an unwillingness to seek out 'independent', 'alternative' viewpoints. Almost a quarter of a century on, one could hardly quibble with his overall analysis. Others (Cooke and Sturges 2009; Mawby 2007) have noted that the police–media association constitutes a series of coexisting relationships that ebb and flow in terms of which organization achieves dominance and control. They suggest that the balance of power differs over time and location and at national and local levels. Taken together, we can conceptualise a constantly changing, developing, mutating but symbiotic relationship between the police and the media.

This assessment of the changing but symbiotic set of power relations becomes more pertinent when one considers the myriad of developments impacting upon the news media industry today, including dwindling media budgets, reduced resources, the growth of low-cost infotainment productions and the proliferation of generalist reporters. Moreover, recent studies into police–media relationships have recognized the growing professionalization of police–media interactions on the part of the police. Police organizations have increasingly moved towards establishing special purpose media units internally, staffed by experts in communications and public relations. This growth in professional police public relations has been highlighted by a range of scholars (for example, Davis 2000, 2003; Leishman and Mason 2003; Lovell 2003; Mawby 2002a, 2002b, 2010a, 2010b) and it is this professionalization that we wish to discuss for the remainder of the chapter.

The development of professionalized police media work

Police media and information services have become established as a regular feature of policing and law enforcement (Leishman and Mason; Mawby 2002a; McGovern 2009; Surette 2001; Wilson 1992). With ever-increasing demands for information being placed on the police by the media and a growing recognition by the police of the strategic importance of information, policing organizations have gradually developed more formal mechanisms by which to manage media requests and information dissemination.

We can trace the emergence of more formal police–media relationships through what can be characterized as the three broad eras of policing, as described by Kelling and Moore (1989):

- The political era, which was characterized by the uncomfortably close ties between the police and politics dating roughly in the US context from the introduction of police into municipalities during the 1840s through to the early 1900s.
- The reform era, characterized by professionalization, and seen as a reaction to the political era. Starting in the 1930s and thriving during the 1950s and 1960s, it began to fade during the 1970s.
- The community problem-solving era, prominent since the late 1970s and 1980s.

Such characterizations are of course reductive. The prescribed periods actually overlap and there are clearly practices from the one period better described by another.[10] Nonetheless, the schema provides a heuristic device to help conceptualize the development of the relationship between the police and the media.

The reform era and the emergence of formal police public relations

Authorized as they were by local municipalities, police of the *political era* in the United States lacked the central authority of the crown to establish themselves with a legitimate, unifying mandate (Kelling and Moore 1988). Informal police–public relations tended to operate through connections to local politicians and street-level policing and public service. While public relations or 'press agents' began to spread from business to government organizations during the first three decades of the twentieth century (Cutlip 1994; Surette 2001), it would not be until the middle of the twentieth century that they took hold in policing in the USA.

Unlike their North American counterparts police departments in the UK did not suffer from the same early political taint during this period. The centralized nature of police organizations in Britain gave them authority and legitimacy – which was generally reflected in media reportage of the times. While the working classes did not necessarily share the same enthusiasm as the influential middle classes and there were instances of ridicule in popular culture,[11] by the early 1900s the Metropolitan Police we being described as 'the best police in the world' (Mawby 2002a). The first police press officer is credited to Scotland Yard in 1919 under the commissionership of Sir Nevil Macready (Leishman and Mason 2003; Mawby 2002a), marking the beginning of a more formalized engagement between police and media, and in a sense marking the beginning of the reform era.

Over the course of the twentieth century policing organizations dramatically changed their approach to their dealings with the media. This can be viewed as part of a broader professionalization strategy during the reform era across all aspects of policing embraced by many Western policing organizations. In the USA this movement towards professional policing was sparked by August Vollmer, a Los Angeles Police Chief. In 1931 Vollmer published the *Wickersham Commission Report*, which came to be known as the professional model of policing (Lovell 2003: 96). Vollmer's model called for dedication in policing, with proficiency in crime fighting and rigorous training for recruits. Tied into this was a focus on efficiency and a strong public relations campaign.

By 1954 in the USA, John Pope had published *Police–Press Relations: A Handbook*. In the foreword to the publication, the then Attorney General of California Edmond Brown states, 'partnership of the police, press and public is paramount for the maintenance of our American way of life' (cited in Pope 1954: ix). Pope optimistically notes that 'crime throughout America, and possibly the world, will be dealt a serious blow when the full potentialities of police and press relations become a fact' (1954: 13).

Police media relations in the interwar periods in both the UK and Australia can be characterized largely by the attempts of top-level police to stem the flow of unauthorized leaks to the press, which they thought could result in 'bad news' (Finnane 2002; Leishman and Mason 2003). Finnane (1999a, 2002) notes that in the Australian context, political sensitivities around industrial and social conflict from the 1900s to the 1940s saw police organizations attempt to tightly control their relationships with the media.

Nonetheless, Australasian policing experienced some moves towards professionalization. For example, the emphasis on better education of police recruits was introduced into the police cadet system within the NSW Police in 1933, which integrated both physical training and legal instruction (Finnane 1994). By the mid-twentieth century, this interest in education led to the development of police colleges (Finnane 1994; Wilson 2008), and the late 1940s and early 1950s saw road traffic campaigns become a site of police public relations work. For children in schools, road safety was not only seen to occupy an important place in safety intervention, but was also regarded as 'excellent public relations work in securing the confidence of children in the Police Force' (NSW Police Force 1950: 10).

The importance of a more productive police–media exchange was recognized in the later 1950s in the Australian context, when then President of the Australian Journalists Association, Mr G. F. Godfrey, declared in an address to NSW Police Detectives that it was:

> The joint task of police and journalists to examine how best they can carry out the functions allotted to their respective professions to develop those aspects on which mutually advantageous cooperation can be achieved and to study any factors on which there may be variance with a view to their elimination.
>
> *(Godfrey 1957: 301–2)*

He went on in his address to assert that 'an atmosphere of confidence and trust must exist in the relationship between the police and the press' so that both parties could rely implicitly upon each other (Godfrey 1957: 305).

Policing in the UK also experienced a movement towards professionalization in this period despite an often fraught relationship with the press (Leishman and Mason 2003). Following a Home Office Committee investigation in 1933, it was determined that England lagged behind other countries in relation to police training and the operation of scientific investigative tools (Emsley 2002). As a consequence of the report, significant developments were made in training, communication between forces and the use of scientific aids.

The postwar period in the UK saw relationships between the police and the media improve. After being appointed Commissioner of the Metropolitan Police in 1945, Sir Harold Scott quickly went about promoting public confidence in the police by maintaining productive links with news outlets (Leishman and Mason 2003), even cooperating with film directors on fictional representations of police such as *The Blue Lamp*, produced by Ealing Studios (Reiner 2010). This period in the UK was also that in which national 'newshounds' would follow Scotland Yard detectives around the country in serious criminal investigations, staying at the same hotels as a detective superintendent and his sergeant and receiving briefings over a beer (Leishman and Mason 2003; Schlesinger and Tumber 1994). However, the 1960 ushered in a period of challenge for that type of increasingly cosy relationship and had implications for policing across many jurisdictions.

The 1960s was a decade associated with social and culture change. These changes impacted both directly and indirectly upon policing (Edwards 2005). Political and social dissent rose to the surface over matters such as involvement in the Vietnam War, Aboriginal Australian and African American civil rights, standards of health and welfare, the equality of women, abortion law reform and censorship matters (Chan 1997; Edwards 2005; Finnane 1987, 1990, 1994). Reiner (2010) suggests this period also saw a 'repoliticization' of the police in the UK where they were frequently used to quell dissent. Across jurisdictions the ability of the police to carry out their roles independently came under increasing public and political scrutiny (Finnane 1999a), and it became common for police authority to be questioned (Edwards 2005). In particular, the ways in which the police dealt with public dissent and protest were closely examined. As Leishman and Mason (2003: 37) put it in the UK context:

> Mass TV ownership and an increasingly motorized society … posed considerable challenges to both policing methods and police image work. A growing counter-culture was emerging, accentuating and accelerating the decline of the automatic deference to authority.

In retrospect we can also see this as a period in which the discretionary actions of the police were placed under more scrutiny by a new technological gaze. Television footage of abuses of police power in the context of street marches and protest was challenging any idealized, institutionally preferred image of policing.

Indeed, technological developments were at the forefront of a number of challenges faced by police organizations throughout the 1960s and 1970s. Many newly implemented policing strategies attempted to merge traditional policing practices with new technological advancements. The effects of such developments, however, often contributed to community alienation from the police through, for example, the removal of foot patrols in favour of auto-mobility in patrol cars (Wilson and Kelling 1982) and the replacement of proactive police–public interaction with reactive approaches driven by police radio technology (Edwards 2005; Garland 2001).

Other authors have focused on the development of formal and professional police–media public relations in the UK and the USA since the 1970s (Cutlip 1994; Leishman and Mason 2003; Mawby 2002a). Here we want to provide a more in-depth case study of these developments in the Australian context – focusing on the jurisdiction of NSW as policing moved into from the *reform* into the *community problem-solving era*.

Formalizing police public relations in NSW: a case study

As a response to political pressure and following the international trends of professionalization, the NSW Police Force moved towards specialization in policing in the 1960s and 1970s. One result of such moves was that the NSW Police Force broadened and focused their media-related activities, introducing the Police Public Relations Branch to deal with media issues (NSW Police Force 1965). When established in 1964 the Branch consisted of three staff: a sergeant, a constable and a female public service officer (NSW Police Force 1965). Its role was the promotion of 'police–public relations', assisting materially in the investigation of serious crimes, not only by publication through the press, radio and television of information relating to cases, but also through the publication of photographs and descriptions of people who were suspected perpetrators of crime (NSW Police Force 1965). It also issued general warnings via the media to the public in respect to crime prevention.

Indeed, in this period the NSW Police Force, led by Commissioner Norman Allan, talked about actively attempting to address some of the 'bad blood' that had existed up until this point between the media and police. In 1965 Allan met with the Australian Journalists Association (AJA) to discuss police–press relations (Finnane 1999b). Following the meeting Allan issued the journalists present with 'new press passes to facilitate reporters passing through police lines' (Chappell and Wilson 1969: 138).

While the Commissioner continued to hold official talks with the press on the need for improvement in relations, in practice little seemed to be being done to achieve this (Chappell and Wilson 1969). When Allan decreed that the only police allowed to speak to the press in an official capacity were the heads of various departments within the NSW Police Force, it did not sit well with many journalists (Chappell and Wilson 1969; Finnane 1999b, 2000). In a further attempt to manage the flow of information from the Police Force, Allan initiated daily conferences from the Sydney Headquarters of the Criminal Investigation Branch, to be held at 7 a.m., 9 a.m. and 5 p.m., where senior police officers were to brief journalists on daily events (Chappell and Wilson 1969).

In order to try to combat this management of the relationship, journalists turned to forming unofficial contacts from within the police, which also came with their own set of problems. They had to be extra careful so as not to reveal their sources when filing their stories, which often resulted in the holding back of some information for the protection of their contacts (Chappell and Wilson 1969). Allan further antagonized reporters when he refused them access to police radios and police communication facilities (Chappell and Wilson 1969). As a result, journalists took to illegally carrying police radios in their cars. While Allan's new system for police–media interactions was seen as a determined attempt to more tightly control the information being given to the media, the effect was detrimental. Without the ability to confirm a lot of what they were writing, journalists were quite often 'getting it wrong'. As one journalist interviewed by Chappell and Wilson, cited in Finnane (2002: 132), stated:

> Press reporting is undoubtedly more hostile in New South Wales than in other states. The press do, on occasions, write stories which are half correct, which show police in a bad light. But the reason for this is that police do not tell them enough.

Allan's actions, rather than fostering better relations with the media, had the opposite effect. The experience of the police–media relationship during this period evidences the continuity in attempts by the police to control their relationship with the media.

The Police Union also stepped into the information void and took on an advocacy role, much to the chagrin of senior police management.[12] Indeed, a range of scholars (Emsley 1996; Leishman and Mason 2003; Mawby 2002a; McLaughlin and Murji 1998; Reiner

2000) have discussed the influential role of police unions internationally[13] in publicly lobbying for the police and influencing government policy. Not only did police unions use the media to advance their own interests during this period (Putnis 1996), police ideologies and moralities also entered the political and public arenas (Freckelton 1988: 58–60). As Reiner (1978: 151) acknowledged in the UK context, the Police Federation was 'not seen as effective in conveying a good public image of the police' and was not 'a suitable vehicle for this' type of activity.

In 1965 the first of many 'law and order elections' in NSW signaled both this general politicization of policing and an increasing public concern about crime (Finnane 1999a; Tiffen 2004). In March of that year Robert Askin and the Liberal Party defeated a longstanding Labor government on the back of favourable press for his call for greater police protection (Puplick 2001: 445). During the election campaign Askin promised to increase police numbers by one thousand in his first term in office if elected (NSW Police Force 1965; Puplick 2001).

Notwithstanding Allen's actions and union activities, by 1970 the NSW Police Public Relations Branch not only informed the public on matters of crime prevention and detection, but also assisted in tracing missing persons, gave traffic control advice, addressed community groups, produced crime prevention pamphlets and cooperated with the news media, authors, feature writers and film producers in preparing material depicting police activities (NSW Police Force 1972). Again, many of these activities reflected international trends. In 1972 the NSW Police Force presented a 'new look' Public Relations Section, which was touted as already making 'a favourable impact on the public image of the Police Force' (NSW Police Force 1972: 364). At this time the Branch was expanded both in activities and staff levels, with twenty people working on 'presenting a better Police image to the media and the public' (NSW Police Force 1972: 364). Duties of the staff within the Branch ranged from administration and editorial duties, to research and promotion. The changes were reflective of the fact that by the early 1970s many police organizations gradually came to the realization that the less they tried to resist or manage their relationship with the media, the easier it actually became to communicate with them and subsequently with the public (Finnane 2002).

As well as continuing to produce daily radio scripts, leaflets, booklets and posters about the police, the Branch also purchased a semi-trailer display unit which, with two specifically allocated staff, travelled the state 'promoting interest in the Police Department' (NSW Police Force 1972: 364). This development displayed a greater focus and effort on the public relations aspects of policing.

Further developments made within the Public Relations Branch during 1972 included press releases covering a wider spectrum of stories and twice-daily press conferences that aimed to give police roundsmen[14] regular briefings on daily activities. Attempts to foster a more positive image within the media were so significant that the Branch began to maintain a 'clipping service', whereby items of interest to the police were collected in daily and weekly editions of Sydney publications, in an effort to monitor the trends in public and press attitudes towards the Police (NSW Police Force 1972: 364–5). The Force was so confident in their 'new look' Public Relations Branch that they were able to state later that:

> [T]here is a marked and noticeable trend towards a more favourable public image of the Policeman being reflected in the media over the past three months.
>
> *(NSW Police Force 1974: 365)*

Consideration of an in-service training programme to enable more personnel to liaise with the media across a number of formats was further evidence of the importance placed on police–media interactions during the early 1970s. By this time the Public Relations Branch also saw its duty as pertaining to the dissemination of 'authentic information regarding crimes, the Police Force and its members, etc., to members of the public' (NSW Police Force 1976: 28), commencing a trend towards the establishment of both external and internal legitimacy building activities.

In 1975 a three-day conference was held in Sydney that brought together police public relations representatives from police forces across Australia (NSW Police Force 1976) demonstrating growing interest across Australian jurisdictions. By the end of the 1970s in NSW, staffing levels in the Public Relations Branch had increased tenfold on the previous decade and operating hours were extended. Unnamed 'reputable public companies' had also, by 1978, begun to link with the Public Relations Branch, offering support and sponsorship to 'matters of community interest' (NSW Police Force 1979: 33). In addition, the Branch also launched *Police File*, a weekly television programme on Channel 10, a precursor to *Australia's Most Wanted*, detailing unsolved crimes, incidents and wanted criminals (NSW Police Force 1979). This was essentially the Australian equivalent of *Crimewatch* broadcast in Germany since 1967 (Leishman and Mason 2003) and adapted for the UK context in 1984.

These Australian developments, however, did not somehow just happen at the insistence or acceptance of the police. The reform of policing (Drew and Mazerolle 2009), and the institutional reassessment of the relationship between the police, media and public, was also driven by an array of public inquiries and royal commissions and their resulting managerialist-style reform agendas. Many of these inquiries, in particular the Woodward Royal Commission in NSW (1977–80), the Fitzgerald Inquiry in Queensland (1987–9), the Wood Royal Commission in NSW (1994–7) and finally the WA Police Royal Commission (2002–4), uncovered entrenched levels of police misconduct, political influence or incompetence. Other inquiries, such as those of Lusher (1981) and Lee (1990), dealt with issues that had direct and indirect consequences for how the police and media would come to interact with one another. These inquiries and the plethora of reforms that have followed uncannily mirror the UK context of reform, or what Reiner (2010) refers to as a cyclical synthesis of reform strategies chosen from the coercion–consent spectrum, from Scarman (1981) to MacPherson (1988–99) as Reiner (2010) puts it, referring to the two public inquiries into policing that he sees as optimizing the reform agenda in the UK.

When Nevil Wran was elected as the NSW Labor Premier in 1976 his political strategy was to not let apparent corruption issues within the NSW Police Force intrude on his government and cause electoral damage (Tiffen 2004: 1178). However, there was a general feeling among the community that there was inaction by the police and government on a number of corruption issues that pervaded the NSW Police Force. It seemed that 'a series of scandals and crises had more or less taken up permanent occupancy on the front page of newspapers over recent years' (Bradley and Cioccarelli 1989: 9; Tiffen 2004: 1179). This led Premier Wran to write to the Police Commissioner in 1977 to arrange an independent examination into the methods and philosophy of the education and training of the police (Bradley and Cioccarelli 1989). In 1979 the Justice Lusher Inquiry into New South Wales Police Administration commenced.

The Lusher Inquiry was particularly significant as it included an investigation into the role of the Public Relations Branch. Lusher was scathing in his criticism of their ad hoc approach to dealing with the media and public. The Inquiry went on to make a number of recommendations in relation to the Public Relations Branch, some of which were:

- The Public Relations Branch should be responsible for, or at least have, a coordinating role for all public relations activities undertaken by the Force.
- The Branch should produce a public relations programme and forward plan developed on the basis of specific objectives and measurable targets.
- An itemised budget for public relations projects should be part of the Police Force estimates.
- Each activity should be regularly evaluated in terms of its cost-effectiveness having regard for the objectives and the number and nature of people influenced by the activity.
- An increased emphasis on training in dealing with the media, including the legal and privacy implications of any comments made by police.
- The Police Force should ... adopt a policy of openness in respect of its operations, policies and procedures.

(Lusher 1981: 660–1)

However, it was not until the mid-1980s, when Commissioner John Avery was appointed, that many of these recommendations were acted upon. Simultaneous to Lusher's findings being handed down, Avery (1981), not yet Commissioner, published his book entitled *Police – Force or Service?* (1981), which shared some of Lusher's criticisms and argued for a community service model of policing – an indication of the gradual embracing of the *community problem-solving era.*

The appointment of a journalist to the re-branded Media Liaison in the early 1980s was seen as a significant step in the professionalization of police media communication systems (NSW Police Force 1983). Avery, who was installed as NSW Police Commissioner in 1984, was of the belief that if police wanted to establish good relationships with the public, which was important to the success of a growing commitment to community policing initiatives, then they 'must display an openness and frankness with the press and the public', as defensiveness only encourages suspicion (Avery 1981: 89). This appointment was also significant as one of the key roles of the journalist was to improve police–ethnic relations and educate the non-English-speaking community on various aspects of the law (NSW Police Force 1986).

Drawing on successful overseas operations, community-based policing and initiatives such as Neighbourhood Watch, Operation Noah,[15] Safety House[16] and Crime Stoppers were also developed and introduced via Media Liaison, in collaboration with other sections of the NSW Police Force such as the Crime Prevention Unit. This constituted a clear commitment to proactive media work. The importance of community relations was further evidenced by the introduction of a Public Service Community Relations Media Coordinator to the Media Liaison Branch in 1986 (NSW Police 1986).

This service mentality flowed through into police–media relations when in 1990 the former Media Liaison Branch, now renamed the NSW Police Media Unit (PMU), conducted a 'Media Effectiveness Survey' of twenty individuals from the newspapers, magazines, television, radio and the Australian Associated Press (NSW PMU 1990). Results from the 15 questions suggested that, overall, respondents were pleased with the level of cooperation and service they received from the PMU. In terms of cooperation, those surveyed found the PMU to be much more cooperative when making inquiries than other units within the NSW Police Service. Ninety per cent of respondents found the cooperation with the PMU satisfactory, compared with the mere 45 per cent who were satisfied with other branches within the police (NSW PMU 1990: 17). Police media relations were thus a professionalized component of the police service that has continued to develop to the present time – albeit with the service reverting back to the use of the name NSW Police Force in the 2000s.

Such developments transformed the way in which police have since chosen to engage with the media, with modern-day forces continuing to emphasise the importance of a productive relationship. For example, the 2011 NSW Police Force Media Policy states that '… the media should not be viewed as an obstacle but as a tool we can use to help achieve our goals' (NSW Police Force 2011b: 4).

Police, control and media

Despite moves away from some of the overt forms of control of the media discussed above, control is still a prominent theme in these modern formal mechanisms. Rather than trying to restrict access to information, however, these new forms of control operate through the provision of information from police media relations offices or media units. That is, police media units now serve as a channel through which almost all information and communications about police activities and the like are managed and disseminated. Finnane (2002) suggests that police are in a position whereby the degree of control they are able to exercise over information is verging on monopolistic, and as such it may be argued that they have developed a number of routines in an attempt to manage the flow of this information, including the establishment of police media units (McGovern and Lee 2010). Indeed, policy statements from the past decade have clearly articulated this theme of control through information provision. For example, in their 2002 Media Policy, the NSW Police Force stated 'providing media with regular information helps to contain them and allows the facts to be reported' (NSW Police Force 2002).

They also recognize that interactions between the police and the media, and the exchange of information between the two, have become increasingly central to policing priorities not only in Australia, but across Western policing organizations, particularly when we consider how important perceptions of crime, and the police themselves, are to the success of these organizations (NSW Police Force 2008, 2010a).

The role and function of the public relations departments of police organizations have grown dramatically over the last decade. Where initially such departments played a role that saw them primarily communicate to the public, via the media, on matters of safety and the occurrence of crime, today's departments play a much more active role in creating the news, as alluded to earlier in this chapter. For example, as well as responding to media inquiries and informing the public about day-to-day crime incidents, these departments now also deliver media training to operational police, develop policy guidelines and regulations around media contact, attend public events to promote the organization, consult with television and film producers who make use of or depict police organizations in their broadcasts or films, and run their own multimedia units which produce footage for distribution to traditional media outlets and online news sites. While some media departments still operate with minimal staff and resources, others see their staff numbers approaching three figures, with public relations and communications specialists making up the bulk of the personnel. As Lovell notes:

> Police are now beginning to maintain media-relations offices staffed by public information officers trained in media communication and journalism whose primary responsibility is to engage the news media to advance the goals of the police organization.
>
> *(Lovell 2002: 2)*

With image and perception being equally as important to police success as arrest rates, police media departments now play a vital part in fostering public consent, confidence and trust through the reproduction of positive images of policing (Lee and McGovern 2012, 2013). For example, a number of Australian police departments have developed relationships with television production companies, resulting in the development and broadcasting of observational documentary television programmes depicting the 'day-to-day' activities of police officers. Likewise, the regular dissemination of press releases detailing the 'good work' being carried out by policing agencies helps remind the public of policing success. This growth in proactive police media work has dramatically changed the way in which police conceptualize their image and how this is communicated, which has implications not only for the way the police relate to the media, but also the ways in which the police now interact and communicate with the public.

Police media and public information officers: the who's who

As noted above, dedicated police media officers, or 'public information officers' (PIOs) (Surette 2001), cemented their position in criminal justice agencies in the late 1960s. While much of this book focuses on the roles of media officers, here we want to explore their background and what experience they bring to their roles.

Little has been documented about the career backgrounds and trajectories of police media office staff, yet their role is central in contemporary police–media relationships. A small number of existing studies offer some insight but are somewhat dated and relevant primarily to the USA context (e.g. Chermak and Weiss 2005; Surette 2001; Surette and Richard 1995). While the work of Surette, Surette and Richard, and Chermak and Weiss, described below, focuses on the role of PIOs in law enforcement agencies in the USA, only cursory attention was given to the career backgrounds of these officers.

In 1993 Surette and Richard (1993, cited in Surette 2001; see also Surette and Richard 1995) surveyed 66 PIOs who belonged to the Florida Law Enforcement Public Information Officer Association (FLEPIOA) on the characteristics of PIOs and the agencies they worked for. They found that:

> The typical PIO in Florida is a forty-year-old Caucasian Anglo male who is a sworn officer and has attended college. They average just over five years' experience as PIOs. Two out of three are men, three out of five are sworn officers, four out of five are Caucasian and Anglo, and nineteen out of twenty have attended college with more than one-half having at least a bachelors degree. The fields of criminal justice and communications dominate their degree areas.
>
> *(Surette and Richard 1995: 327)*

They also found that about half of the PIOs had prior media experience, most commonly working for television, radio or newspapers. This media experience was more common among civilian PIOs than those that were sworn officers.

Their study also revealed a clear division between sworn and non-sworn media officers: sworn PIOs tended to have little or no media-related experience prior to being media officers, and were more likely to be males with educational backgrounds in criminal justice (Surette and Richard 1995). Civilian PIOs were more likely to be female and to have substantial media-related experience and educational backgrounds in communications (Surette 2001: 108).

Surette's survey of PIOs in Florida was conducted again in 1998, this time with a sample of 127 and including both those who belonged to the FLEPIOA and those who were not members of the association (Surette 2001). He found that the demographic characteristics of PIOs had changed little since 1993, with a typical respondent remaining a 'forty-two-year-old male, sworn, college-educated individual'. The educational background of PIOs had, however, changed during this time, particularly among those PIOs who belonged to FLEPIOA (primarily civilian PIOs).

In 1993, communication fields slightly dominated the background of PIOs, and only a handful of PIOs had degrees outside of criminal justice or communication. By 1998, association PIOs had shifted away from communication degrees (five out of ten in 1993 to three out of ten in 1998) to other varied degree fields such as law, public administration, sociology and psychology. It is now thought that only about three out of ten FLEPIOA member PIOs hold criminal justice degrees. In sum, the professional member PIO group is becoming much more interdisciplinary with less concentration in either criminal justice or communications.

This was not the case, however, for PIOs who were not members of FLEPIOA (primarily sworn officers), among whom six out of ten were still educated in criminal justice (Surette 2001). Surette (2001: 111) concludes that 'while developing as a specialized career field, the criminal justice PIO is simultaneously evolving as a multidisciplinary field, especially among its professional association members [e.g. primarily civilian PIOs].'

Chernak and Weiss (2005) surveyed 203 PIOs from law enforcement agencies in American cities with populations over 100,000 about their roles and responsibilities. They found that PIOs were drawn from various ranks within law enforcement agencies and had an average of 4.3 years public information experience and at least 50 hours formal training in the police–media relations field specifically.

Our own qualitative research into police media offices in each Australian jurisdiction found, like Surette (2001), that broadly speaking police media officers (PMOs) typically come from either operational policing (e.g. sworn) or media (e.g. civilian) backgrounds. Importantly, however, there appear to be two discrete groups within the media background cohort: those from journalism/reporting backgrounds, and those from what might be called media relations backgrounds. Those from a journalism or reporting background had worked in a wide variety of positions – in television, radio and print journalism – and on a variety of topics, including mainstream news, crime reporting and sports reporting. Those from media relations backgrounds had often worked in roles and/or environments similar to police–media relations in other sectors. For example, a number had worked as media advisors to politicians, with emergency services or with large international non-government organizations.

This is an important distinction, as such media relations roles bear a much closer resemblance to PMOs' roles than those of journalists or reporters. Reflecting this distinction, two respondents we interviewed who had come from journalism backgrounds described moving into police–media relations as akin to entering a different world. One described a colleague who had come from a journalism background by saying 'he's worked on both sides of the fence'. Another described his own move to police–media relations by saying 'I made the move to what journalists call "the dark side".' This presumably stems from these PMOs' sense that, while as journalists their role was to obtain information from the police, they are now the gatekeepers of that information. But it also offers an important and impartial insight into the ways journalists view PMOs.

Only a small number of PMOs we interviewed had backgrounds in both policing and media roles, or had an interest in or education that covered both areas. One claimed: 'I had tertiary education basically in journalism and law and I particularly specialized in media law – defamation, privacy, contempt – they were the areas that interested me' (WA Police PR Respondent 1).

Another of our interviewees, an Acting Assistant Director in Media and Corporate Communications of the Victorian Police, had substantial experience as both an operational police officer and in both journalism and media relations: 'I was actually a police officer up in Queensland for six years and prior to that I had 14 years as a journalist and media advisor and media director with Emergency Services.'

As might be expected, given the seniority of those we interviewed, respondents typically had extensive careers in police or media roles, with many years' experience as these responses demonstrate. One noted: '[I am a] police officer and have been for the last 25 years' (NSW Police PR Respondent 4). Another suggests: 'I've been in the police force for 26 years' (Vic. Police PR Respondent 1) and a third recalls: 'I had most of my career at Channel Nine, starting there in 1977' (NSW Police PR Respondent 1) while a fourth states: 'I'm a journalist of long-term standing, 30 or 40 years' (WA Police PR Respondent 1).

The amount of experience being pooled in these positions attests to the relative importance placed in high-level public relations staff by policing organizations. For larger organizations, the level of recruits that are being lured to these positions do not come cheap.

However, for some PMOs from operational policing backgrounds, the role was not something they had necessarily coveted at all. Rather, they came to it as a result of unexpected events or opportunity. One noted: 'How I came to be here was quite by accident' (Vic. Police PR Respondent 3). Another suggested: 'My background is very much operational policing ... What led me to this job was opportunity more than anything' (Vic. Police PR Respondent 1).

For one PMO from an operational policing background, the move was not initially a happy one, although he did grow into the role somewhat:

> I'm an operational police officer. I've come up through the ranks – half my career in uniform, the other half as a detective,

and I was asked to come to this … I did not want to come to this spot. I thought this was the last place on Earth I would be involved in.

(WA Police PR Respondent 2)

For those PMOs from operational policing backgrounds, the shift into police–media relations was often a temporary one:

I came into this role 12 months ago, in a relieving capacity. Something happened and the Commissioner asked me to come here and I've been here for just over 12 months … I'll have to stick it out until the Commissioner says I [can] move on.

(WA Police PR Respondent 2)

One PMO described the demands of the role being responsible for the temporary nature of many working in the field. It was seen as quite a high-pressure environment: 'It's quite a high turnover in the sense that it can be quite stressful and demanding so people tend to do three to five years' (WA Police PR Respondent 3).

In all our cohort of higher-level police public relations staff indicates that police organizations in Australia, especially the larger ones, are investing heavily in having well trained and experienced media officers. Many are able to think like journalists and have numerous journalist contacts on 'the other side'. The police media officer is now certainly a profession.

Conclusion

Every policing jurisdiction in Australia now hosts a professionalized public relations/media branch within its organization. The establishment of such branches reflects an international trend where police public relations have become both professionalized and mediatized. Media units, public affairs branches and communications departments have become major vehicles for the promotion of the police profile as well as more general police–community relations. As noted by the former NSW Police Force Director of Marketing and Media, Sue Netterfield (1994), in the past the media had been used by the police in a reactive way to announce details rather than to proactively promote issues. Police nationally and internationally have thus broadened their scope and usage of communications, which has allowed 'the Police Service to retain strategic control of the agenda and the key messages' (Keelty, 2006: 3). The concept of control is a cornerstone of much police public relations work – control, or at least attempted control, over the information disseminated and the police image.

As Lovell (2003: 139) notes, '[t]oday, media relations units have become central to both the police organizational structure and the daily function of routine police work'. Indeed, the larger Australian police forces have departments that operate 24 hours a day, seven days a week, staffed with 'experienced journalists, public relations specialists and police officers' (NSW Police Force, 2004a: 5) and guided by well-developed media policies and strategies. They play an integral role in a range of reactive and proactive media activities, and their directors are often situated in influential positions in the organizational hierarchy. Whereas police media departments of old, as previously discussed, were more interested in disseminating information about crime events or communicating road safety messages, the departments of today engage in a wide range of activities, including but not limited to:

- media liaison and communications strategies;
- media training;
- media monitoring;
- multimedia filming and production;
- digital and social media; and
- film and television production liaison.

The range and scope of media activities now being undertaken by most, if not all, police media departments in Australia and many Western nations is demonstrative of an increasingly professionalized and strategic approach to the way in which police interact and deal with the media. In the following chapter we explore in more detail the logics that drive contemporary police engagement with the media.

Notes

1. See, for example, Ericson et al. (1989), Ericson et al. (1991), Fishman (1981), Hall et al. (1978), Kelly (1987), Mawby (1998, 2003), Reiner (2002, 2003).

2. Threshold, predictability, simplification, individualism, risk, sex, celebrity, proximity, violence, spectacle, children and conservatism.

3. She argues that in today's more risk-oriented times, news stories have become more about the victim and concerned with notions of vulnerability and fear.

4. This refers to both spatial and cultural proximity according to Jewkes: spatial in terms of geographical proximity, which will vary according to the nature of the media (local, national, international) and whether the story involves a celebrity, and cultural, which refers to the apparent relevance of a story to a particular audience.

5. Jewkes argues the attachment of children to a story gives it a prominence that a story may not otherwise have received, for example the disappearance of Madeleine McCann in 2007.

6. The unusual, bizarre and shocking, wealth and crime, celebrity, malpractice, scale/magnitude, attractive white people, a 'good' victim, young people (especially when involved with anti-social behaviour), graphics, violence (though this was relative to the geographical location), human interest, and relevance to readership ('It could be me').

7. This model argues that the media directly and immediately influence the behaviour of consumers (Marsh and Melville 2009; Jewkes 2011).

8. For example, the online edition of the NSW-based *The Daily Telegraph* (2013) encourages readers to 'send in your news', while the *Sydney Morning Herald* (2013) online edition asks readers if they have 'missed anything', urging readers to alert them to any 'corruption, problems or issues' and to send in 'photos, videos and tip-offs'.

9. For example, the diversity of mainstream media in Australia has shrunk in recent years with the dominance of key players such as the Murdoch owned News Limited.

10. In only slight contrast, Mawby (2002a) outlines three British periods of image work: informal image work (1829–1919); emergent public relations (1919–72); and embedding public relations (1972–87).

11. See, for example, Mawby's (2002a: 10) discussion of the *Pirates of Penzance* and *Punch*.

12. See again Brogden (1987), Emsley (1996), Finnane (1999a, 2000, 2002: 137–9), Mawby (2002a: 46–51), McLaughlin and Murji (1998), Reiner (1978).

13. The Police Federation, the Chief Police Officers' Staff Association (CPOSA), the Association of Chief Police Officers (ACPO) and the Police Superintendents' Association (PSA).

14. Reporters who exclusively report police-generated news.

15. Operation Noah was an annual police and government campaign where the community is urged to phone a special hotline and 'dob in' people they suspect of manufacturing or supplying illicit drugs within the community.

16. Safety House was a campaign run nationwide providing education, particularly in schools, about personal safety. One of the hallmarks of the programme was the Safety House scheme, whereby children were encouraged to seek refuge in advertised 'safety houses', marked with a yellow triangle, if they were lost or in danger.

2

THE LOGICS OF POLICE MEDIA WORK

Introduction

In Chapter 1, we outlined a brief history and the changing dynamics of relationships between the police and the media. This chapter explores the logics that drive contemporary police engagement with the media. By logics we refer to the rationalities that underlie modes of media and public engagement by police. The chapter draws on empirical research from Australia and related literature and research from the UK and the USA in particular to illustrate these logics.

Reaching back as far as the architects of modern policing such as Sir Robert Peel, sophisticated police leaders and elites have realized that policing is as much a matter of symbolism as substance (Reiner 2003). In this sense public support or consent for policing appears to rest as much on what the police are perceived to be doing as what they actually do. Contemporary research and reports on relations between the public and police in liberal democracies such as the UK and Australia indicate relatively high levels of support for, or satisfaction with, the police.[1] Putting aside normative arguments as to what an acceptable level of satisfaction might be, public satisfaction with the police, and consent for policing, has historically waxed and waned (Emsley 1983; Finnane 1987, 2002; Rawlings 2002; Reiner 2010).

Indeed, the legitimation of policing has involved, and continues to involve, the careful construction and reconstruction of image (Mawby 2002a, 2002b; Reiner 2003). It is not surprising then that in the late twentieth and early twenty-first centuries, periods of significant cultural, social and importantly technological change, we might expect to find reconstructions of policing images, changes in the ways in which police disseminate information, and a reorganization of the ways in which the police, the media and the public communicate (Mawby 2010a; Surette 2001). As Tyler (1997) has argued, in such a period of change the legitimation of policing and police activity should not to be taken for granted, a proposition supported by the history of police media relationships discussed in the previous chapter.

One significant factor in this changing set of conditions has been the development of professionalized and centralized public relations and media units within police organizations. As we saw in Chapter 1, the proliferation of professional units over the last thirty years (Lovell 2003; Mawby 2002a, 2010a; McGovern and Lee 2010; Surette 2001) has transformed the ways in which the police do business with the media and, by extension, the public. Moreover, these emergent professionalized units have seen the recruitment of an increasing number of professional public relations personnel to their ranks (Surette 2001) with backgrounds in journalism, public relations and even political advising. Alongside these developments, there have also been moves towards the adoption of increasingly formalized media policies that seek *inter alia* to provide clear guidelines for police interactions with the media (e.g. NSW Police Public Affairs Branch 2010). This also constructs the capacities for breaches of such guidelines or policies.

Unpacking the logics of police media engagement

It would be easy to suggest that police engagement with the media is about only two things: the release of relevant information to the public and institutional attempts to cast the police in a positive light. However, it is clear when we begin to dissect police–media relationships that intersections between the police and the media, and indeed the public, are much more complex than this might suggest.

As Mawby (2002a) has noted in the British context, with 'image work'[2] a defence was assembled against unwanted reform and indeed unwanted criticism. However, there was also a new level of engagement made with the media, and concerned police leaders genuinely attempted to address the state of the institution and the police–public relationship; that is, they genuinely attempted to improve the legitimacy of the organization. This indicates both a multifaceted relationship between policing and the media, but also illustrates the fluid and perpetually changing and contingent nature of the relationship. Put succinctly, the positive representation of the police to the public 'involves the continuous reconstruction and reinterpretation of the nature of policing as matters of social order, conflict and authority change' (Reiner 2003: 259).

Indeed, an initial point can be made here about the relationship between the police and the media that we will later elaborate on, that is that the traditional gap between the police and the media has all but disappeared, as was evidenced in the make-up of media officer personnel discussed in the previous chapter. In contemporary times the police are also media organizations and, as such, they are media organizations that engage in and facilitate the business of policing. For now though, we will concentrate on teasing out the key logics of police media work.

One overarching logic is self-evident and goes much further back than the development of police media units and public relations, that logic being engagement with the media as a form of simple information dissemination about crime and criminal activity. This also extends to the release of crime statistics in many jurisdictions. However, such information is never value neutral. It originates in the organizational, cultural and political context of policing and/or is solicited by a mass media within the well-discussed range of media constraints, practical, ideological and organizational (Chibnall 1977; Jewkes 2011). As such, information and stories are always mediated. Indeed, the politicized release of crime statistics in Victoria in 2011 claimed the scalp of the then Commissioner Simon Overland.

Taking this to be the case, the simple sharing of 'information' or 'stories' by the police can never be conceived of as completely

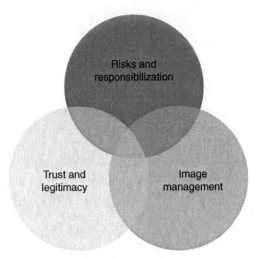

FIGURE 2.1 Interrelation of key logics

independent of what we identify as the three key logics of contemporary police engagement with the media. These are:

- the management of public *risks* and the *responsibilization* of the public;
- the *management* of police *image* – or 'image work';
- attempts to increase confidence or *trust* in policing, and in the *legitimacy* of police organizations.

While these logics can be analysed as empirically discrete, in practice they inherently overlap, mutually reinforce and influence one another – and all influence and are influenced by the modes through which information passes from the police to the media. We conceive of these logics as being interrelated, as represented in Figure 2.1.

Such logics are clearly themes for those that work in police public relations. When asked about the work of the PMU one of our research respondents from the NSW Police Public Relations Branch expressed very succinctly:

… we're a communications organization and we've got to communicate with the community and we do that for a whole
bunch of reasons, obviously in terms of investigations, assisting
with the investigations, warning the public, I guess raising
awareness of dangers and things of that nature. So you're constantly communicating that kind of thing and you've got to
communicate it in a way that the community is going to listen
so that's always been done through the media, I guess you know,
these times we have other opportunities of course. There is a
notion of pure public relations that's simply about reputation
[…], corporate reputation is pretty important for the cops
because we know from our own research, or research conducted
on our behalf … if community confidence in police declines,
community reporting of crime declines therefore the cops can't
do their job. So that I often wonder about people's cynicism
about corporate public relations when it comes to the reputation
of the police force because it's actually fairly important.

(NSW Police PR Respondent 1)

Here the respondent notes the way each of these logics interlink,
overlap and in some ways mutually reinforce one another. Moreover,
he also alerts us to the new or 'other' communications opportunities
available in contemporary times, and the capacities of policing
organizations to take advantage of these in (operationally) meaningful ways.

These logics are also readily identifiable in police media policy.
For example, the NSW Police Force's Public Affairs Branch is driven
by the following key objectives:

1. Maximize assistance and information from the public to help
   solve crime.
2. Correct or clarify information in the community.
3. Warn people of dangers or threats.
4. Create discussion in the community and/or among criminals
   during investigations.
5. Deter criminal activity by increasing the perception of detection.
6. Highlight good police work.

7. Increase police visibility.
8. Reassure the community and reduce the fear of crime.
9. Provide transparency and maintain community faith in policing and our system of justice.

Adapted from: NSW Police Force Public Affairs Branch (2013: 6)

Here we can again see the self-evident category of information communication listed at the top in objective 1 (and overlapping with objective 2). Objectives 3, 4 and 5 (as well as part of 2) could be seen to all fall largely under the category of logics of risks and responsibilization. Furthermore, objective 6 and part of objective 7 fall under the logic of image management, while objectives 8 and 9 (and part of 7) fall under the logic of trust and legitimacy.

Similar themes are expressed in the media objectives of the ACT Police:

- Build community relations and confidence in the police.
- Increase the accountability of ACT Policing to its stakeholders.
- Reduce fears of crime within the community.
- Ensure perceptions of crime are representative.
- Prevent crime by raising public awareness of potential risks and police operations.
- Deter crime by raising awareness of law enforcement measures.
- Assist in the successful resolution of operational outcomes.

(Australian Federal Police n. d.)

What these media objectives demonstrate is a clear acknowledgement within police media departments of the need to undertake a range of media activities above and beyond simple information dissemination. The other point to make about these logics and the objectives that modern police organizations seek to achieve in their interactions with the media is that they are increasingly proactive. As the former Commissioner of London Metropolitan Police, Sir (now Lord) John Stevens, stated with regards to proactivity:

> We therefore need to take a new approach to our working with the media by developing more effective and positive

relationships with journalists. This is a job for us all, not just the Directorate of Public Affairs. Over the years, I have seen the Met become increasingly cautious in its media relations and become far too reactive. This cautiousness can breed suspicion and contempt, while an open approach tends to breed confidence and respect. If we are to gain the goodwill, confidence and support of the general public and achieve our aim of making London a safer place, we need to re-engage with the media and seize every opportunity to be much more proactive. I want to see Metropolitan Police officers and civil staff representing the Service through the media, speaking up about their achievements, correcting inaccuracies and just as importantly, explaining why things may not have gone as we would have liked.

(Cited in Filkin 2012: 11)

While many police organizations are guarded – and less than open – about their media objectives, these examples offer an insight into the logics that drive contemporary police engagement with the media.

In the remainder of the chapter we will expand on examples of each of these logics along with the component rationalities that inform them. We begin with the logic of risks and responsibilization, before moving on to explain the logic of image management and then finally the logic of trust and legitimacy.

Risk management and responsibilization of the public

Ulrich Beck's (1992) 'risk society' thesis suggests that risk thinking has become pervasive across numerous organizations, including the police (Hudson 2003). Indeed, the police are one of a number of agents that put themselves forward as advisers on risk reduction and management techniques (Chan 1999; Ericson and Haggerty 1997; O'Malley 1996; Rose 2000). Police organizations not only govern through risk logics and make claims to special expertise in risk management, communication and reduction; they are also increasingly *governed by* risk logics which, among other things, circumscribe what, when, by whom, and to what ends information can be released to the media and public.

Thus risk thinking occurs internally and externally to policing organizations and is a constant theme of contemporary policing practice.

Contrary perhaps to the Beckian model of risk, the management of risk and the responsibilization of the public is not a new theme in policing. Indeed, one very early policing model that was 'loosely risk based' (O'Malley 2010) was the prevention of crime through intelligence-led policing and public information. This model can be traced to the earliest articulations of policing by figures such as Colquhoun and Peel (Colquhoun 1796; Gilling 1997), and while the construction of police as crime fighters superseded risk-based prevention models in the public and organizational imagination in the nineteenth and early twentieth centuries, risk-based prevention was never completely absent.

In the 1950s, for example, the NSW Police Force initiated a 'Safety First' campaign managed by the Traffic Branch, whereby weekly safety broadcasts were conducted on two radio stations (NSW Police Force 1950). Over time these broadcasts widened to include a number of other stations and by the mid-1960s over two thousand radio sessions were being broadcast across metropolitan and country areas (NSW Police Force 1964). Such strategies were aimed at enlisting and responsibilizing the public with the aim of reducing the road toll. In this way, the communication of risk and the dissemination of educational messages about road safety became key media activities for the police.

Thus, while not new, risk logics have expanded in importance in recent decades, along with the notion that the police cannot be seen as simply a crime-fighting instrumentality. The birth of television and other forms of media, as well as the development of an increasingly literate population, has only intensified the capacity of police organizations to communicate and manage public safety through risk reduction and responsibilization. O'Malley (2010) argues that the emergence of risk as a governing logic, together with a neo-liberal political climate, has seen risks passed from the state and government back to private citizens. Citizens thus become 'responsibilized' to manage their own risks of victimization and new communication technologies make it increasingly possible to 'govern-at-a-distance' – this is in a sense a hallmark of policing in the community problem-solving era. As such, by making use of media platforms, the police are able to engage a project of public self-responsibilization.

This process was evident in the UK by the early twenty-first century when the Home Office explicitly pushed for policing to be informed by 'active citizens'. As they put it, policing would deliver community safety through the active involvement of communities and citizens (Home Office 2004). Likewise, staff working within the NSW PMU clearly recognized the role they play in notifying the public of potential risks and encouraging behavioural change. As this respondent suggested:

> I think public information and public risk is possibly, I think the most important prevention strategy, […] … because it feels like you're actually doing something positive to help … [For example, with] the Inner West rapist [we have] duty of care issues. We have a big duty of care consideration in the Unit, in sexual assaults, if somebody has been sexually assaulted and there is a random nature to it, as the Inner West rapist has, we publicize it as duty of care, to warn people to be aware, we try and put out the images, put out descriptions, we warn people, we put out media releases saying protective strategies, 'don't walk home by yourself after dark', 'women try and walk together', that sort of stuff. All those things; provide spokesmen to go on radio, we have a whole situation like when those pack rapes were occurring in 2001, we did a really positive thing then because we needed to warn people.
>
> *(PMU Staffer 1)*

Evident here are the dual strategies of risk management through communication and attempts at the responsibilization of the public.

The ability of police organizations to define risk, to both media and public, has the capacity to help govern public safety. However, having the expertise in risk management and the capacity to define public risk brings with it the ability to exercise power. As Peter Slovic (1999) has argued, those who control the definitions of risk are also able to control what appear as rational solutions to the problems at hand. Defining risk one way also helps define the most cost-efficient, safest or best solution to this risk. Defining it another way will provide a different ordering of solutions. 'Defining risk is thus an exercise in power' (Slovic 1999: 19).

As NSW PMU Staffer 2 related:

> [We act as a] conduit of information from NSW Police to the public on our activities, what we do and what will affect the public ... the community has an expectation that they will know of the events and incidents that impact upon them.

When asked to explain the most important thing the PMU was trying to achieve when communicating with the news media, the same staff member said:

> It's to assist [police] investigators to elicit information from members of the public who might have witnessed [a crime], who might have seen something ... and through that we're assisting the investigators, and ultimately the community by solving a crime. So we're reducing fear in the community one, by showing we can solve these crimes, and two, we want them to be confident in our ability to solve those crimes, and three, it's providing that information to the media ... So, one, it's meeting their needs, meeting the community needs, and it's meeting the police needs.
>
> *(PMU Staffer 2)*

As evidenced in the quote above, the NSW PMU plays an active role in informing the community of risks and responsibilizing citizens to act in ways that minimize risky situations, a role that similar departments around the world are increasingly playing.

Image management

As suggested at the beginning of this chapter, the contemporary police preoccupation with image is anything but new. Even during the first days of the London Metropolitan Police Service (MPS), beyond presenting a positive image to the public, every element of the police image was subject to management. Police were meant to act in a 'quiet and determined manner' so as to 'excite the well-disposed of the bystanders to assist him, if he requires them' (Critchley 1978, cited in Rowe 2007). Police uniforms were to play a symbolic role, in both identifying officers and setting them apart from the military at a time when suspicion about the role and motives of the 'new police' ran high.

The management of image is the second key logic of police engagement with the media. This includes attempts to filter and manage stories involving the police and the desire to present positive policing stories. According to Manning (1978), one of the drivers for this image management is the contradictory mandate of policing – protecting public order while upholding individual rights. Such a contradiction means the police have to continually resort to managing their public image, which will inevitably be damaged from time to time by contravening one or other elements of the mandate – negative police–citizen encounters are easy, positive encounters are far harder to engineer. It also means police organizations do their best to define the indexes that measure accomplishment as external indicators inevitably cut across their contradictory mandate.

Since the 1980s criminal justice organizations have increasingly had to deal with the blending of public and private service provision in a range of fields, including policing. As Garland (2001: 117) argues, this blending has had consequences for the ways the crime control field operates, particularly in relation to questions of legitimacy and decreasing public confidence. In response to the 'customer relations' philosophy touted in private industry, organizations such as the police have increasingly shifted their focus away from grander 'public interest' principles towards reacting to public opinion demands (Garland 2001).

Police media units (PMUs) and public relations departments play an important role in reacting to and shaping these public opinion objectives. For example, one of the most important roles NSW Police Force PMU staff saw themselves playing was that of promoters of positive police images, and the relationship with the media was naturally instrumental in distributing such messages. As one PMU staffer mentioned, it was important that they gave positive messages to the media:

> We have to get a certain message out to the media to focus the message we're giving to the media on the positives of what the police are doing ... I think in the higher ranks and especially in the executive positions, the officers upstairs understand the importance of the media and having them onside and getting information out that they need to and that it can be used as a positive tool.
>
> *(PMU Staffer 5)*

Another former staffer noted that the PMU was a vital element in ensuring the police, and significantly the Police Commissioner, continued to be represented in a positive light despite negative press:

> There was a very public campaign of criticism of what [the Police Commissioner] was doing, so my main job was to try to break through, to pierce the veil of that criticism to make sure that the Police Commissioner was still being seen in a positive way. It was up to me to make sure that I tried to do that.
>
> *(Ex-PMU/Other 2)*

Attempts at disseminating positive stories and images of policing are not, however, the sole territory of police media units – not at least without broader institutional support. The London MPS has championed something they call 'the Good News Box'. As they put it:

> Despite the considerable amount of proactive work undertaken by the DPA[3] and the MPS generally there are still many items of good news that are not reaching colleagues within the Service or – through the media – the wider public. To enhance the gathering of positive news, for both an internal and external audience, an e-mail account with the internal address GoodNews@MPS has been set up. All MPS staff are encouraged to e-mail details of good news that they consider warrant publicity. DPA will assess this information and pass it to the relevant member of our staff to pursue – for instance, one of the Area Press and Publicity Officers or The Job newspaper. The Good News Box is designed to capture positive news and stories that may otherwise go unreported. Most boroughs and MPS departments already liaise

with their relevant press office or DPA unit and pass on positive results and the Good News Box is designed to be an additional line of communication, not a replacement.

(MPS 2011)

Here police officers themselves are to be responsibilized with the aim of producing positive stories. Effective media relations also entail effective relationships within the organization.

Journalists are aware that the police and their media units try to utilize them in getting these positive messages out to the public:

> It is always in their interest to publicize police and make them look good, so if there's been a particularly good arrest or something, they're going to want the whole world to know, because it's important for them […] that the perception of crime, not in a twisted propaganda like way, but they want people to know that police are dealing with things out there … And that's what the Police Media Unit does.
>
> *(Journalist 13)*

Not that it has necessarily stopped journalists from also reporting on contentious matters. Perhaps for this journalist, as Savage and Tiffen (2007: 83) see it, the 'bank of goodwill' built up by reporting the positive stories helped to overcome the pressures faced by only focusing on the bad:

> I found myself looking at a new tactic, and that was to get a call with the offer of a good police story. It might be small, it might be medium sized, on an exclusive sort of basis, you know, 'oh the Commissioner's doing this this week, you know, we'll let you go in and do it, you know, this is all good, it's positive it's worthwhile' and all that. And I was happy to do that, so I'd go and write those and I'd write my next negative story as well. So, you know, I think they pretty quickly realise they might be able to get among the good stories, but they were still going to get the bad ones too.
>
> *(Journalist 5)*

And again, the importance of the Commissioner's image was important: 'Everything that comes through has to look good for the Commissioner and the police department' (Journalist 1).

Many journalists, however, feel there are hidden agendas behind the police's provision of positive policing stories to the media, agendas beyond simply assisting the police themselves to look good: 'There's a certain spin on things, and it's the job of the Media Unit to enhance the corporate image of the police force. And anything that reflects badly on it, it's not going to get a run. There is a distinct lack of candour' (Journalist 2).

The importance was in recognising that agenda:

> You've got to keep in mind though that this sort of information is part of an agenda, which may be to create generally a good news story for the police, it may be a story that shows that they're being, you know, tough on crime. It might be a story that shows that the Commissioner was taking a hard line in respect to something. It may be a critic of the police is cast in a bad light, it may be any number of things. But it's got a hidden agenda, and the problem with that is sometimes those stories make good stories, but you get the effect whereby these stories are being spoon fed and you know, I suppose it's open to the idea that this is spin.
>
> *(Journalist 5)*

The logic of image management for policing agencies could be simply seen as the use of spin. The police image is certainly fundamental to the exercise of police power; however, it is also important for both the organization and the public that the image of the police is positive. As Yim and Schafer (2009) have demonstrated, even job satisfaction for police officers is linked to their perceived self-image. Moreover, lack of public trust and subsequent lack of public cooperation with the police is likely to significantly hamper any policing efforts (Tyler 2006). This brings us to the third and final logic of police engagement with the media.

Trust in and legitimacy of the police organization

Our final logic of engagement with the media intersects closely with the previous two. A 'public confidence agenda' has come to be a key element of modern policing in many jurisdictions – indeed from 2009 the UK Home Office made public confidence *the* key indicator of police performance (Mawby 2010a).[4] Similarly, in 2010 a new customer service charter, informed partly by a public satisfaction agenda, was implement by the NSW Police Force (Burn 2010). As Fleming and McLaughlin note:

> In Australia, where eight police jurisdictions manage their citizens in their own way, there is still common ground to be identified in an ongoing concern with customer service, the need to engender and improve public confidence, particularly in 'hard to reach groups', to identify security concerns, and to build trust. And this when public opinion surveys across the country consistently report high levels of support for and confidence in police.
>
> *(Fleming and McLaughlin 2010: 200)*

For policing agencies concepts such as satisfaction, public confidence and legitimacy have become normative. By normative we refer to two elements. One, as we have seen, they have become accepted as goals for many policing organizations. Two, they have become concepts which are measurable and measured. Increasingly time series data are available on such measures for specific policing organizations and accepted levels of these concepts have developed. Moreover, while such concepts have been discussed in policing historically, and more generally in political science, they have now been ascribed empirical justification from an organizational and academic perspective.

A range of concepts and interrelated theories have recently been developed to help explain and analyse public perceptions of criminal justice agencies in general and the police in particular. Such concepts are often spoken about as measures of legitimacy, trust, satisfaction or confidence in justice.[5] It is worth noting that quantifiable measures of these concepts emerge as part and parcel of the late twentieth-century predilection for key performance indicators, reform agendas and the proliferation of public opinion polling. It is also fair to say that there is some conceptual confusion around many of these ideas (Bottoms and Tankebe 2012); nonetheless, researchers have attempted to identify and disentangle the component conceptual elements of these

(Bradford and Jackson 2010). While the idea of public confidence in policing is something of an umbrella term rather than a specific concept, we see the concepts of *legitimacy* and *trust* and their interrelationship with *compliance with the law* particularly pertinent to the police media agenda. These concepts are central to understanding the motivations of police media work.

Legitimacy

To be effective, policing requires the ongoing support, consent and voluntary cooperation of the public. Such public support and cooperation rests upon the police organization and the power it exercises being perceived as legitimate (Tyler 2006; Sunshine and Tyler 2003). Social scientists have generally looked to Weber as the starting point from which to study the question of legitimacy. Beetham (1991), however, has noted that we need to take analytical care with Weber's (1964) key insight that power is legitimate when those exercising it and subject to it believe it to be so based on accepted laws and customs; that is, legitimacy is seen as essentially equivalent to a public belief in legitimacy. This we might call an *empirical* legitimacy (Bradford and Jackson 2010). However, in expanding on Weber's characterization, Beetham (1991) adds that legitimacy should also be understood as the legal validity of both the acquisition and exercise of power and the justifiability of the rules governing a power relationship in terms of the beliefs and values current in the given society. Such a refiguring of the concept implies a *normative* element where a measurable objective external standard might be met. Thus the concept is often measured by the extent to which citizens are willing to defer to authority. In this sense legitimation fosters an obligation to comply with the law and obey authority because it is the *right thing to do* (Bradford and Jackson 2010). One may not necessarily agree with a particular law yet one will still feel an obligation to abide by it.

Bottoms and Tankebe (2012) have recently drawn attention to the *dialogic* nature of legitimacy. They suggest there are two interrelated dimensions of legitimacy: *power-holder legitimacy* and *audience legitimacy*. They also note that the criminological research agenda has focused almost exclusively on *audience legitimacy*. Both are important, as we will see in later chapters. As Barker (2001: 35) puts it:

[w]hen rulers legitimate themselves, they give an account of who they are, in writing, in images … The action creates and expresses the identity. The identity at one and the same time legitimates the person, and is confirmed by the person's manner of expressing it.

Attempts at securing *audience legitimacy* then are something of an extension of expressions of *power-holder legitimacy*. They are two sides of the same coin and both rely on positive image management.

Trust

While institutional legitimacy is seen to be important for maintaining public consent for policing, a second-order interrelated concept, trust, has been used to explain the public's willingness to approach police, report crime and assist in policing agendas. Trust is fostered, according to Bradford and Jackson (2010), where there is: (1) effectiveness to address the crime problem; (2) fairness in police citizen encounters; and (3) a demonstrated moral alignment between police and community, and officer and individual. Trust then captures perceptions of procedural and distributive fairness, including the beliefs that officials can be trusted to act in one's interests and that officers have appropriate motives and competencies (Tyler 2006). Trust simplifies risky situations and encounters brought about by the freedom and discretion of the various ways an officer might act (Jackson et al. 2011). It is argued that the development of such trust can subsequently also lead to a police organization being granted legitimacy by those it governs. As Murphy et al. (2008: 16) also argue, '[p]olicing by consent encourages public trust in police, which thereby facilitates an ongoing interchange of information between the public and the police and voluntary compliance with the law' (see also Skogan 2006).

Compliance with the law

Legitimacy and trust in turn increase compliance with the law and cooperation with authorities (Tyler 2006). Hinds and Murphy (2007: 35) suggest '… people are more likely to assist police when they perceive police are treating the public with procedural justice' (see also

Hinds 2009). Using a normative/moral values model of criminal social regulation, Hough et al. (2010) suggest procedural and distributive fairness and the perception that police are effectively fighting crime leads to a sense of trust in both the interpersonal relationships between individuals and police officers on the one hand, and with a police organization on the other – although these are conceptually and empirically different and might not necessarily coexist.

There is some debate in the international literature as to whether police/citizen encounters can result in any significant increase in citizen trust (cf. Bradford et al. 2009; Indermaur and Roberts 2009; Skogan 2006; Tyler 2006). However, Hohl et al. (2010) argue that police-initiated leaflet information campaigns can positively affect public trust. Whatever the case, the weight of evidence suggests citizens that have the greatest satisfaction with the police are those who have no direct contact with them (Bradford et al. 2009) and form their opinions from information they acquire elsewhere. This mirrors much of the literature that states that most people gain their knowledge of the criminal justice system, not through personal experience or interaction, but through other media (Marsh and Melville 2009; Mason 2003). Boda and Szabó (2011) recently found that while exposure to 'reality' crime television and tabloid media could increase fear of crime and punitive attitudes, it also had the surprising effect of increasing trust in the police. This is supported by our own research discussed in Chapter 6. In this case, it is hardly a surprising supposition that policing organizations may be well served to have a robust and proactive communications apparatus available to them, particularly as such communications units can potentially bypass the sometimes problematic nature of direct police/citizen encounters.

As the above discussion suggests, the logics of trust and legitimacy is now supported and reinforced by a growing body of academic literature that progressive policing agencies actively deploy. The NSW Media Unit Director articulates the importance of the logics of trust and legitimacy for a range of audiences:

> We're here for operational police and the community so it's providing that flow of information in an efficient, quick way that works best for all so if the policeman in the field sees us

doing that well they'll have confidence in us and if the media see us doing that well they'll also have confidence.

(NSW Police PR Respondent 3)

His comments reflect the desire to secure the trust both of peers in the organization as well as the media and public.

In Victoria corporate reputation was similarly equated with gaining the confidence of the public. This was to be achieved though targeted measures:

> [It] … comes back to our general reputation and public confidence and that's something which at the moment we're really trying to attack through our proactive area. And we've got a particular project running at the moment called engaging the community where we have identified where public confidence is lowest geographically against certain crime trends.
>
> *(Vic. Police PR Respondent 1)*

WA respondents were more likely to couch reputation in a discourse of professional integrity. As they put it:

> We want to make sure that the community can relax and feel safe in the knowledge that this is a professional investigation that's being done thoroughly and properly and they don't have to worry, or they can sleep at night knowing there's somebody guarding the walls for them, and the big thing is enhancing … not enhancing but protecting the integrity of the Police Service itself and its professionalism.
>
> *(WA Police PR Respondent 1)*

They also articulated the challenge they face in attempting to balance a reputation as open and transparent alongside the needs and requirements of operational policing:

> Oh from our point of view here, our priority is to maintain public confidence in the police force, or police service 'cause once you start losing that then you end up with controversy

and Royal Commissions into corruption and all that, so we're so open about just about everything. If we've got internal affairs investigations we tell the media about it; if a police officer gets charged with an offence we make a point of making a media release about that. We don't hide … the only things we actually keep from the media are sensitive ongoing operations that might tip off the criminal element that the police are investigating. So there are obviously sensitive operations, but even a homicide investigation, the media will be right across it and pushing for information all the time, so we have to withhold; we can't tell you that yet because we don't want the suspect to know. So anything that's out there is stuff we want out there.

(WA Police PR Respondent 1)

So here we get the sense that the trust/legitimacy agenda, and an accompanying 'openness', can guard against reform agendas by conferring legitimacy on the organization. This also reaffirms Mawby's (2002a) claim that defence against unwanted reform agendas can be an important driver of the emphasis of police media work.

NSW respondents were also quick to point out that communicating the odd negative story, particularly when a police officer has been charged with an offence, was important in terms of maintaining reputation:

… if a police officer is charged with an offence [w]e have a policy now to ensure transparency, to ensure that the public doesn't think police, that no police officer thinks they're above the law, and that the public don't think the police think that as well. We put that out as a proactive media release as soon as we become aware of it and yeah, that's a negative story that we're proactively pushing out there but that's important that we are transparent and showing that we have no hesitation in charging our own officers.

(NSW Police PR Respondent 3)

Victorian respondents also noted the challenge of managing corporate reputation against the dissemination of 'bad news':

Issues where Victoria Police might have stuffed something up or the media are onto a particularly bad story about something Victoria Police have done, and trying to manage that in order for us to come out looking as good as we can. Not to say we're spinning it, but acknowledging mistakes where it's appropriate and informing the media and therefore the community about what we're doing to address and improve systems and not make the same mistakes again.

(Vic. Police PR Respondent 1)

Overall our examples indicate the fine line in maintaining trust between police and the media – and by extension the trust of the public. In particular this involves the careful protection and cultivation of a trusted corporate reputation – fostering this trust could, drawing on the above conceptual framework, provide something akin to the protection of organizational legitimacy. Without this, the concern for police often is that the message might not get through. Thus the logic of trust in and legitimacy of the police organization overlaps with our first two logics.

Conclusion

Policing organizations have to engage the media; they always have and always will. None of the logics of this engagement are necessarily novel. Police have always been risk communicators, image has consistently been important to policing, and the trust of the public and public legitimacy being conferred to policing organizations is vital to effective policing. However, in today's multi-mediated society, where diverse publics interact in differing ways with policing organizations, police engagement with the media has become more formalized, more professional and perhaps more important to effective policing.

Image management is spin, it is pure public relations and it is about the exercise of power. As the police are expert knowledge brokers in relation to law and order issues, the exercise of power is an inevitable element of policing. However, to suggest policing organizations should not engage the media, or should refrain from image management, would be to the detriment of both the police and the public. The question is not whether they should engage, but rather whether policing organizations can actually live up to the positive images they seek to disseminate.

Notes

1. For example, the most recent Australian Productivity Commission report suggests between 60 and 70 per cent of respondents (depending on state jurisdiction) were 'satisfied' or 'very satisfied' with police performance (Steering Committee for the Review of Government Service Provision 2011). Likewise, in the UK the Institute of Customer Service (2011) found that 67 per cent of people were satisfied with their local police service.
2. Mawby (2002a: 1) describes image work as 'all the activities in which police forces engage and which project the meaning of policing'.
3. Department of Public Affairs.
4. Although it appears this agenda is being reconsidered under the policy direction of Britain's current coalition government.
5. See Bradford and Jackson (2010) for such a review.

3

'SIMULATED POLICING'

Framing contemporary police media work

Introduction

The previous chapter explored the overlapping logics that inform police interactions with the media. We argued that while there is an overarching logic of the dissemination of information to the public, within this three key logics could be empirically identified: risk management and responsibilization, image management, and assuring trust in and the legitimacy of the organization. Further, we suggested that these logics, while not necessarily new, had emerged as key platforms of policing in today's multi-mediated society.

In addition, the first two chapters also outlined the symbolic function of policing and discussed how the management of image and reputation has always been of central importance to policing organizations. As Reiner has also noted, '[t]he role of the police … was always more important for its dramaturgical function, symbolizing social order, than for any instrumental effects in successfully controlling crime' (Reiner 2008: 691). Yet, to suggest that crime control or operational policing can easily be separated from the symbolic function of policing would to overlook a basic fact – the two are intimately linked. While this is not new, in the early twenty-first century this has become even more central to policing. As we have illustrated, police public relations have played an increasingly important part in police 'image work'. Beyond this function, however, we suggest it also plays an increasingly important part in crime control and operational policing objectives in and of themselves.

Indeed, police public relations professionals now see themselves as an integral part of operational policing. Despite this, in many policing organizations the relationship between operational police and the newly professionalized police public relations personnel has been strained at best. Operational police have traditionally been suspicious of these newcomers, these outsiders, and in some cases believed them to be political appointments aimed at 'containing' the political fall-out from policing activities, or worse, mouthpieces of the government of the day. These new public relations professionals have, however, endeavoured to try and campaign internally, working to legitimate their own positions by arguing that their activities, rather than being public relations 'spin', have much to offer operational police work. This development will form an integral part of our discussion in this chapter.

Moreover, this chapter explores and develops a range of theoretical frameworks that allow us to conceptualize contemporary police, media and public relations analytically. As we will argue, public relations and image work are now no longer bounded by the limits of the traditional mass media. Rather, contemporary information technologies and the emergence of social media have created a new landscape in which policing takes place, and opened up a range of possibilities for both image work and operational policing. We explore this by proposing a framework that uses the concept of simulated policing in the context of the viewer society and contemporary cultures of control. We conclude the chapter by examining the converse of these new opportunities and cultures of control. We suggest that this new mediatized policing has also opened up increasing spaces for resistance and we outline a conceptual framework for understanding these.

The viewer society

Criminology has a long history of researching and discussing policing cultures (Chan 1997; Waddington 1999a), images and popular media representations of policing (Manning 2003; Reiner 2003) and the relationships fostered between news journalists and police (Freckelton 1988; Mawby 2002a; 2010; Surette 2001). However, the place of the police as 'knowledge brokers' (Ericson and Haggerty 1997) within media discourse and public representation has, for the past decade or so, been going through a significant transformation. The changes to which we refer are not simply a rebirth of police media relationships: that change began in the 1980s with the development of profession-alized police media and public relation units, as we have demon-strated in the preceding chapters (also see McGovern and Lee 2010). Rather, we are experiencing a period where police–media–public relationships have become liquid, continually shifting, folding in on themselves – policing, news and popular culture are colliding, feed-ing off one another, being reproduced and re-presented in ways Baudrillard (1983) could have only imagined thirty years ago. Today Scotland Yard employs ex News Corporation staff to manage their media profile; (supposedly) routine policing becomes reality televi-sion entertainment; and police organizations are popular Twitter and Facebook friends. To cite Ferrell et al. (2008: 81), criminology needs to make sense of the 'blurred line between the real and the virtual' where 'mediated processes of cultural reproduction constitute the experience of crime, self and society under conditions of late moder-nity'. Policing has become hyperreal.

In our contemporary world image is paramount; we soak in images. And while image has always been important for the legiti-mation of policing organizations (Emsley 1983; Mawby 2002a; Reiner 2010) there is now a significant difference in the ways in which images are produced and circulated (Manning 1999). Three recent developments in policing strategies are illustrative of these changes:

1. Police engagement with social media – Twitter, Facebook, YouTube and blogs.
2. Increasing police engagement with reality television – so called 'ob docs' or 'observational documentaries'.
3. The introduction of police 'multi-media units' or what are essentially in-house television production facilities.

In many ways this expansion is not so surprising (Lee and McGovern 2012; Mawby 2002a; McGovern and Lee 2010). After all, police agencies have come under increasing observation from a population and media hungry for stories and information about crime, and a 24-hour media cycle desperate for images, stories and print. When we factor in the growth of the Internet and other communication technologies we would argue that the police are perhaps the most watched organization in the world, in a panoptic/synoptic relationship; that is, while the few watch the many, the many also watch the few (Mathiesen 1997). It is not just the size of the expansion of the police public relations apparatus that is significant; it is also its form.

While the managerialist turn in policing that began in the 1980s is central to understanding some of these changes (Loader and Mulcahy 2003), so too is the way in which these organizations themselves have become subject to increasing public visibility. It could be argued that there is something of a dialectic relationship between police organizations using the media to promote policing, and the media and public wanting to produce and consume images of policing. In the UK Mawby (2002a) has highlighted how this increased 'police visibility' developed hand-in-hand with a new push to manage 'policing images'. He suggests that the contemporary multi-mediated environment in which policing takes place constitutes an example of Mathiesen's (1997) 'synopticon'. According to Mathiesen, the synoptic gaze is reciprocal to Foucault's concept of the panopticon; the synopticon is where the many watch the few (also see Welch 2011). Mathiesen's argument is that panoptic and synoptic dynamics operate simultaneously in the 'viewer society':

> The many see and contemplate the few, so that the tendency for the few to see and supervise the many is contextualized by a significant counterpart... the total system of the modern mass media. Corresponding to panopticism, imbued with certain basic parallels in structure, vested with certain reciprocal supplementary functions ... and merged with panopticism through a common technology ... it is possible to say that not only panopticism, but also *synopticism* characterises our society.
>
> *(Mathiesen 1997: 219)*

While Mathiesen's concept referred mainly to the role of the mass media and was, as Doyle (2011) has argued, somewhat top-down and instrumental, we expand the notion to include the public gaze that can operate through social media and other avenues that circumvent the traditional mass media. So, ironically, as policing has developed increasingly sophisticated modes of surveilling the public, 'the police service has become one of the most watched institutions in our contemporary society' (Mawby 2002a: 37).

The reasons for this increasing visibility are many and varied; police are a valuable and reliable source of stories for media outlets; police stories are popular with media consumers; police 'reality' television programs can be made relatively cheaply; new managerialist public accountability measures require public visibility as part of customer satisfaction measures; and police organizations need media coverage and public cooperation to police effectively (e.g. see Innes 1999). All this has created a context whereby regulation and control can occur not just through the panoptic gaze, but reciprocally, through the synoptic gaze where 'appropriate' behaviours are performed and or displayed to the many by the few.

Doyle (2006) alerts us to the ideological nature of televised police images. In terms of the synoptic gaze, we can see these ideologies play out on a regulatory continuum from discipline to control and from institution to public and back. Doyle's example of a roadside traffic stop by a police officer perfectly illustrates our point:

> Now consider how the social situation would change if such a police traffic stop were to be captured by a TV camera and broadcast to a wide television audience ... [...] the police officer's behaviour might be affected, the officer may start playing to the camera, for example, letting the driver go with a warning lecture that is also aimed at the TV audience, or, alternatively, deciding to 'throw the book' at the driver, given the high profile of the situation. As well, the experience would almost certainly be altered for the driver herself. For example, she might experience the traffic stop as much more punitive because of the shaming effect of TV... [...] Furthermore, if such police traffic stops were televised on a regular basis, this

might lead to wider changes, changes beyond those particular situations that are broadcast. Indeed, the standard operating procedures for conducting traffic stops might well change, given that they would have become high profile events. And the televising of traffic stops might also lead to wider changes in how traffic policing was institutionally organized. For example, more political attention, more resources, and more expertise might be committed to policing speeding drivers. Finally, the television audience might become players themselves in new ways in the new social situations that were created. For example, viewers might be able to phone a hotline to turn in speeders to a TV program.

(Doyle 2003: 6–7)

Doyle's point is that the camera, the TV and the viewing assemblage not only produce a representation of this situation; their presence and the process has the potential to change the behaviours of all involved; from the practices of individual viewers, to actors in the scene, to procedures involved in policing, and through the broader social body. Doyle also draws on Altheide and Snow's (1979) notion of 'media logics', which suggest that institutions actively reshape themselves to fit media needs. In a general sense there is little doubt policing organizations have been reshaped in this way. However, we would argue that in the contemporary multi-mediated world new communications technologies, the World Wide Web and social media create a much more diffuse and dispersed relationship between institutions, the media and the public. As such, a much broader conceptualization of both 'media logics', and the 'viewer society' in which such logics might play out is required. Institutions are not bounded by the constraints of the old mass media *per-se*, and as such institutional change as a result of media logics could be conceptualized as a much less direct and instrumental process than might be suggested by Altheide and Snow, writing in 1979.

As their media activities highlight, today's policing extends beyond the bounds of having more visible police on the beat or more direct police–citizen encounters. Indeed, police media work has become one of the primary ways through which police organizations are able to communicate to the public about the work that they do. While television is one way in which the police are harnessing the traditional media to do this, other forms of media are similarly important in communicating the work of the police to the public. For example, new media strategies, via social networking sites, are being deployed, aimed at delivering information in a range of new ways:

> The community always says they want more police and want to see more police, etcetera. But visibility doesn't have to actually be a physical presence. You can be visible in other ways … So out of that … and I distinctly remember, we were talking, I think, about Facebook or something. You know, we could improve our Internet site; we could do … 'You could do YouTube.' That's right. And then somebody mentioned, 'What about Twitter?' And nobody had heard of Twitter, at that stage.
>
> *(NSW Police PR Respondent 4)*

In today's expanded and more diffuse 'viewer society' there are increased opportunities to promote a particular public image for police institutions. There are thus greater opportunities for control, regulation and responsibilization. However, such developments also come with dangers for police organizations. Being subject to the synoptic gaze will inevitably bring with it forms of resistance, public scrutiny and change. Even the minor exercise of police discretion can be subject to synoptic facilitated criticism. The 'viewer society' is, then, a double-edged sword for policing. Police organizations can, and indeed need, to put themselves on display, but in doing so open themselves up to potential criticism and resistance.

Cultures of control

Conceptually, our framework seeks not only to account for the context of mediatized policing in a broadly conceived 'viewer society'; we also need to be able to account for the scope and socio-cultural context of institutional attempts to control both the content and flows of information from police to public and back. David Garland (1996, 2001) has outlined what he refers to as the sometimes contradictory 'cultures of control' that emerged through the 1980s and 1990s. We believe it is possible to theorize contemporary police, media and public relations with regard to these emergent 'programmes of crime control' and within the broader context of the 'viewer society'. Garland refers to the two key emerging 'cultures of control' as *the criminologies of everyday life* (incorporating the *criminologies of the self*) and the *criminologies of the other*. These, he broadly suggests, were responses to the crisis in penal modernism and the normalization of high rates of offending towards the end of the twentieth century.

Looking at these more closely, the *criminologies of the everyday life* refer to a complex array of responsibilizing and partnership strategies that seek to produce active citizens who subsequently govern the self and can thus be 'governed at a distance'. As Garland (1996: 452) argues, in regard to the criminologies of everyday life:

> ... key phrases are terms such as 'partnership', 'inter-agency co-operation', 'the multi-agency approach', 'activating communities', creating 'active citizens', 'help for self-help'. Its primary concern is to devolve responsibility for crime prevention on to agencies, organizations and individuals which are quite outside the state and to persuade them to act appropriately.

Such criminologies are optimized in programmes and strategies as diverse as Neighbourhood Watch and private crime audits – indeed many of the key components of community problem-solving policing. They are exemplified in such examples as insurance policies that make reporting property crime to the police a prerequisite for insurance coverage. They are signified in the move from policing agencies that once trumpeted their capacity to 'serve and protect' to those, like the contemporary NSW Police Force, that provide a 'safer community' 'with your help' (NSW Police Force 2009). This suggests a shift towards less intervention with a more limited role for the state as citizens take on the role of crime prevention and risk reduction – *the criminologies of the self* where we all become our own criminologist.

Most significantly for the discussion here, these criminologies require information networks through which risks and responsibilities can be communicated, passed on, identified and avoided or guarded against (Ericson and Haggerty 1997). They require avenues of risk communication between agencies as well as the production of specific discourses about crime aimed at activating these partnerships and self-governing prudential subjects (Lee 2007; O'Malley 2010). We see it as no great accident then that the professionalization of police public relations generally, and the emergence of police media and public affairs departments specifically, began to appear historically – at least in their current and more sophisticated and professional form – towards the end of the 1980s. They take shape at a time when strategies of responsibilization also began to emerge as a then unrealized or incomplete governmental programme. At the same time as these departments emerged, police became more active crime prevention advisers, managing and defining risk. This role reflects Garland's (2001) idea that policing organizations moved away from placing an emphasis on their role as crime fighters, preferring instead to assess their performance through internally focused endeavours.

For Garland, these forms of risk governance and responsibilization tactics – cultures of control – are also a response to historically high crime rates in the 1980s. They are in essence an attempt to define down the capacities of policing to be able to reduce crime. As he puts it:

> Modest improvements at the margin, the better management of risks and resources, reduction of the fear of crime, reduction of criminal justice expenditure and greater support for crime's victims ... become the less than heroic policy objectives which increasingly replace the idea of winning a 'war against crime'.
>
> *(Garland 1996: 448)*

It is not just the police facing such circumstances, however. Criminal justice agencies more broadly have had to 'adapt to failure'. They adapt to the notion that these 'historically high' recorded rates of crime are difficult to shift, that clear up rates are low and workloads are high and that community trust in policing is, at best, tenuous.

Garland (1996) suggested this ushered in a new set of managerialist strategies aimed at making organizations more efficient and 'customer focused'. Such responses to systemic overload and failure have seen the introduction of new strategies of system integration and monitoring, seeking a level of process and information management that was somehow seen as lacking (Garland 1996: 455).

And while organizations might be managed more like budget-conscious businesses, they are required to adhere to stricter reporting mechanisms and to meet a new range of key performance indicators (KPIs). Garland sees this as attempting a 'taming of the system'; it indicates the desire for orderliness, control, the management of risks, the imposing of administrative controls and regimes of regulation and monitoring. Such taming has increasingly impacted upon late modern policing organizations and the ways in which they operate (Garland 2001). Professionalized police media departments can be seen as a manifestation of the governmental project to 'tame the system', whereby they function in such a way as to filter, manage and tame information flows. Public relations is itself also 'tamed' by administrative and managerial oversight, media policies and guidelines, and political demands.

This 'taming of the system' again requires lines of communication for information, and new strategies of bureaucratic management, to pass information to, from and within the police organization. The public must be made aware of the 'successes' of policing.[1] Moreover, as consumers, citizens provide both feedback on satisfaction with the agency[2] and data on meeting its KPIs. For example, many police websites proudly display performance indicators for Police Assistance Lines, showing the average length of time in answering calls, the total number of calls answered and the percentage of calls answered in 27 seconds or less, the latter being a performance indicator for the grade of service signifying both police responsiveness to the public and bureaucratic efficiency. One of the consequences of this is that many police organizations are now 'increasingly subject to state-imposed standards and guidelines, and are closely monitored and inspected to ensure they comply' with these reduced mission statements (Chan 1999; Garland 2001: 120). In NSW this has, for example, entailed meeting the performance indicators set out in a State

Plan (2011), which include a 15 per cent reduction in property crime by 2015. In this way, government essentially increases its strategic management of the agency through a range of structural and managerialist changes.[3]

The expansion of communicative technologies itself also impacts the policing organization. Media policy, for example, limits who is able to say what, when, and to whom. As Ericson and Haggerty (1997: 388) put it:

> ... communication technologies also radically alter the structure of police organizations by levelling hierarchies, blurring traditional divisions of labour, dispersing supervisory capacities, and limiting individual discretion. In the process, traditional rank structures of command and control are displaced by system surveillance mechanisms for regulating police conduct.

Public relations and media offices are demonstrably part of this expansion in managerialist and communication technologies just as they obviously have a role in communicating 'successes' to the public.

Yet at the same time as these new rationalities of governing crime have developed and, as we have argued, professionalized police public relations have developed along with them, we have seen a ramping up in the punitive rhetoric and actions of governments. There has been, for example, a continual emphasis on 'tough on crime' credentials (Hogg and Brown 1998; Weatherburn 2004). These 'law and order' policies often involve a 'cynical manipulation of the symbols of state power and of the emotions of fear and insecurity which give these symbols their potency' (Garland 1996: 460–1). These are the *criminologies of the other*. By the criminologies of the other Garland refers to criminologies that engage in images of the 'other'; the marginalized, the criminalized, the feared. Emotion, rather than careful analysis, is evoked. It is a politicized discourse of the unconscious (see also Douglas 1992).

Yet these contradictions in crime control provide no great impediment to police public relations work that can both enlist citizens as 'partners' in crime control at the same time as they reinforce the tough crime-fighting credentials of police organizations. Using the cultures of control thesis then allows us to analyse the exercise of power both internally and externally of policing organizations, and has the capacity to let us see the role of police public relations and mediatized policing more generally in this assemblage. We must, however, refrain from seeing these control strategies in too instrumental a fashion. As our own research has indicated, the practices that constitute these strategies are often ad hoc, misjudged, unplanned, ill-conceived, underfunded and contingent. So while we might be able to identify cultures of control at the broad sociological level – and we think we can – we would also expect many examples of police–media–public interactions that run counter to, resist and confound such cultures.

Moreover, while Garland's thesis indicates a paring back of state police responsibilities, we accept this characterization with some caution. It is also possible to conceive of an operational policing that is changing form, adapting to mediatized contexts, rather than folding back with the neo-liberal state – and we're not just taking about the more punitive inclinations of the criminologies of the other here. Rather, operational policing is finding new spaces of expression, and as we argue throughout this book, becoming networked, virtual and perhaps more far reaching. We would suggest this is more than Garland's *criminologies of everyday life* might have indicated. Yes, it is governing at a distance, but it is more than that. The 'distance' has collapsed; it's policing but not as we know it. This is simulated policing, which we see in the context of an increasingly 'viewer [based] society' and contemporary, if contingent, 'cultures of control'.

Simulated policing

Pat O'Malley (2010) has outlined what he argues are new forms of 'simulated justice', which include 'simulated governance' and 'simulated policing'. Simulated justice, he notes, is the space where the real and the virtual converge, as we explain below. Further, he argues that there are two varieties of simulated justice: the 'hard' and the 'soft'. The 'hard' zone is illustrated in forms of risk-based actuarial justice, offender profiles, electronic anklets and the like. It tends to be directed at those 'dividuals', drawing from Deleuze (1995), labelled as difficult to govern. The 'soft' zone of simulated justice for O'Malley tends to be a monetized justice, aimed at those who have proven themselves governable. For example, the traffic fine seeks to govern those who opt into a traffic licensing system – and are thus governed through their freedoms. At various times individuals will morph from one zone to the other and back, particularly if they refuse or resist simulated governance (O'Malley 2010: 805–6).

Soft 'simulated justice' is a form of governance operating at the level of 'the bar code reader at the supermarket, the freeway, the passport gate, the ATM, the baggage carousel, [which] all exist to govern and police without touch, and thus to maximize good – desired – circulation and interfere only with "bad" circulation' (O'Malley 2010: 796–7). Such policing indeed governs-at-a-distance. It '… governs distributions and complements individual discipline' and 'simultaneously expands the reach of policing while at the same time reducing its unit cost and visibility, and minimizing the friction imposed upon "good" circulations' (O'Malley 2010: 797). He notes how this policing focuses on 'dividuals' and its almost infinite potential for the expansion of depersonalized, anonymous and remotely administered policing and justice (O'Malley 2010: 801). While O'Malley alludes to, but does not expand upon, other forms of 'soft simulated policing or justice', we wish to extend this notion through the concept of 'simulated policing'.

Quite obviously the mediatized policing techniques to which we refer here are quite different in nature to those outlined by O'Malley. We are not looking at a growth in 'telemetric' policing, or indeed a reduction in the 'visibility' of policing – quite the opposite in some cases. Instead, we want to identify a simulated form of policing that we believe has grown in chorus and which complements the simulated processes and strategies outlined by O'Malley. We can see these operating in the cultural realm, a space not explored by O'Malley. Moreover, like the policing processes outlined by O'Malley, the techniques we wish to identify also rely on a swathe of new technologies.

The simulated policing to which we refer means a number of things but first and foremost it refers to the fact that policing is increasingly

occurring at the level of the policing image, through simulated representations of policing. While, as noted above, the Peelian model of
policing has always relied on the image and representation of policing
to legitimate the institution of the police (Emsley 1983; Reiner 2010),
the difference is that now the representation of policing *is* policing –
or at least a simulation or simulacra of traditional policing. The image
not only represents policing, but increasingly the images of policing
and actual operational policing are inseparable – they are, for all
intents and purposes, the same thing. Rather, policing is occurring
through often disembodied image work, and this image work is also
occurring though policing.

A second point about this version of simulated policing is that
those engaged in its production and reproduction believe in its
authenticity, its operational utility and its capacity to increase confidence in policing and the legitimacy of the police organization.
Public relations professionals are engaged not just in image work or
information dissemination, they are actively working with operational police to identify and apprehend offenders, to deliver public
safety messages and to receive intelligence through their 'networks'.
They are present in cyberspace answering questions, giving advice
and debating. Moreover, they are projecting the police onto our TV
screens so we can watch their work, observe decision-making processes and empathize with the challenges of the job.

Simulated policing is not just about (re)presenting images of
police work, although it does this too. Rather, policing operates
virtually. As such, this simulated policing is more than a cynical
attempt at spin produced by increasingly professional and savvy
public relations units – although it most certainly is this at times.
Instead, it insinuates itself into the public consciousness through an
ever increasing number of virtual media formats. This policing takes
place not on the beat or in the patrol car or even at the police station.
Rather, the policing we identify here occurs in virtual cyberspaces,
on televisual 'observational documentaries' and through the lens of
the police digital video camera as reproduced on the nightly news
bulletin. Yet while these forms of simulated policing rely on a swathe
of new technologies, they are traditional in nature. That is, they
generally seek to achieve traditional goals of public policing such as

the deterrence of crime, social control, compliance with the law and the securing of public consent for policing.

The third point about simulated policing is that it has a potentially unlimited public reach – much as O'Malley (2010) identifies in the soft simulated policing practices to which he refers.

Where traditional public policing is temporally and spatially confined to public spaces and private spaces in particular circumstances, the continuous 24-hour cycle of police shifts and the limitations of staffing levels, simulated policing enters the private and public spheres through the Internet, the television, the phone application, the tablet or the iPad. It is not big brother watching; it is rather more like a continual reminder that police are there on your behalf for the law-abiding, that you can interact with them at any time and that they are doing, 'something', as one police public affairs director told us. Watching, interacting with and being entertained by policing (the synopticon) (Mathiesen 1997) simultaneously operates as a form of bio-power aimed at regulating freedoms (Foucault 1977; Rose 1999).

In this way, we now see policing organizations take new approaches to the way they operationalize interactions with the public. Increasingly, these simulated interactions are being seen as just as important as many of the personal interactions an individual may have with the police. There is an assumption built into this approach that police-public encounters, whether physical or virtual, can be generally positive in building trust. While international research tends to suggest that police encounters with the public have little or negative effects on satisfaction (Skogan 2006), or indeed if they are well handled only minimally positive effects (Bradford et al. 2009), much less is known about how 'virtual' encounters impact on public satisfaction levels. Recent research by Hohl et al. (2010) has shed some light on this question, finding that the police in select areas of London were able to enhance public perceptions of the police, including trust and confidence, by directly communicating with the public through local newsletters. While Hohl et al. (2010) were interested in more traditional methods of communication, their work does reveal something about the importance of the police proactively communicating their activities to an increasingly faceless public.

The divide between operational policing and police media work is collapsing. Policing organizations are putting representations to work for them in ways that not only aim to improve their corporate image, but which seek to increase the legitimacy of the organization, deter potential offenders and increase public compliance and cooperation. This has resulted in the line between policing, the media and popular culture becoming increasingly blurred and fluid.

Strategies, tactics and resistance

As we have flagged in the discussion so far, an increasingly mediatized policing also opens up new sites and possibilities of resistance. Strategies of control that attempt to create some dialogue, some exchange – and simulated policing must do this – create within them the possibilities for their contestation. The work of Michel de Certeau provides a useful framework to understand both the operation of strategies of surveillance and social control, and indeed how tactics of resistance operate in the face of technologies of power. His work provides a number of conceptual tools that can be deployed to understand the expansion, rationalities and strategies of police public relations and indeed resistances to these.

De Certeau argues that any analysis of television representations (to use his example) and of consumers' viewing habits should be complemented by a study of 'what the cultural consumer "makes" or "does" during this time and with the images' (1984: xii). In short, we need to know about the 'ways of using' the products imposed by any dominant social order (1984: xii). That is, as opposed to just knowing what these products *are* and how they are *intended* to be used (understanding their logics or mentalities), we need to assess the complex reality of their *actual* use in practice.

His analysis, drawing on a military metaphor, delineates two sets of actions that should be subject to such analysis: *strategies* and *tactics*. Strategies, he suggests, are 'the calculation or manipulation of power relationships that becomes possible as soon as a subject with will and power … [in our case police public relations organs] can be isolated' (1984: 35–6), that can find a site of power from which to operate as it were. That is, such an entity develops a base from which to operate separating it from its *Other* that it then seeks to manage. In this broad sense all policing, and police media work, entails strategies, strategies that seek to manage, to control and to delineate the parameters of knowledge and discourse about policing and social order. The exercise of power through strategies is bound by its very visibility. Policing requires strategies of visibility: policing must be seen. This is amplified in the case of mediatized and simulated forms of policing.

On the other hand, a tactic, de Certeau suggests, is an art of the weak. The use of tactics are afforded by occasion, and are thus temporal in nature. Where strategies operate over delineated spaces or places of power, and seek only to manage the erosion of time through the security of space, tactics rely on the 'clever utilisation of time, of the opportunities it presents and also of the play it introduces into the foundations of power' (1984: 38–9). In this sense, many of the tactics we assess in the following chapters are momentary, fleeting, yet they use the precise platforms deployed by police strategies.

De Certeau argues that ordinary people frequently reuse opportunities, subverting the rituals and representations that institutions seek to impose. As he puts it, the 'circulation of a representation … [by elites] tells us nothing about what it is for its users. We must first analyse its manipulation by users who are not its makers' (1984: xiii). We must, as he puts it in a sympathetic critique of Foucault, understand what 'popular procedures … manipulate the mechanisms of discipline to conform to them only to evade them …' (1984: xiv). Following de Certeau, then, we must get beyond both panoptic and synoptic readings of power to understand how the dominant representations are manipulated, subverted, resisted, misread and interpreted in everyday life.

As Ericson and Haggerty (2006: 20) note, resistance is generally not 'motivated by desire to eliminate or modify systems, but to evade their grasp'. As such, most resistance 'leaves the surveillance system intact, although resistance can become so widespread that specific surveillance initiatives are withdrawn' (Ericson and Haggerty 2006: 20).

Marx (2003) suggests that there are eleven generic strategies or 'moves' where resistance and subversion can occur in the face of surveillance. These are *switching, distorting, blocking, piggybacking, discovery, avoidance, refusal, masking, breaking, cooperation* and *counter-surveillance*. All could be understood in the context of de Certeau's tactics of the weak. Counter-surveillance, or counterveillance, sousveillance and other forms of resistance can be understood in de Certeau's terms as *tactics* (1984: 36). A tactic must play within the terrain imposed upon it and 'organised by the law of a foreign power' (1984: 37). 'It does not have the means to keep to itself … it is a manoeuvre … within the … enemy's field of vision … and within enemy territory' (1984: 37). So tactics will generally by nature be visible to the system or strategy they seek to resist or subvert.

This is not to suggest that all tactics or forms of resistance are somehow good. Nor would we want to suggest that somehow the expansion of what we might call simulated policing is all bad. This book attempts to avoid such normative judgements. Rather, if we accept Mathiesen's (1997) characterisation of the synopticon, it is clear that policing organizations will have little choice but to play the image games of the viewer society. However, we would want to avoid totalizing judgements about these activities. Coleman and McCahill (2011), for example, draw our attention to the ambiguities of resistance. They give examples of resistance by privileged road users, the conservative press and motoring organizations to speed cameras, and how 'Copwatch'-style sousveillance filming can lead to the police dispensing with the discretion not to charge in favour of the clear application of the law.

What is clear is that tactics of resistance play within the field of power. They are themselves expressions of power, albeit often circumscribed and limited plays. In the viewer society a range of sites for resistance have opened up even where strategies of control seek to limit these. The complexities of contemporary police public relations can only be fully understood by paying close attention to such resistances.

Conclusion

What we might think of as the most watched of institutions, police organizations, are revelling in the virtual and media spotlight and developing new capacities for taking advantage of their capacities as knowledge brokers for crime and justice issues. As the Director of the NSW Police Force Public Affairs Branch put it in relation to the increasing police use of YouTube:

> We put [examples] on YouTube [of] not just our successes but we'll put on these appeals, we've got crime prevention tips and if there's a statement by police to be put out we put it up through that various ways. So YouTube's used – we've got about 108, 109 videos up I think on YouTube at the moment under the police channel website, and I look at the number of views we get – we're into the many thousands of views, it's equivalent of LAPD. It's certainly equivalent of LAPD and rivalling New York in some other ways, and they've been in that space a couple of years longer than us.
>
> *(NSW Police PR Respondent 1)*

Images of policing are no longer simply re-presentations. Policing itself is being altered by its engagement in these virtual fields, these simulations. On one level this is a more democratic model of policing, with constant public feedback and (virtual) interaction – a more 'transparent' model of policing. On the other hand, it demonstrates how the police, as knowledge brokers, have increasing capacities to produce and disseminate preferred narratives and images. It extends the cultures of control even while opening up spaces for resistance, scrutiny and uncertainty. Performance measures are not just based around reductions in crime, or even emergency line waiting times; policing success is also being conceived in terms of the number of Facebook friends, Twitter followers or YouTube views established.

While some traditional news media formats – newspapers in particular – have less resources through which to hold policing agencies to account, the proliferation of media outlets since the 1980s and subsequently the democratization of the World Wide Web has ushered in a reassessment of the way police organizations communicate through the media at both an organizational and technical level. Currently the police–media relationship could be said to:

> ... operate within a framework where the media have less resources and the police have more, but this is balanced by technological media changes that mean the police remain under scrutiny. Albeit this may be a scrutiny that matches our media age in that it can be instant, snapped by protesters and passers-by, rather than accomplished through the work of a well-resourced team of investigative journalists.
>
> *(Mawby 2010a: 136–7)*

Policing has become increasingly mediatized. This mediatization has intensified over the past two decades and even more so with the advent of social media in the early twenty-first century. New techniques and technologies being deployed by policing organizations signal a significant intensification of police engagement with the media and the public. While in many senses these strategies are simply extensions of traditional forms of media and public engagement, and indeed traditional forms of public policing, the examples we discuss in the following chapters all take place in newly emergent virtual and televisual contexts. These are representations of policing that simultaneously *constitute* policing: they are 'simulated policing'. These strategies break down the boundaries between popular culture, policing culture, operational reality and fictional entertainment.

However, such policing is open to resistance, to subversion. In the next three chapters we will discuss these examples of simulated policing in more detail, guided by the frameworks developed here. Following this, the final three chapters of the book will look more closely at practices of resistance.

Notes

1. For example the NSW PMU webpage proudly displays performance indicators for the Police Assistance Line, indicating both the responsiveness of the police to the public and bureaucratic efficiency. These include the average length of time in answering calls, the total number of calls answered and the percentage of calls answered in 27 seconds or less, the latter being a performance indicator for the grade of service – 74 per cent on our most recent viewing, April 2013 (NSW Police Force 2013).

2. For example, NSW Police Force Annual Reports routinely display the latest 'high' results from the National Community Satisfaction with Policing Survey, a 'key indicator in the delivery of policing services' (NSW Police Force 2009: 28). The results are also followed by a disclaimer which states that 'Survey estimates are subject to sample error. Perceptions are influenced by many factors, not necessarily related to police performance' (NSW Police Force 2009: 29).
3. For example, the NSW State Plan features heavily within recent NSW Police Force strategies.

SECTION II

Simulated policing

This section of the book explores three discrete fields of simulated policing drawing on the conceptual framework and policing logics outlined in the preceding chapters. In exploring each of these fields we draw on a range of empirical research projects undertaken by the authors over a ten-year period. While each of these projects focused on police media and public relations in the context of Australian police organizations we also draw on broader research and literature in order to place our examples in an international context.

Chapter 4 explores the ways in which the interface between the police and the media is changing, particularly the changing dynamics of the media release. The information police release to the media (and public) is becoming, perhaps contradictorily, both increasingly controlled and yet more transparent. While the media have access to more information from the police, the mediums through which this information is disseminated have become more sophisticated and targeted.

Chapter 5 discusses the ever more important role of social media in police public relations. In the past four years social media has become a centrepiece of police public relations and is increasingly imploring police organizations to significantly alter the way in which they communicate with the media and the public. The success or failure of the policing of the future may well be predicated on the popularity an organization can achieve on social media.

Chapter 6 explores the emergence and significance of law enforcement reality television. The recent investment in these programmes has not only impacted the viewing habits of consumers, it has also affected the way in which the public have come to understand police activity. Importantly this genre has also provided new opportunities for police organizations to disseminate preferred images of policing to an audience hungry for stories about crime and criminality.

4

POLICING THE PRESS RELEASE

Introduction

Today many police organizations are in a position to release information to the media on a continual basis. Technological advancements to communications systems, among other things, have created new opportunities for the police to control the dissemination of crime-related information. Gone are the days of 'free-to-air' police radio channels, where emergency services communications were openly accessible to anyone with an (albeit illegal) scanner, criminal, journalist and curious citizen alike. Instead, we have ushered in a new standard, whereby outdated analogue technology has been replaced by encrypted digital systems, restricting access to emergency services radios to all but those with official approval.

This chapter deals largely with the ways in which news about crime and justice is sourced, produced and distributed with regard to the changing media and technological landscape, and increasingly media savvy policing organizations. We begin by exploring the nature of the information police organizations release to the media and the actors involved in this process. We then examine how the media receives such information, paying particular attention to the perceptions of journalists involved in these exchanges. Finally, we discuss the increasingly sophisticated ways in which police are able to produce and frame the information they release to the media. As we will demonstrate, while most of the news about crime, justice and policing we read in the daily newspapers or watch on prime time news begins with the humble press release, this is increasingly being coupled with a complex mix of mediums, platforms and multi-media productions, many of which are managed by the police with the express intention of either making it 'easier' for journalists to meet their media imperatives or bypassing journalists altogether.

Policing information

The digital encryption of police, fire and ambulance radios in many jurisdictions has transformed the ways in which journalists are now able to access information about real-time crime incidents.[1] Instead of the traditional practice of journalists monitoring emergency services radios for breaking news and incidents, the current situation in NSW, to take an example, is that 'approved' media representatives are now allocated access to a new system of emergency services monitoring, the Police External Agencies Transfer System (PEATS).[2] On the one hand, systems such as PEATS allow journalists to access significantly more information than would be possible via radio scanners – up to 6,000 incidents a day, much more than any one individual could reasonably keep track of. As the manager of the NSW PMU, who oversees the PEATS system, told us: 'There's, like I said 6,000 jobs going across the CAD[3] system and the PEATS system every day. So there's no end to content I guess for media and getting information out to the public' (NSW Police PR Respondent 3).

On the other hand, this system of information transfer has drawn complaints from journalists sceptical of police motivations in implementing such a system. Of particular concern has been the potential for information to be withheld from journalists, something difficult to achieve over a non-encrypted system. Further, some journalists (e.g. Morri 2010b) have complained that the system provides less detail on individual events, making it more difficult to filter and identify priority news events than was possible in the pre-encrypted police radio era. A number of journalists have even gone so far as to accuse the police of covering up serious crime incidents by using vague or inaccurate descriptors on events logged (Morri 2010a, 2010c; Morri and Jones 2010). In short, journalists with limited resources to sift through the mountains of information delivered by PEATS have argued that the system is information overload, to the benefit of police and detriment of news outlets.

Despite the introduction of new ways in which to impart information to the media, policing organizations still regularly make use of more traditional communications methods in what may be seen as a scattergun approach. This is not to suggest that their processes are chaotic or unmanaged – quite the opposite really. Rather, what we are now seeing is a recognition by police organizations that a range of communications strategies are needed in order to ensure information is received by multiple audiences through different mediums – each audience with different journalistic priorities, interests and practices. One example of a long-established tradition in police communications activities is the broadcast system. These information systems are installed in police media departments, enabling police to notify 'approved' journalists and media outlets of events, stories and police press conferences. In NSW the system is called the 'disseminator', and police media officers use it around twice a day to notify journalists of key events in the state. While this system may seem superfluous, given the range of other communicative options available to police and journalists, it does allow some insight into what the police may see as priority issues of the day. As one journalist put it:

> They have a disseminator which basically is a hotline to every newsroom in Sydney, whether it's radio, TV, print, anything. They can get on it and with one dissemination they can let you know that there's been a significant arrest, something's going on, there's a fire, there's a murder, there's a bridge collapse, there's something happening, the Commissioner's going to say something. So they will use that disseminator maybe once or twice a day and failing that we will be in constant contact. It's a very symbiotic relationship.
>
> *(Journalist 6)*

Other Australian states, reflecting global trends, are also increasingly moving resources into online information systems. South Australian Police (SAPOL), for example, have transferred much of their media information release systems online. Such systems provide journalists with unique login access to the SAPOL website[4] where they can source a range of information about cases, press conferences, safety campaigns and the like:

> [Our website is] not just a public interface but also a great tool for journalists as well. They have their own separate log in area and when we launched we got everyone – I sent everyone on our usual mailing list, our old-fashioned mailing list, and got them to reapply as such for access to the news website. So we've got a database of 200 plus journalists that we regularly deal with across the state and nationally across all the main-stream media outlets and whenever we do a media alert – which is 'just for information we will be speaking about 11 o'clock in relation to the murder of …' or 'for information we will be releasing statistics on this certain time' for media alerts – they will be alerted and they'll get an email that's been updated automatically any time you access any of the stories and press releases as well.
>
> *(SA Police PR Respondent 1)*

The benefit of newer online systems is that journalists are able to access up-to-date information about crime events while they are out 'on the road' via Internet-enabled mobile technologies, such as smart-phones and iPads. In this way, the police are not only adapting tech-nologies to their own advantage, but also responding to the demands and imperatives of journalists. The disseminator, PEATS and the police website are just three localized examples of the ways in which the ever-symbiotic but fluid relationship between the police and tra-ditional media are shifting with new modes of communication.

Producing and reproducing the press release

In Chapter 1 we outlined the scope of the growth of police public relations departments generally and police media officers more specifically. There is little doubt that this growth has also impacted upon the ways in which police and journalists interact. Things are much different now from the 'bad' (or good, depending on your view) old days of informal meetings at local hotels, where information passed from police working on a case to the journalist eager for a scoop over a beer or two (see, for example, Chappell and Wilson, 1969) – although that is not to suggest these things do not happen, as we will discuss in Chapter 8. However, as the discussion of the PEATS system above indicates, new technologies, reform agendas, police and police public relations professionalization and shifting media and political environments have changed the nature of the relationship. And while the PEATS system or its equivalents may produce a constant stream of information for journalists, the formal press release is still the key method of information delivery used by the police for journalists to initiate most media stories that focus on crime, policing and justice.

Official press releases, delivered these days via email and social media among other mediums, are the bread and butter of police media work. Police media and press offices around the world dedicate a large part of their working time to the press release, which has gone hand in hand with their role of responding to incoming media inquiries. The form and style of press releases has changed over the years and become more formulaic, but it is still one of the simplest ways of communicating crime news to the media and the public. While it could be argued that some police organizations flood the media with such releases, the benefit for journalists is that such releases not only contribute important information for lengthier news articles through the provision of basic factual details that such stories require, but they also provide good pre-packaged filler material for media outlets experiencing 'slow news days'. It is the latter practice which also signals some potentially worrying trends for the reliance on official police information.

The almost mundane reproduction of police press releases in the mainstream media could be viewed as largely innocuous when seen in isolation. The breadth of such reproductions, however, provides us with a telling picture of just how, and by whom, stories regarding law, order and criminal justice are framed. We have previously demonstrated the scope of this reproduction and (re)presentation in our own research (McGovern and Lee 2010), highlighting the scale of reliance on these official press releases in the daily press. By tracking every police media release distributed by the NSW Police Force over a one-month period, and following the crime stories published in the two key Sydney metropolitan daily newspapers over that same period – *The Daily Telegraph* and *The Sydney Morning Herald* – we were able to establish that a large percentage of crime news in these key daily newspapers was simply reproduced, often word for word, from NSW Police Force press releases.

During a one-month monitoring period[5] by the authors (McGovern and Lee 2010) it was revealed that the NSW Police Media Unit produced an astonishing 260 press releases, an average of 8.5 per day. From our more recent discussions with the NSW PMU we know that some six years later this figure was more like 15 per day. This volume of information provides a glut of potential crime stories for media outlets should they deem them newsworthy. These daily stories also speak to Chibnall's news value of *immediacy* – the event must have just occurred and the news must be fresh. Over the monitoring period we found that *The Daily Telegraph*[6] and *Sunday Telegraph* published a total of 119 crime-related articles and *The Sydney Morning* and *Sun Herald* a total of 111. For *The Daily Telegraph* and *Sunday Telegraph*, it was calculated that 69 per cent of all crime-related articles were derived from releases, with the remaining 31 per cent emanating, as far as we could ascertain, from sources unrelated to official NSW PMU releases.[7] Similarly, calculations showed that 67 per cent of articles in *The Sydney Morning Herald* and *Sun Herald* were connected to official press releases, with 33 per cent being unrelated.

From these analyses we can conclude that a high percentage of published news articles were simply paraphrased or copied verbatim from the content of NSW Police Media Releases, with 35 per cent of all *Telegraph* crime stories and 33 per cent of all *Herald* crime stories falling within this category. It should be noted that although it was not the aim of our analysis to assess the narratives of the stories, it was clear, in most cases, that the stories closely mirrored the media release and generally followed the discourse being presented in the release, painting the police in a positive light. In sum, over two-thirds of crime stories came from police press releases, with well over half of these being directly reproduced or heavily paraphrased.

The heavy overall reliance on the police press releases as a source and the fact that journalists were relatively unlikely to seek out other sources does raise serious questions about the impartiality of reportage and the power of police organizations to influence, frame and control both the flow and content of crime news. It also raises questions about journalistic integrity and the impact of shrinking resources available to the maintenance of high-quality investigative news journalism vital to liberal or social democratic societies. Our analysis identifies what may be described as a lot of 'churnalism' (Davies 2008) and much less journalism.

As UK reporter, Nick Davies, stated during the recent Leveson Inquiry in relation to the replication of police-produced content:

> Close to that also is press officers posting stories on websites, their own websites, for journalists to put into the paper, and there's a big reporting problem with that, because you're allowing the police force to make all of the editorial decisions about what should be reported and with angle and language and quotes … it's not being done for malicious motives. It's about shortage of resources cuts …
>
> *(Davies, cited in Leveson 2012: 766)*

So while many new and innovative ways of communicating news and information to the media and public are being trialled and implemented by police worldwide, traditional methods of information dissemination, such as the humble press release, still have the capacity to be highly effective in helping police to communicate their key organizational messages.

Press releases and journalism

We argued in the previous chapter that news and information about crime and policing have facilitated, and been facilitated by, a panoptic/synoptic relationship between the police and the public. In short, mediatized news about policing is attractive in the viewer society – as a source of information, of risk management and of entertainment. Applying this overall framework, as well as Chibnall's (1977) notion of newsworthiness as discussed in Chapter 1, we can understand both the demand for, and the relative mundane reproduction of policing news as detailed above, but that does not make it journalism.

Research interviews conducted with journalists in NSW revealed much more about the ways in which they interpret both their roles in reporting the content of police media releases and their relationship to police media and public relations more generally. Indeed, journalists freely admit to the utility of a centralized media unit and the reproduction of press releases as being instrumental to their reporting roles: 'Oh yeah, look let's face it, any of us in our job, if we can just sit down and get a phone call to complete that job, you'd do it, I mean you know, I don't blame the journo's' (Journalist 9).

Most journalists suggested that they used PMUs regularly. Nevertheless, they were cognizant of the PMU's role as a public relations mouthpiece to put a 'positive spin' on police activities. As one journalist suggested:

> It's a siphoning unit in a very positive way ... it saves me having to ring around every single [local area command] to see what's gone on overnight. At the same time they [the police media unit] can filter what is sent out to us because obviously their function is to not only get the news out there, but to make sure it's all good news. [They are] essentially a PR firm.
>
> (Journalist 1)

As staff at the NSW PMU put it, their role was 'to try and portray the police always in a good light'. Such statements no doubt reflect the policy that guides the Unit,[8] but they also tells us something of the staff's self-awareness of their roles. Journalists, they suggested, often phone the PMU hourly in order to update the latest 'news', check that 'nothing's going on' or simply call in the hope of being first to report major events. The constant communication between journalists and police media professionals indicates that our content analysis only scratches the surface of the true quantity of information that moves from police media officers to journalists on a daily basis – this is further discussed in Chapter 8. Again this highlights the police as a source of not just *novel* or new stories, to use Chibnall's characterization, but also indicates its privileged position as an institution with *structured access* to crime news.

This in itself presents an interesting question: does the existence of police media departments now often operating 24 hours a day, continually circulating media releases, holding regular press conferences and contacting journalists with information on various matters, make it easy for journalists to overlook the critical investigative function of their reporting? Grattan (1998: 42) argues that 'spin can encourage lazy journalism and distorted journalism', where material is accepted uncritically from 'spin factories'. Jiggins (2007: 204–6) similarly has likened journalists to 'lapdogs' more so than 'watchdogs'. Some journalists seemed to agree with this assessment:

> … The police could offer cheap sensation to journalists and journalists would be like Pavlov's dogs and they would salivate at this and they would say 'I got the scoop' but they wouldn't think about what was the motivation of the police officer giving them that.
>
> *(Journalist 12)*

When other journalists and police media professionals were questioned on the issue of lazy journalism they were almost unanimous in their response. Some questioned the investigative capabilities of many journalists and the expectations of roles of the simple police 'roundsmen': 'I don't think many police reporters do original investigations at all. You know, the investigation doesn't really go beyond the coppers that will give them a bit of information' (Journalist 3).

Others felt that that there were journalists who simply overlooked their investigative responsibilities for an easy story. They noted, however, that such practices would only take the reporter so far in their career: 'I think most media outlets expect a bit more than press releases and soundbites, sometimes they need, you know, harder information than they are going to get from a press release' (Journalist 4).

While the checking of alternative sources for a story was seen as an issue, some journalists saw it as more acceptable to cover the smaller stories without going to other sources. They suggested that if the story was important enough they would follow it up:

> Yeah, in particular with the smaller stories, like you know, if the Media Unit puts out an armed hold-up or something, and they've got the information there for us, we just write briefs from the information they give us. So that helps us out a lot, but it also means that we don't need as much staff there because they're making it so simple for us for the small things.
>
> *(Journalist 5)*

This estimation reflects Reiner's (2002: 222) view that many crime news stories are just 'routine fillers' following 'a clearly established paradigm', thus conforming to a similar pattern of presentation only with different names and dates according to the event. Indeed, one only need look at many of the press releases sent out by police themselves to see this routine formatting. It is of course reasonable that police media should provide stories on a standardized template, for legal and authenticity considerations if nothing else. However, this also demonstrates the capacity of police media officers to provide easy *simplification* of *conventional* stories, making them very attractive 'briefs' (Chibnall 1977). While police media departments are seen as important sources for up-to-date, *accessible* and *novel* information, there has been some circumspection about the quality of the information one is likely to receive. The journalists we spoke with, for example, appeared to have conflicting views over the role and influence of police media departments, noting their capacity to reduce the quality of reportage while also celebrating their ability to provide *immediacy*:

> It breeds lazy journalists. But it's also very convenient, particularly for some aspects of the media like radio, where we need information quickly. Without it you are required to go to

different sources, and in a sense it legitimizes the cowboys of the industry who are prepared to go to print without having checked as many sources as possible or legitimizing it through some officially sanctioned authority.

(Journalist 6)

Others thought the reproduction of press releases and reliance on police sources was simply indicative of a culture that was spreading across the board, where 'spin doctors' increasingly played a role in news reporting:

That doesn't just happen because of the Police Media Unit, that happens because of spin doctors everywhere, I mean that's perfectly accurate, yeah … if you're lazy … But yeah there's always people who undoubtedly get things from the Media Unit, type it in as a press release, and let it go.

(Journalist 7)

Literature concerning the 'PR state' (see Deacon and Golding 1994) tells us that this is a common feature of contemporary state institutions, not just the police. Governments increasingly look towards public relations professionals to ensure that the media carry forward their preferred messages to the public – to secure public legitimacy in the organization and its activities.

Importantly this highlights a significant shift in police–media relationships, from police as sources of information to police organizations as actively framing and constructing crime narratives. Analytically too this demonstrates the limitations of Chibnall's (1977) instrumentalist analytical framework of news values, and necessitates a change of register so as to interrogate the socio-political and cultural significance of contemporary police media relations. Modern day police do not just supply information in response to crime events; they proactively produce news stories. As the manager of the NSW PMU put it 'we also do a lot of things proactively to try and educate the community on policing initiatives or operations and results' (NSW Police PR Respondent 3). Moreover, as is illustrated by the following discussion, police media professionals also have a role in 'taming the systems' internal to policing organizations, as well as taming external systems of communications.

Taming the system

As we outlined in the previous chapter, Garland's (2001) cultures of control thesis is a useful framework through which to understand the ways in which state institutions such as police organizations are increasingly seeking to micromanage both themselves and their interactions with others. With progressively more detailed internal media policies and guidelines stipulating how, when and by whom public statements on crime matters can be made by the organization, police media branches and press officers facilitate the controlled release of information. These attempts to control or tame the system can often cause consternation within journalistic circles.

Indeed, many journalists were of the belief that police media offices sometimes reward particularly helpful reporters with 'scoops' or 'exclusives' providing incentives to publish the police angle. This practice was highlighted by the Leveson Inquiry, that noted instances of 'the press turning up at incidents or at newsworthy occasions' and the problem of 'unhealthy relationships between individual officers and members of the press' (2012: 744). The inverse, however, may also occur. In particular, journalists could be disadvantaged should they make it known they were in disagreement with the police position. As one disgruntled investigative reporter told us:

> There's no doubt that there was a conflict between the *Herald* and counter-terrorist type people and the Police Media Unit [two nights before an operation] and the *Herald* was out of the loop and *The Daily Telegraph* got a leak that there was an operation, you know, 'stand by for an operation', and so did *Channel Nine*.
>
> *(Journalist 2)*

The key point here is that there is capacity to tame those journalists who are in conflict with police organisations by either withholding information or providing preferred access. Of course key to taming the system is to have the organization painted in a positive light. Not that journalists are naive to what some saw as the 'real' role of police public relations in producing 'spin' and publicizing the police positively. Indeed, many are mindful of being 'spoon-fed' a police 'agenda':

> You've got to keep in mind though that this sort of information is part of an agenda, which may be to create generally a good news story for the police, it may be a story that shows that they're being, you know, tough on crime. It might be a story that shows that the Commissioner was taking a hard line in respect to something. It may be a critic of the police is cast in a bad light; it may be any number of things. But it's got a hidden agenda, and the problem with that is sometimes those stories make good stories, but you get the effect whereby these stories are being spoon-fed and you know, I suppose it's open to the idea that this is spin.
>
> *(Journalist 5)*

Another put it in terms of the contradiction between information dissemination and information control, suggesting that we have seen the development of sophisticated 'propaganda' tools:

> I suppose, in an ideal world they are there to provide information, and to be as transparent as they can within the bounds of operational security and that sort of thing. I think they've now evolved into an extremely sophisticated propaganda tool … I think, there's a difficulty between drawing the line between public interest and public information, and police spin.
>
> *(Journalist 11)*

It has also been suggested that one of the 'unwritten' roles of police media departments is to attempt to smother negative stories about the police, a 'taming of the system' whereby sensitive interactions are 'referred up'. This practice was highlighted by the Leveson Inquiry (2012) and the Filkin Report (2012), where evidence was heard of police reluctance to release information that may reflect negatively on the force. One British journalist claimed that he 'found the MPS to be defensive and protective of its image and reputation' (O'Neill, cited in Leveson 2012: 772). However, it was suggested that journalists often came to this position because of the increasing difficulty in developing informal contacts within police forces. Taming the system then can have perhaps unintended consequences of getting journalists further offside than they need be, or indeed giving them the impression of an organization being overprotective.

Journalists' claims of information suppression speak to the increasingly sophisticated internal guidelines for police–media interactions. Such guidelines obviously provide legal and ethical safeguards, but they also manage police–media relationships in more circumscribed ways. This also opens police public relations work up to claims from journalists that it is overprotective of the organization:

> I think the reality is that they are meant to provide a limited amount of factual information regarding any story of interest and general stories of interest and certainly any operational story of interest to journalists. Over and above that I think their unwritten role is to smother negative police stories, full stop. I don't think that individuals within the Unit are employed with the express purpose of trying to trip journalists up, hide things from them, you know, to go out there and choke the life out of negative coverage of police, but, they are only given a certain amount of information themselves and if something becomes problematic, they are told to refer it to someone more senior and then a different process begins again.
>
> *(Journalist 5)*

Indeed, many journalists in Australia and the UK conceptualize police media units as more like 'gatekeepers' to police organizations and indeed to information relating to the organization's operation: access controllers who tame the delivery and mediate information. Of course journalists, looking for a scoop, would also be understandably critical of a bureaucratic gatekeeper that they might see as undermining their capacity to get a good story. Some have even gone so far as to suggest that media units actually impede the flow of information: 'Often they [PMUs] sort of serve a counter-purpose really in restricting the flow of information ... They can give out much more information than they do I think' (Journalist 7).

Along the same lines, journalists have clearly articulated the argument that control is a key element of the work of media units – control of information, but also control of image more generally:

> They [PMU] want to be in control of it [information], they want to know exactly what's going on in their organization, so that ... Their main purpose is look after the image of the police service, look after the Commissioner ...
>
> *(Journalist 1)*

However, journalists are also aware that attempts to control media output can be more complex than they first appear. In particular, controlling information flows can involve doing deals with certain outlets or media commentators (Leveson 2012).[9] However, the consequence of this can be that police have to surrender some control in return:

> I think one of the consequences of media units, be they in the government or police ... has been a kind of surrendering of control in an ironic way because when you start doing those deals with people like Alan Jones,[10] you have to, by definition, give them power too. And then when they start saying 'but if you don't do this, we'll do this' then you do wonder who's in control.
>
> *(Journalist 3)*

But quite apart from attempts at controlling what may or may not appear in the mass media, police public relations professionals have also had the challenge of actually taming the systems of information delivery. Notwithstanding the rather Orwellian picture painted by some journalists, attempts to tame systems of information delivery are often much more sporadic and ad hoc than we might expect. As one NSW public relations respondent noted:

[When I started here] that system of delivering electronic media releases out to that database … all it was was a list of email addresses. We didn't have any other information about these people getting the media releases. Someone was tweaking something at the back end of the website and doing some testing and just put out a test message, 'Arrest everybody' and that database got that message and you can Google it. It got run in the *Sydney Morning Herald* I think and suddenly the IT people went, 'Oh we can make changes to this' and realized that there was a glitch in their systems, a weakness and suddenly came on board very quickly to developing a new system and a new database which they developed and developed quickly and we've now got a good system where we've got a database of 2,000 people, about 1,200 of which want to receive our media releases so they are subscribed. The others are just sort of contacts and phone numbers for us but getting that – the system sends out a media release as well as puts it up on our website automatically.
(NSW Police PR Respondent 2)

So while technological advances and changes to the media environment more generally have created opportunities for the police in terms of the delivery, format and content of information dissemination, it has also had the effect of putting more pressure on police organizations not only to manage this plethora of new systems, but also to become savvy in the knowledge of how such systems work, and the implications and issues they bring with them. Manning (1988, 1992) has noted the complexity and challenges of such technologies for policing organizations: like contemporary society more generally, police organizations both operate through, and are swamped by, information.

Logics of the media release

In Chapter 2 we outlined what we saw as the logics of police engagement with the media: the management of image, risk management and responsibilization, and improving the trust in and the legitimacy of the organization. These logics can be identified as informing much of the communications around police media releases. Clearly journalists too understand these logics and, as one journalist we interviewed suggested, being seen to be dealing with crime was vital for police, and constitutes a key communications priority for police public relations:

> They want people to know that police are dealing with things out there … And that's what the police media unit does. They will contact us if there is a court story we may be interested in, and they will always contact us for things like appeals or press conferences.
>
> *(Journalist 13)*

In this sense, journalists too understand that part of building trust in policing, and confidence in the police organization, is the police being seen to do their job. As this journalist explains:

> Yeah, they do [contact me] from time to time if they've got, and it's on a couple of levels I guess, there are sort of like, I don't know 'good news' stories like, say, if they have trained up a new police dog … They might also contact you because they want to release information about a certain crime, say there's a rapist on the loose or something … But sometimes they do contact you and say 'we've got this story for you', that usually happens if you've been asking questions about it. Say, if I've been asking about a particular case and showing a particular interest in a matter … So then you would go and see the detectives in charge or the officer in charge, probably with the police media person being present, and they would give you a briefing. And their reason for doing that is they want publicity for their case, for a particular reason. There are operational reasons why they might do that, but they want a suspect to read the paper or to see the TV and get a reaction from that person, which may be over the phone, or maybe they'll do something.
>
> *(Journalist 10)*

As the above demonstrates, police media work today has become multifaceted, linking with a number of different logics that are all ultimately aimed at helping the police meet their stated media objectives.

While many journalists give accounts of being subject to drip-fed news from police media officers, police public relations and media officers suggest that important stories are often ignored by journalists, despite police beliefs of the importance of their dissemination for investigative purposes; the application of news values in action. It has also been noted that the location and readership of a media outlet has a significant effect on whether a story is picked up. This disparity between local reporting and the sorts of stories that are more likely to make national headlines was highlighted in the Leveson Inquiry and was noted by our own interview subjects:

> [I]f we are putting a press release out it might sink without a trace in the metropolitan media but it will certainly get used I'd say – I'm not going to put a figure on it – the suburban and local newspapers would pretty much run most things that we put out. Sometimes we'll put out a media release and not receive one follow-up phone call but then you'll see the press clips come through and it gets a run all throughout regional papers or in that local area. Sometimes a media release goes out and we get a lot of interest from all the metro media and requests for stand-ups or images.
>
> *(NSW Police PR Respondent 2)*

While police organizations can never be sure whether a story will be picked up by media outlets, their growing media professionalization means that police now have a greater capacity to give a story the best chance of running, particular when the vast majority of staff working in the larger police media offices have come from journalistic and communications backgrounds. As the Leveson (2012) report noted, the scope for communications activities by the police has broadened now, meaning that the mass media are no longer the sole vehicle through which the press can disseminate important messages to the public. As we have demonstrated, police organizations are now acutely aware of this.

Proactive police media

> ... our intention ... is to become an organization which is
> attempting to break news ourselves rather than just feeding it
> to media.
>
> *(Vic. Police PR Respondent 1)*

One significant shift in the way in which police organizations are
dealing with the media and are attempting to get their preferred narratives and images circulated more generally is through being proactive. That is not to say that police organizations have not been
proactive with the media in the past; as our example of traffic risk
reduction in Chapter 3 indicates, police have been always somewhat
proactive in their approach to the media. However, the emergence
of more formalized police media units, media officers and public
relations professionals has broadened the scope and enhanced the
possibilities of this proactivity. Being proactive now takes many
forms from carefully managing the release of information to serve
investigative and other purposes, to producing completed crime narratives for newspaper and radio, editing video footage for television
networks to air and hosting large-scale events that demonstrate the
good work that the police do. Proactivity is also regularly deployed
for operational reasons:

> Occasionally I will get a call from the PR person who exclu-
> sively looks after the state crime command, these are the major
> crime squads, Homicide, Robbery, Drug Squad, blah, blah,
> blah and say 'look, we've got something we think that would
> be a good Sunday story' they'll say, 'we think now that it will
> help us as well if you could write it, it would be good, we're
> looking for the publicity'.
>
> *(Journalist 5)*

In this way the seed of a preferred and perhaps 'exclusive' story can
be planted by the policing organization, with the journalist provided
just enough information to execute the story in a manner in which
the media outlet or journalist feels they have ownership or author-
ship. At the same time, the police have not only acquired their media

story, but they have also been able to exercise a level of control over the content and direction of the story, all in the name of operational considerations. This should not necessarily be seen as a negative development in police management, however; in fact, it demonstrates our very point about the capacity of police media work to fulfil a 'simulated policing' role, aiding in the actual operational capacity of police organizations.

As we have demonstrated, Chibnall's (1977) work gives us the tools to assess the production of stories at an instrumental level, which goes some way to explaining the utility of police media professionals and specialized media units to journalists – and vice versa. However, we believe these units demonstrate something of a broader shift in both governing rationalities and technical capacities.

Over two decades ago Grabosky and Wilson were able to suggest that journalists only use police media units as a 'starting point' in the construction of news stories (Grabosky and Wilson, 1989: 37; Wilson, 1992: 171); this series of interview data suggests it is now much more than this. In many cases the media unit story *is* the news story. Indeed, what our respondents demonstrate is that policing itself is increasingly mediatized.

Police and multimedia production

Perhaps the most obvious example of police organizations moving into the full production of news is the recent phenomenon of multimedia production units operating within policing organizations. Such units are becoming an essential element of the larger and better-resourced organizations. This development sees police organizations now managing their own in-house video production crews who can, among other things, be available to film, edit and produce a high-quality vision of police activities, from news stories made for television to police raids and vignettes about the behind the scenes of the organization for online broadcast and consumption.

An example of how these capacities are being used is evidenced in the arrest of a 67-year-old Sydney man in 2010. The man, charged with 31 sexual offences against three young boys, was filmed by police cameramen being arrested at his home and escorted, hand-cuffed by police, to a waiting police van. The footage was then cut, edited and produced by police multimedia staff and placed on YouTube, linked to the NSW Police Force website and social media accounts, and eventually delivered to the various television networks in time for the evening news. Television viewers would have been forgiven for thinking that the network journalists reporting on the high-profile arrest were on the scene, camera's ready, providing live commentary on the action. In truth there were no reporters present at the time of the arrest. Similarly, the detailed reports of the arrest in the daily papers the following day were primarily taken from care-fully crafted media releases distributed by the police to coincide with the arrest and distribution of footage.[11] As one of our police public relations respondents explained, access to two full-time camera oper-ators and specialized media staff within the force gives them great capacity to carefully prepare their media approach with these sorts of events:

> … we have a News Projects Officer who proactively goes and seeks those jobs that haven't happened yet where we might be going to an arrest phase of an operation or raiding a hydro house or a drug syndicate and seizing drugs or guns or what-ever it is. That News Projects Officer liaises with those police and gets on the inside of that operation so we can get our cameras there and get footage of things that the traditional media would be not able to authorize to do and then we can release footage in a way that suits the operational police to see that we've now locked up these people.
>
> *(NSW Police PR Respondent 3)*

These kinds of multimedia production units are gradually finding their way into more and more police services. As Ferrell et al. (2008: 184) put it, 'police shoot more images than they do people'. As a result, we are seeing that increasing amounts of the images broadcast on the evening news bulletin or in the daily newspapers have been shot by police camera crews. Not only that, but in many cases this vision has been edited in house, and the story presented as a completed news item, leaving very little for news organizations to do when it comes to the news-making process. Thus, often what viewers perceive as an objective news story is actually one completely framed, produced and delivered by a policing organization via its media staff.

On one level this is not so surprising. As we argued earlier in the chapter, police media releases are often reproduced in newspapers verbatim (McGovern and Lee 2010). In this sense a more sophisticated video production unit is simply an extension of the already existing police media apparatus. However, the primacy of the image in contemporary culture means that this extension is significant.

Being able to film and edit footage at events and incidents gives police the capacity to ameliorate a range of risks, particularly in the face of sometimes questionable actions from journalists. As inquiries such as Leveson (2012) and Finkelstein (2012) have shown us, the media often show themselves to be irresponsible in the face of trying to get the next exclusive tip. The Leveson Inquiry, for example, evidenced a number of occasions where media presence during police operations and the subsequent airing of police raids resulted in legal action (Leveson 2012). Under the possibility of such risks, police in-house filming crews overcome many of the potential legal risks that a media free-for-all can cause. On top of this, in-house filming can also serve to ensure that evidence is not damaged by the media, victim dignity is maintained and unwanted disclosure avoided, mitigating against future legal problems. As this NSW respondent indicated:

> … we'll pixelate that and legal it before it goes out. We want to make sure we frame out or edit out any police who are working in a covert capacity that can't be seen so it's a much safer and secure way of doing it well in a way that the media can still get access to these jobs.
>
> *(NSW Police PR Respondent 2)*

A similar sentiment was expressed by a WA Police PR respondent:

> There are some things that happen just so quickly that some-one will say … '[is our cameraman around], can he shoot out

for this? I don't want to allow the media there 'cause there's kids and there's other families there and there's people who are undercover', so our bloke will go out and shoot everything just like a TV crew would, then we'll cut out the undercover cops or something, so their lives aren't put at risk because the media's there.

(WA Police Respondent 1)

To return to the news story that began this section of the chapter, the NSW Police Corporate Communications Director noted these very concerns in his discussion with us:

… we shot some video today of a chap arrested in Northbridge this morning for some crimes where he has assisted Dolly Dunn way back when in procuring young lads for child sex assaults … it sounds like a bit of a mastermind in this sort of area, so he's about to face something like 200 charges this afternoon, a 67-year-old. Now we shot some video of his arrest … it's not all about us just shooting the videos and releasing it to the media but it is about protecting the neighbours, there may be family involved. If you tell the whole media to be there at the same time you do the collateral damage to the case; it could be quite large. So in this case we would shoot it but the media would know a whole lot of other background information by other ways, through fact sheets and stuff like that, or depending on the nature of the story we might get them in and have them there soon after the arrest. So the actual arrest part is protected in the sense that we're not allowing things that are going to allow cases to fall over later on for legal reasons.

(NSW Police PR Respondent 1)

Where once police would have relied on providing media tip-offs and preferred journalists to get the coverage required to get their story to press – and this can and still does occur – the expanded communications capacity of police, and more detailed media policies that frown upon favouritism in media access, make such scenarios far less likely. In today's environment, police now have the capacity to control these stories in ways that their predecessors could only have dreamt of. And with the expansion of police media activities and more proactive approaches to communications, what does not make the news will almost certainly be disseminated through police social media.

As noted, the increased multimedia activities of police organizations, while partly about image management, also allow police media work to play much more crucial roles in operational policing outcomes. As Western Australian police media officers explained to us:

> … we might hold back for a couple of hours on something. Sometimes we'll hold back for a whole week because we know something is about to happen but we plan a big media strategy around it, so when it does happen on the night … We've got our own cameraman, we'll go out and shoot stuff, edit it and give it to them and say, 'Oh we had a big series of drug raids last night, we arrested 20 people …' and blah-blah-blah, 'And here's all the vision to go with your story.' They love that.
>
> *(WA Police PR Respondent 1)*

In other cases the use of police multimedia resources are justified in terms of privacy and/or the comfort of a victim or member of the public:

> The other thing that we have done just recently is we had a triple murder and a police officer was shot, etc., in a siege – very high profile here and the media were really desperately after trying to talk to our victim. We actually sent out and set up and recorded our own [footage] … as in SAPOL recorded an interview and a statement from the victim in the privacy of this woman's home where she was hiding away from the media and then released it with her consent. That was her way of delivering of the message. She didn't want to go through the trauma of speaking directly with the media and getting questioned, etc., so we are sort of being very I guess proactive and diverse, open to different sort of ideas and thoughts on how we actually do this.
>
> *(SA Police PR Respondent 1,*

Police multimedia activities in this case reflect a greater recognition of the impact of the media on victims of crime and their families. Growing concern over the impact of the media on victims (Victims Services 2011) has seen the development of guidelines for victims and reporters.

In this new professionalized police media world, some journalists are astonished at the improved capacities of police to both produce the information and images they are disseminating, as well as the strategic intent behind much of this information. In reference to this, one journalist related his experience:

> They gave reams of footage you know, and they all had titles, there was footage that said what was seized in the cells, you know it was all there for the picking, I mean it was just amazing really.
>
> *(Journalist 11)*

Recent improvements in the capacities of multimedia production and the quality of output has also significantly increased the likelihood of these images and stories being taken up by media outlets, as police media staff, specialists in media and communications themselves, play the news-making game, aware of what is needed to get prime-time positioning on the nightly news:

> … so they've got A-grade quality product, now, whereas, before, their quality wasn't great. And so the TV networks, 'Well, the quality is not good so we're not going to show it'. But now the quality is there.
>
> *(NSW Police PR Respondent 4)*

As one of our WA Police respondents also put it, new deadlines and the development of newly sophisticated equipment has changed the business model as it were:

> … we've now got a Video News Media Officer who spends his whole time going out to crime scenes, shooting vision, putting that vision up on the website in an edited format.
>
> *(WA Police PR Respondent 3)*

Police media professionals noted that the multimedia production of televisual stories for news outlets has increased the chance of coverage significantly. Aside from traditional broadcast routes, footage is also being uploaded and viewed on a range of online platforms including YouTube and dedicated police news websites. For police, the benefits are obvious:

> Yeah, that certainly increases the chances of getting a run on television without a doubt but also the websites take that footage as well, the news.com and smh.com so they love it but yeah, if you've got arrest shots, a stand-up and people before the court where facts are tendered, it's pretty much all the ingredients that the media needs to cover it, so yeah, it's a very popular service and you'll see it sometimes on the nightly news where sometimes they might say police vision, other times they'll roll the police vision and not put police vision.
>
> *(NSW Police PR Respondent 2)*

The capacity of the police to essentially become media producers and outlets is significantly changing the processes under which policing images are manufactured and produced. These processes are increasingly rendering crime news hyperreal. The link between mass media news and image production is broken. The policing we increasingly view is thus simulated policing – the images of policing, produced by police, have become policing.

Mediatized policing

As the examples above illustrate, since the emergence of professional public relations and dedicated media branches, the relationships between the traditional mass media and police organizations have been ever changing. Policing has become mediatized to the point that police organizations and their work are not simply the subject of media attention – rather police organizations are actively framing and producing stories. Whether under the guise of the traditional media release or in more contemporary modes such as sophisticated multimedia production, police organizations have become proactive media organizations in their own right.

This proactivity allows police organizations to pursue agendas largely in line with the logics we have outlined: information can be disseminated that helps the police image, that attempts to manage risks and responsibilize the public, and that endeavours to build trust in the police and legitimacy in the police organization. The increasing professionalization of police media activity also enables police organizations to have more effective control over this information and its dissemination. Clear media policies and procedures mean that over time journalists have been channelled towards using the preferred policing modes of information dissemination. Observations made by journalists of 'control', 'spin' and 'propaganda' emanating from media units are further suggestive of these attempts to control information (see Feeley and Simon 1992; Garland 2001; Jiggins 2007; Lovell 2003; Mawby 2002a).

Despite such claims, Cavender (2004) has criticized Garland's account of the development of *cultures of control*, suggesting that he downplays the media's role in agenda setting and framing debates.[12] By his account the professionalization of police media communications should not be seen as simply being *driven* by new political rationalities or logics; they should also be seen as a *response* to changing media landscapes, capacities and technologies.

The media landscape has thus also changed. The need to fill 24-hour news channels with (new) content, the collapse of the traditional print media and new online platforms for news have all played a part in changing the traditional relationship between police organizations and the media. Yes, there may be new cultures of control that have emerged, but they have done so within broad sociocultural and economic contexts – not simply because of police attempts to manage the media.

Thus it would be overstating things to suggest that the power relations between police and the media were all top-down or unidirectional. One of the central messages to emerge from our data has been the unpredictable and dynamic nature of the relationship police and journalists have with one another, and the frequent power struggles that each felt they were faced with in their ongoing exchanges. These findings reflect similar themes discussed in other jurisdictions by researchers such as Mawby (2002a) and Lovell (2003). As Foucault has argued, the issue of power relationships is one that traditionally conjures up notions of power as a repressive force; rather, he argues that power is productive, producing domains of objects and rituals of truth (Hunt and Wickham 1994: 16). We similarly would argue that the power relations in police media exchanges are productive (as distinct from positive or negative). This symbiotic relationship produces domains of truth about crime, social control and justice. As knowledge brokers police are able to exercise significant power, but it operates through and is mediated by the media and indeed increasingly by citizens – as we will see in Chapter 7.

The filming of an arrest as described above, for example, will make the 7 p.m. news broadcast because of its newsworthiness – clearly it meets many of the criteria outlined by Chibnall. However, with the police having the capacity to film, edit and produce the story, it can also carry preferred images of the police and messages of deterrence to would be offenders. Additionally, it can convey a message to the public to be vigilant in the identification and reporting of such offenders. That is, it can encompass the range of media logics we outlined in Chapter 2.

Here we can also see the slippage between operational policing and police image work. Narratives and images captured and produced by police public relations teams fulfil the demands of the viewer society where police stories are sought after as a form of infotainment. But they can also play a role in the identification and arrest of offenders, the identification of victims, the deterrence of future crime, and in building trust and legitimacy in policing. In short they provide the capacity for forms of simulated policing. The news story on the 7 p.m. news is not just information – it *is* policing as well.

Conclusion

As our interviews and reviews of other current research demonstrate, police media branches play a pivotal mediating role in the construction of news regarding crime, justice and policing. Over-reliance upon police media and public relations offices as sources of information evokes important questions about journalistic independence at a time when shareholders in public media corporations are being

appeased by editorial staff cuts and leaner, more productive journalistic staffing arrangements. With print media in particular in serious
(if not terminal) decline, the attractiveness of media releases and professionally produced, proactively ready-made stories cannot be
understated. Indeed, policing organizations are increasingly filling an
information void, framing and presenting stories to media organizations in ever more creative ways. The danger in this climate is that
with a largely compliant and uncritical traditional media and the
capacity of policing organizations to control much of the flow of
information, police organizations have the ability to set the agenda
on a high percentage of narratives about law and order and policing.

To draw from Garland, professional police media branches are
constitutive of another domain through which new political rationalities are deployed to 'tame the system' and 'manage' both the police
organization and what 'news' is disseminated. Their operation also
needs to be analysed as part of a range of logics that seek to control
the agenda of crime stories as strategies of image work, risk management and the conferring of trust and legitimacy. These intricacies of
the police–media relationship, transformed by the professionalization
of police media communications, signal the need for a change in the
way we think about and analyse the crime–media nexus.

Notes

1. See Pearson (2005), McGovern (2009), Morri (2008), Morri and Jones
   (2010), Hollins and Bacon (2010).
2. PEATS is a computer-based information dissemination service providing
   pre-screened media representatives with basic information on the latest
   events and incidents that have come to police attention.
3. CAD refers to Computer-Aided Dispatch used by emergency services
   to manage emergency calls and assist in the dispatching of services to
   particular locations and events. These systems also integrate with other
   emergency systems to collate, store and retrieve information.
4. http://www.sapolice.sa.gov.au/sapol/home.jsp
5. From 1 March 2006 to 31 March 2006.
6. All references to the *Daily Telegraph* in this article refer to the Sydney-
   based Murdoch publication and should not be confused with the British
   newspaper of the same name.
7. It is important to note that not all information disseminated by the
   NSW PMU is represented on their website in the form of a media

release. Rather, NSW PMU staff have constant communications with journalists at which point follow-up information may be disseminated and interviews with relevant police might be organised. Thus there would be a significant amount of information our study would not capture. This caveat is clearly illustrated by the fact that some years ago the NSW PMU released much more in-depth stories on their site. Currently, however, stories are generally only one paragraph in length.

8. It is suggested to all NSW Police that by following the policy officers 'will play your part in building positive public opinion of your work and that of your colleagues' (NSW Police, 2004: 4).

9. For example, Leveson (2012: 744) noted the giving and receiving of 'off the record' briefings. Again, the risks here are pretty much self-explanatory, but apart from the obvious lack of transparency the person doing the briefing will often have an agenda and each party will be hoping for, if not expecting, future favours.

10. A Sydney-based right-wing conservative radio announcer or 'shock jock'.

11. For example: http://www.smh.com.au/nsw/sydney-paedophile-ring-arrest-20100622-ytu1.html#ixzz1SdFcGl9x.

12. See also Sparks (2000) for a discussion of this.

5

POLICING SOCIAL MEDIA

Introduction

In the last chapter we examined the ways in which traditional police media activities were being supplemented by new modes of communication, including the development of multimedia formats that enhance the ability of police to disseminate and communicate preferred messages to the public. In this chapter, we will explore this expansion further, examining how social media platforms in particular are being deployed by the police in the pursuit of key police media and public relations objectives. The chapter will begin by outlining the context within which the developments have occurred, followed by a discussion of the rationales and policies driving the police use of social media, and ending with some examples from practice and our research interviews exploring the ways in which the police are engaging with social media to meet their stated aims.

As the previous chapter discussed, police organizations of today are actively engaging with a range of media formats in order to meet particular operational and public relations objectives. With the emergence of social media, police have new opportunities to extend their media activities in innovative ways. Moreover, if we accept the core argument of Mathiesen's (1997) notion of the viewer society, they have little option but to do so. Over a relatively short period of time, social media has led to a reimagining of the police–media–public relationship.

Until the end of the twentieth century it could be said that the relationship between the police and the public was mediated through quite formal structured communications activities. That is, the media primarily facilitated the police–public relationship through the reporting of police activities to the community. Similarly, reporters negotiated their own relationship with the police in a variety of ways, which included direct approaches to police or, more recently, through police media departments. However, the interaction between the police, the media and the public has been fractured by the increasingly prominent role of social media. Today's police–public relationship, in particular, has taken a new and arguably less 'formal' turn. Moreover, as discussed in previous chapters, the police–media relationship has changed too. These developments now see the police regularly communicate with the public through modes previously unimaginable, which can bypass the traditional media altogether. Similarly, the notion of direct police–public communications, once something that only occurred in personalized contexts such as 'on the beat', are now relationships that citizens can experience or be subjected to in the privacy of their own home, without a uniformed officer in sight.

In part, changes to the police–public interface can be attributed to the many technological developments and new media platforms that have become part of the everyday landscape; society more broadly has experienced a significant change in the ways individuals communicate as a result of such developments. When examined in the context of the professionalization of police media activities more specifically, such changes make possible the expansion of a range of governing logics that drive contemporary policing public relations activities. The reimagining of the police–media–public relationship has come at a time when policing agencies themselves have actively sought out more direct contact with the public, a proactive, more regular and 'transparent' approach to public relations and communications. So, while many of the changes we are seeing in police media work – and social media activities more specifically – have been facilitated by technological advancements, the fact that police are exploring innovative forms of engagement is something of a logical step in police public relations given the role of social media in both the commission and investigation of crimes.

Background and context

A decade ago Leishman and Mason (2003: 41) observed that, '[t]he Internet provides the police with many useful opportunities to promote their activities, not least in terms of updating press releases and "controlling the context" of such information.' In the decade since this observation was made the Internet has, for many police organizations, grown to become one of the most powerful tools in the police's media and public relations toolbox. In even less time, police organizations have emerged as leaders in social media application, praised within government and public sector circles as demonstrating best practice for the integration of social media into departmental routines. More than any other state agency, police organizations have managed to successfully harness social media as an effective communications tool, recognizing early on its significant potential to meet a range of police public relations objectives. Many of the earliest examples of policing forays into the social media realm were developed with little awareness or consideration of the potential legal, operational and managerial implications of social media engagement. Today, however, many police forces have developed quite sophisticated approaches to their social media environments. Indeed, strategizing around social media has become a priority within media and public affairs branches of police organizations. As a result, platforms such as Twitter, YouTube and Facebook have experienced growth in usage by police organizations eager to reap the rewards of carefully planned social media agendas.

As we have noted in the previous chapters with regards to police proactive strategies more generally, police moves onto social media platforms come at a time when the media landscape is shifting, creating uncertainty and instability within more traditional media outlets and formats. For example, dwindling budgets, decreases in advertising revenue and an increased focus on cost-effectiveness within media organizations has had implications for staffing levels and access to resources (McGovern and Lee 2010; Putnis 1996). The impacts of this have been felt worldwide, with a number of large media organizations being forced to downsize news departments, leading to the retrenchment of staff in an effort to offset losses in revenue.[1] The expansion of the Internet and other new media platforms has served to further challenge these traditional media formats in a number of ways. The demand for immediate news content and ceaseless deadlines means that media outlets are now operating within 24-hour news cycles (Goldsmith 2010; Lewis et al. 2005; Mawby 2010b), with bottom of screen 'news tickers' giving instantaneous updates. Competition for stories is fierce, and the Internet more generally has become a convenient source for breaking news and events for cash-strapped news organizations and the public alike. In addition, the proliferation of public relations and marketing specialists across the board has impacted upon the type and sources of content available to media outlets, and when coupled with the aforementioned reductions in staff, the move towards cheap media content and the decline of specialist reporters, the implications for news content can be significant (Cottle 2003; Davis 2000).[2] The resultant over-reliance on official sources and press releases created by these PR and marketing personnel, as discussed in Chapter 4, has become commonplace (McGovern and Lee 2010).

For criminal justice agencies themselves, such changes to the media landscape have wide-ranging implications for the ways in which they interact with the media and public. New technologies and social media platforms are increasingly playing a significant role in the communication priorities of criminal justice agencies, and it has become apparent that the police are taking the lead in this regard. Not only is this apparent in the introduction of systems such as PEATS, detailed in Chapter 4, but perhaps more significantly in the rate at which police organizations are engaging with the online environment through social media. For many organizations, not only has social media become a useful way of expanding the police repertoire when attempting to communicate with more technologically savvy audiences, but it also means that the police no longer need to rely solely on traditional media formats to engage with the public, allowing for more direct and intimate connections with a public whose approval they so desperately seek. It provides a new conduit between the police and the public.

The social media experiment

Policing organizations globally are increasingly cognizant of the benefits of social media to their communication and operational priorities. With pressure on the police, to increase public confidence and reduce community concerns over crime, social media has emerged as a valuable tool for proactive police communications strategies. The uptake of online tools and platforms by policing agencies globally is growing daily, as is the audience for such media (see, for example, National Police Web Managers Group 2010). Having moved into this space, the police, as we will illustrate, acknowledge the benefits of this new form of engagement.

Consequently, social media has now become firmly embedded within the communications strategies and objectives of many police departments worldwide. Social media platforms such as Facebook, Twitter, YouTube, Tumblr, Flickr, Weibo and Pinterest are just some examples of those being embraced by police organizations and, no doubt by the time you are reading this, the space will have expanded to include further, hitherto unforeseen, platforms – such is the speed of this communications and information revolution. Each platform can potentially perform a different role for the organization and is deployed in convergent and divergent ways depending on the aims, objectives and resourcing available to each organization. It is almost impossible to predict the direction or scope of future social media developments – as one media unit manager stated, 'I guess we're waiting for the next big thing along the way' (NSW Police PR Respondent 2). However, one thing that is certain is that social media, and their associated technologies, have become integral to police corporate and media communications activities. Indeed, they have joined traditional media platforms as important methods of public engagement. As one of our respondents noted:

It's really important as we move forward into this new world of social media that … these two groups [traditional media and social media] are complementing each other and they really do. The social media is just another way of getting our message out and *in many respects it's bypassing the formal media and in some respects it's bypassing the filters that the normal traditional media can put on our information.* Absolutely the traditional media are still the most powerful thing in terms of reaching eyeballs and ears and the millions of people watching the nightly news but obviously that, the number of people seeing these via websites and Facebook and Twitter and getting their information that way is absolutely increasing and absolutely vital and who knows how much the volume of people and the way they get their news, how that's going to change in the future but social media will grow and some might say traditional media will decline.

(NSW Police PR Respondent 1)

As such, rather than superseding the traditional police media activities social media is becoming another strategy on top of police's traditional media activities. However, there is a stark difference. As our respondent noted (as emphasized above), it is a strategy that offers the police much more control over content than previous endeavours, at least in terms of initial dissemination. This is information mediatized by policing organizations themselves.

However, this is not just about trailblazing and the control of information dissemination – albeit the latter is a key advantage of the platforms. West Midlands (UK) Police Inspector Mark Payne has acknowledged this nexus between traditional and new forms of media, saying: 'This is not about abandoning the traditional ways … More and more people are using social media to communicate and, if that's where people are talking, that's where we need to go' (BBC News 2009). As such, police organizations are actually following the trend rather than creating it. Similarly, the Toronto Police Service in Canada has promoted its use of social media by saying that it 'is taking an active role in participating in Social Networks as a means of extending our reach to all members of the community' (Toronto Police Service 2013).

This is a sentiment that has been echoed repeatedly in interviews conducted with police media professionals across Australia. SAPOL, for example, recognized the important role that social media platforms have grown to play in their communications objectives.

> I recognized the need for SAPOL to take a leap into the twenty-first century and take advantage of what they considered 'new' technology, even though social media has been around for some time. So one of my roles when I first started was the need to actually assess how we could use social media and how we could better engage with the public directly rather than perhaps using mainstream media.
>
> *(SA Police PR Respondent 1)*

Even smaller agencies, for whom staffing and resourcing such initiatives can be inhibiting, are aware of the many positives to be gained from moving into these spaces. As one interviewee from the Tasmanian Police Force, which consists of just over 1,200 officers policing a population of less than 515, 000,[3] expressed:

> I'm putting up a proposal to the Corporate Management Group to basically start out with Facebook and Twitter as a first iteration and then possibly moving to YouTube. I mean, obviously the department can see the benefits of it and I'll obviously be selling it quite heavily to the department, the bosses, because we've seen in the Queensland floods how the Queensland Police Service used Facebook and how successful that was in getting the messages directly out there.
>
> *(Tas. Police PR Respondent 1)*

As it currently stands, police organizations that have embraced social media have spoken positively about the experience. SAPOL, for example, were pleased with their move into the 'Twittersphere':

> We're happy with our Twitter, what we're doing there. We just use it as a push mechanism rather than a response mechanism, but we notice a lot of people are re-Tweeting our

messages and we feel we've got a really good social spider web
or network, or whatever you want to call it, out there.

(SA Police PR Respondent 1)

Twitter is one good example of how social media is being used as a
mode of information dissemination. The Victorian Police Force, for
example, found that Twitter was a useful tool for sharing information
about the police training and recruitment experience when in 2010
police recruit Stephanie Attard was enlisted to tweet about her experiences while training at the Victorian Police Academy. Attard's account
was slated as an unedited account of 'the good, the bad, the tough and
the sad' side of recruitment training, thus improving public awareness
and understanding of the process of training recruits (McGovern 2011;
News.com.au 2010). Similarly, numerous individual police officers
across the UK have been granted official licence to use Twitter in the
line of duty, employing the platform as a way of informing the community about their day-to-day activities, whereabouts and specific
local crime issues. This formula has been very successful in establishing
grassroots connections between the police and the public. However,
the platform has not been without its problems for UK police organizations, with the Metropolitan Police investigating 75 officers for
misuse of the platform between 2009 and 2012 and finding complaints
proven against 38 of these, resulting in three sackings (Halliday 2013).

Like Twitter, Facebook has also become a popular social media
tool for the police. While some organizations have been using the
platform for a number of years, others have hung back, waiting to see
how the platform has worked for these early adopters. When SAPOL
launched their Facebook site in February 2011, much later than
many of the other state police organizations, they were pleased with
the response. Waiting until they had a clear strategy that developed
on the back of experiences of other jurisdictions, they noted:

> We've had some huge successes. We're up to 23,846 Facebook
> fans and it's growing; not once has the number dropped off
> and since February, to grow to that number is quite phenom-
> enal. NSW Police are about six months ahead of us, they're on
> 50,000 in relation to their state of six to seven million, and

we've got a little old population of about 1.5 million and we're nearly at 24,000.

(SA Police PR Respondent 1)

The uptake of social media has not been without some scepticism though. Some organizations have been wary of taking the plunge for fear of unknown and unintended consequences. As one respondent commented to us during interviews:

We've been fairly slow out of the blocks on new media, per se, because we wanted to watch and see whether these things were gimmicks or real tools ... 99 per cent of the exchanges on Twitter and even website blogs are just complete rubbish. So there is a reluctance by highly qualified intelligent public servants ... there's some doubt about 'do we really want to be in that space?'

(WA Police PR Respondent 1)

These concerns are not unfounded given the potential pitfalls of social media. The NSW Police Force, for example, unexpectedly entered the 'Twittersphere' when a marketing company established a fake NSW Police Twitter account in an apparent attempt to demonstrate to the police the effectiveness of social networking tools (Moses 2009). As a result the NSW Police Public Affairs Branch quickly appropriated the account, embracing the new communications tool and prompting additional wide-ranging developments to their social media strategy. As one of our NSW Police Force respondents stated: 'Twitter had hardly been in the space for a second and fortunately this company who chose to grab our name actually gave us an opportunity to get in early' (NSW Police PR Respondent 2).

The episode is demonstrative of the ad hoc way in which social media have been embraced by many police organizations. This experience, while not common, also raises questions and concerns about the authenticity of police social media sites, a potentially problematic issue. As will be discussed in Chapter 7, 'fake' police pages, or pages set up with the intention of either criticizing or parodying particular police organizations or deceiving the public, are often established on social media by individuals or groups, either as an expression of dissatisfaction or as an attempt at humour. With it becoming increasingly difficult to distinguish such pages from the 'real thing', police need to be vigilant in clearly delineating their presence. In some cases, such parody sites can become more popular than those of the police they are critiquing. Consequently, many police organizations have gone on to develop policies for the use of social media, a topic we will return to later in the chapter.

Another tier of current social media engagement by policing agencies is that of YouTube. With a number of the larger police agencies now running their own multimedia departments, as discussed in Chapter 4, YouTube has become an important tool through which police can disseminate a range of multimedia productions shot by in-house camera crews. Furthermore, YouTube allows the police to broadcast a diverse range of messages to the public, as experienced in NSW:

> We put on YouTube not just our successes but we'll put on appeals. We've got crime prevention tips and if there's a statement by police to be put out we put it up through that … I look at the number of views we get – we're into the many thousands of views, it's equivalent of LAPD.
>
> *(NSW Police PR Respondent 2)*

SAPOL reported similar successes:

> The YouTube channel has been a good success for us as well … we use lots of CCTV and we've had some great successes right across our social media in terms of actually helping solve crimes; great successes in terms of pushing out the CCTV and people ringing up Crimestoppers and actually identifying people.
>
> *(SA Police PR Respondent 1)*

As well as the fostering of closer police–public relations, and perhaps even because of these closer relations, social media platforms are also increasingly seen as a beneficial investigative tool for the police. The

Internet is littered with news stories of how the police use of Facebook, in particular, has assisted in solving crime as a result of either information posted on the social networking site or information garnered from the public via the site. For example, the *Townsville Bulletin*[4] in 2012 reported that social media led to the recovery of more than 20 stolen cars across the city due to residents posting tip-offs on Facebook (Armistead 2012). Its use in an evidentiary sense was also well established following the 2011 London Riots (Daily Mail 2011; Greer and McLaughlin 2010).

The investigative potential of YouTube to help solve crime was shared, something experienced by a number of jurisdictions. In NSW, for example, one instance stood out for media staff:

> There's one great success story we do have which was in YouTube. So in YouTube land we put up a bit of video a few months ago, some CCTV; it was an Asian crime. In other words, Asians on Asians outside a karaoke bar where the guy was, I think, killed in a stairwell or outside. Local police had some good CCTV of it and [asked via the internal communications systems] did we know who these people were. So we've edited that [CCTV footage] up, placed it into YouTube land ... Anyway, a comment came on YouTube and you couldn't identify who the person was but their comment was 'Oh the guy on the right in the white is [Suspect One]. His girlfriend is so-and-so, she owns the hairdresser shop in Sussex Street. The guy over there is [Suspect Two], he went back to Hong Kong on Monday'. Named all four people in there and it was like the most amazing amount of information. Now obviously from our point we said 'Thank you very much', didn't post it, obviously online, and passed it onto the investigators who said 'Thank you very much' . [T]he information was completely accurate and that led to a couple of arrests.
>
> *(NSW Police PR Respondent 2)*

Such accounts leave little question of the capacity for social media to facilitate in enlisting public support for policing operations. In the following section we discuss in further detail the logic of this engagement with these social media platforms.

Social media logics

Evidence so far suggests that policing agencies in Australia, the US, Europe and Asia are engaging with social media in convergent and divergent ways, experimenting with different modes of social media in an attempt to align their use with broader police media and communications objectives. As Denef et al. (2012: 13) have noted, '[f]or most forces, social media remains a new topic, and strategies and practice thus continue to emerge and mature'. However, despite the differences in engagement, the overall deployment of social media platforms within communications objectives largely align with the logics that we have outlined in Chapter 2. As Chan et al. (2010) and Ericson and Haggerty (1997) have argued, new technologies have extended the capacity of the police to communicate (Chan et al. 2010: 655). Not only has the Internet created a new space through which police organizations can now share information and communicate with their 'stakeholders', but it has also enabled a greater capacity for the police to respond to never ending demands for information and content from the public and the media on issues of crime. As one interviewee related, 'We have to be ready to promulgate information because of the huge thirst for information within the community' (SA Police PR Respondent 1). This is an important insight, as it highlights again that the social media revolution in policing is not simply a top-down exercise in police colonization of information, there is also this public thirst, this synoptic gaze, where the many want to watch the few. As one respondent noted, 'we have the whole digital social media world giving us opportunities for direct communication' (NSW Police PR Respondent 2).

Logics of image management

Clearly the customer service agenda has been important for the move by police organizations into social media. Customer service is an example of the police image being managed in a way that situates policing as a 'responsive public service'. As Garland has noted the police represent themselves less as crimefighters and more as 'a responsive public service, aiming to reduce fear, disorder and incivility and to take account of community feeling in setting law enforcement priorities' (Garland 2001: 18).

Social media provides a perfect platform for the extension of this 'service'. This was clearly articulated by a NSW Police Force respondent, who stated that: '[t]he move to more of the social media – Twitter, Facebook – that all came out of customer service, originally' (NSW Police PR Respondent 4).

Image work on social media platforms not only demonstrates the dramaturgical nature of policing, but it also indicates the increasingly blurred line between operational policing, public relations and entertainment. The synoptic gaze is attracted by the drama, interest and the 'experience' the public might have in engaging with the police in cyberspace. As this respondent notes about Victoria Police's Facebook site and the need to improve it:

> I think we probably need that two-pronged approach that we're promoting it and we're profiling it but we're giving people a great experience when they're there, whether it's looking at what we do, giving them an insight into policing, having some vision there, having some expert commentary around things, and talking about things that are topical so it's not just corporate speak there or it's not boring or it's not just about recruitment, but we're actually talking about things that are topical as well.
>
> *(Vic. Police PR Respondent 2)*

But the world of social media is also crowded. Police organizations are by no means certain of getting their message to the public. This is one reason for the panoply of platforms currently being deployed. Policing through social media then is akin to firing a scattergun. The more platforms used, and the greater styles of communication employed, the more chance of reaching the desired audience. As one interviewee stated:

There's a lot of competition out there and I guess a lot of contradictory information, which is why it's important that we communicate in a way that people actually get. So we use humour for example, where appropriate so you know, people are actually interested in what we're saying and we're not just a voice that's lost amongst all the other social media that's occurring.

(Vic. Police PR Respondent 2)

The beauty of social media is, of course, other users can be enlisted in supporting the organization through sharing, reposting and re-Tweeting. While this is true of enlisting help with solving crimes, it is equally true when it comes to general image work. In this sense some police organizations will use social media just to push messages to the public – with genuine interaction through the platforms sometimes subordinated to information delivery. This is more likely to be the case with smaller or less resourced organizations, where monitoring social media pages is beyond the scope of the staffing level. While this logic of image work is a key driver of the expansion of police social media use, it is not the only one.

Logics of risk communication and responsibilization

During and following the UK riots in August 2011, the police were able to harness social media to communicate with the public and seek assistance in identifying alleged rioters. A number of British police agencies, including West Midlands, took to Facebook, Twitter, Flickr and YouTube to allay public fears and concerns over safety during the riots, call for information, publish photographs and descriptions of alleged rioters in an effort to identify suspects, and assure the public that justice would be served (Hartley 2011; Van Grove 2011). In the aftermath of the riots, Greater Manchester Police made further use of Facebook and Twitter to 'name and shame' those convicted of riot-related offences, although this particular strategy was met with mixed reactions from the public (Van Grove 2011).

The far-reaching benefits of social media for policing agencies were also felt in Australia in late 2010 and early 2011 during a series of natural disasters in Queensland. During Tropical Cyclone (TC) Yasi and TC Tasha, the QPS took to their newly established Facebook and Twitter accounts to inform the public about weather patterns and impending threats, safety measures and tips, public transport closures, emergency services responses and, most importantly, 'mythbusting' information aimed at quashing widespread rumours and community concerns (Larkin 2011: 37). According to Kym Charlton, Executive Director of QPS Media and Public Affairs Branch at the time:

> The situation was rapidly changing, and people wanted to stay informed in order to stay safe. The moment our branch received an update, we posted it online. We were live Tweeting from briefings and press conferences, so the public was able to immediately access all the information, not just what the media chose to cover ... While we can't prove that the work done by QPS media helped to save lives, hopefully we at least made the work of front-line officers a little easier by informing and calming the people affected by these disasters.
> *(Larkin 2011: 37)*

Given widespread power outages across the state, many in the community were only able to access information via smart phone. As a result, the up-to-date, informative and potentially life-saving information being disseminated by QPS via Facebook and Twitter saw traffic on these sites increase exponentially. With just under 10,000 'fans' prior to these natural disasters, the QPS Facebook page jumped to 23,000 'fans' during the TC Tasha threat in December, then surpassed this figure in January with the onset of TC Yasi, with the page reaching a staggering 165,000 'fans' (Larkin 2011: 37), a testament to the important role social media played in informing the community during these disaster periods.

These examples demonstrate that social media can play a vital role for police organizations in the dissemination of risk-related information to the public. As 'a responsive public service, aiming to reduce fear, disorder and incivility' (Garland 2001: 18), the police can play an active role in informing the community of risks and responsibilizing citizens to act in ways that minimize risky situations in real time.

That is, once a risk or threat is identified, the police can log into their social media pages and immediately inform the community about these risks and how best to respond to them. Social media then enables the police to strengthen the control over definitions of risk, and indeed the rational solutions to such risks. Policing organizations are thus in an even stronger position when it comes to this exercise of power, becoming primary definers of risk. Their authoritative voice and positioning as 'experts' during times of crisis or concern takes on new meaning in social media spaces. As a result, the police suggest they are able to engender much greater levels of public compliance with the risk-avoidance strategies, particular during these discrete events. Moreover, the public are more likely to see their advice as legitimate (NSW Police Media and Public Affairs Branch 2013).

The power of social media in enlisting public support for policing goes beyond alerting the public of impending existential risks and responsibilizing them to take care or precaution. Like other forms of media work, social media can also be deployed in responsibilizing the public to help in policing matters more generally. The rationale for this may be as straightforward as convenience – it is easier to click 'share' on Facebook or 'reTweet' on Twitter than it is to walk into a police station and offer assistance. What is clear though is that the public often feel more compelled to take some form of action in social media environments than they are in 'real life':

> … There are things that work well on Twitter … What is interesting is how people respond and the things they respond most to is that notion that 'I can help'. So we're looking for this person, we're looking for this mother and her young son, they've gone missing or this is a missing person or have you seen this person because they're wanted in relation to this crime here, here's some CCTV footage on the little link, and the moment people think they can help the re-Tweets start and it goes viral.
>
> *(NSW Police PR Respondent 1)*

Indeed, as Ericson and Haggerty (1997) have noted, risk logic is a key driver of policing activities. In this sense social media can be seen as another tool in a suite of policing strategies aimed at the minimization of risk and the responsibilization of the public. It is a tool over which police, as risk entrepreneurs, can exercise considerable control.

Logics of trust and legitimacy

While police use of social media is gradually becoming an everyday communications strategy, US policing departments in particular are started to recognize the capacity for social media to bridge the divide between the police and the public in meaningful ways. As well as seeking to deter online offending, police departments, such as those in Illinois, are eager to use social media as a way to 'create a healthy dialogue between law enforcement and the community' (Gradeless 2009). In this way, social media is being harnessed not just as a 'push' mechanism, as we have previously outlined, but also as an interactive tool, enabling two-way communications between the police and the public. By demystifying policing and demonstrating to the public that police are 'just like them', social media has broken down many of the barriers between police and community in ways that other communications activities have been unable to. As a number of respondents told us, humanizing the police is very powerful when it comes to fostering public trust.

Police media activities across the UK are also seeing the benefits of regular social media usage. As already noted, there is a distinct trend in the UK now for the police to sanction the use of Twitter by individual officers in the line of duty. For example, Harrogate PC Ed Rogerson gained national (BBC News Online 2009) and international (Gibson and Jacobsen 2010) attention for being 'the most popular' police officer on Twitter. Rogerson, who started using Twitter in 2009, is just one of a growing number of UK police officers who have been encouraged to reach out to the community and engage on a more personal level. Such strategies are increasingly being seen as a way of reintroducing the police to their community. In this way, the bobby on the beat becomes more 'visible', even if it is only in a virtual sense.

With the police being, arguably, the most visible or public face of the criminal justice system and with potentially the biggest stake in obtaining and maintaining public confidence in their activities, it is perhaps not surprising that they are embracing these communications tools in the pursuit of legitimacy. On top of this, many of these new technologies enable the police and their media units greater efficiency in such interactions. Indeed, the organization of time-space – or the time-space distanciation (Giddens 1991b) – on the World Wide Web is something that provides the perfect environment for policing – where the bobby is always present on the beat, even in their absence. These cyber bobbies demonstrate to the public that police are not only doing their job, but they are doing it well.

In this way, these communications platforms can and are being used to enhance the professional status and institutional legitimacy of police organizations, as well as their claims of transparency and public accountability (Chan et al. 2010: 656). Such public relations activities within policing organizations are part of a broader project of governance that sees police organizations engaging in the business of promoting the state's capacity to govern, as well as maintaining their credibility and evoking popular support (Garland 2001). As one of our respondents stated:

> We recognise well in terms of all the social media that's there that it does assist us to reach particularly a younger audience and it allows us to reach them in real time, which is why I love the iPads going down to some of the big sporting events or the big operations and the tweets going out because it's instant and we are reaching people that don't necessarily read the Herald Sun[5] or listen to the ABC.[6] So I think it's an extremely powerful tool.
> *(Vic. Police PR Respondent 2)*

However, the building of trust is heavily bound up in the police image and how to project it. Here, authenticity is important. As one Victorian respondent elaborated: '… one of the things I've tasked the new team leader to do is come up with new and engaging strategies with our social media so it is entertaining as well as informative, to build a bit of credibility there amongst the users' (Vic. Police PR Respondent 2).

Simulated policing, viewer society and taming of the system

In the aftermath of the NSW state election in March 2011, the newly elected conservative Liberal-National coalition government and Police Minister Michael Gallacher looked to make a mark in the party's first term in government since losing the 1995 election. Buoyed by overwhelming public support, the new government embarked on a series of what some may call radical criminal justice initiatives, certainly unlike those implemented by past conservative governments. At the time the NSW Police Force were already putting serious effort into their social media activities. The new government encouraged these police initiatives and a new strategy towards their Facebook communications was developed. By August 2011, the Police Minister and NSW Police Force were ready to launch Project Eyewatch. Eyewatch was promoted as the twenty-first century's response to more conventional Neighbourhood Watch schemes. Key to the Project Eyewatch campaign was the use of Facebook as a tool through which the police, at a local level (LAC),[7] could engage and interact with the public, using the platform as a way of informing the public about local crime issues. Dubbed as a 'local solution to local problems', according to the NSW Police Force, Project Eyewatch was said to be:

> ... about empowering residents with the ability to participate in crime prevention activities to ensure community safety ... [and giving] community members the opportunity to participate in active crime prevention activities online in their own homes 24 hours a day, 7 days a week.

For NSW Police, this new community policing approach enabled them to take their social media activities to another (simulated police) level. The brief of the scheme suggested that:

> Neighbourhood Watch Groups can be mobilized through Eyewatch using social networks and affording them the opportunity to participate with their local police in active crime

prevention initiatives. [Police] will train civilian precinct coordinators and police coordinators at the Local Area Command level to participate in online crime forums and provide accurate and up-to-date information to ensure safety and security. Eyewatch presents an opportunity for residents to be aware of incidents that are occurring in their neighbourhood and provide them with the ability to voice their concerns to police, obtain feedback and to be part of the solution.

(NSW Police Force 2011)

Why we start this section with this example is evident: Project Eyewatch takes the rationale for the very real and localized initiative of Neighbourhood Watch into the virtual world. It is in fact a simulation of Neighbourhood Watch, a hyperreal forum where the local is global. Moreover, Project Eyewatch is a bringing together of operational and communications experts within policing organizations in a way that blurs image work and operational policing. Project Eyewatch is a marker of just how important police agencies (and governments) perceive social media to be to their media logics and operational imperatives.

Project Eyewatch also sees corporate communications specialists in the Public Affairs Branch devolving responsibility of police communications down to the local level. This devolution of responsibility, while common in the UK examples of Twitter use we have outlined, is novel in the experience of Australian police organizations. Indeed Australian police organizations have hitherto been reluctant to pass responsibility away from central public relations personnel. It is also a unique use of Facebook. In the Eyewatch scheme, communications are manifest in the form of regular posts warning local residents of crime risks, alerting residents to recent arrests, updating the community on the latest crime prevention and safety tips and generally creating a perception in the community that the local police are successfully performing their policing role. The difference between this and the usual ways in which police use Facebook is that in this example there is community buy-in: residents who sign up to be part of the virtual Neighbourhood Watch scheme are encouraged to see themselves as part of the solution to local crime problems. This is evident in the rhetoric used by police to motivate public engagement. As the NSW Police Force (2013) explains, there are five key reasons why individuals should feel compelled to become involved:

1. Find out about crimes in your area
2. Get emergency alerts and warnings
3. Help us solve and prevent crime
4. Ask us for advice or assistance
5. Attend Eyewatch meetings (the online version of Neighbourhood Watch).

Clearly Project Eyewatch seeks to achieve the traditional goals of public policing, such as the deterrence of crime, social control, compliance with the law and the securing of public consent for policing.

With over 80 individual Eyewatch pages on Facebook, connecting to each of the LACs in NSW, there is the opportunity for any resident in NSW (with Internet access) to become involved in the scheme, enabling them to participate in crime prevention meetings online from the comfort of their own home (NSW Police Force 2013). The public reach is almost limitless, enabling simulated police to be present in any household at any time. The early successes of Project Eyewatch in NSW have led other police organizations to deploy similar strategies. Victoria Police Force, for example, has already established a number of Eyewatch pages as 24-hour online forums for the discussion of issues around crime and anti-social behaviour (Victoria Police 2013). International police departments too are keenly watching the NSW experience to see its potential utility in their jurisdictions (Stevens 2012).

This Australian example conceptualizes local contact as something quite unique and much more strategic in nature than any of the previously discussed UK examples. Where Hohl et al. (2010), for example, noted the limits of uni-directional 'push' conversation from police to the community, Project Eyewatch entails something more akin to a two-way conversation, whereby the public can 'speak' with the police online. This online approach to community policing also represents a significant shift away from more recent media activities that have seen communication and interactions by the police primarily managed by those working within the specialist realm of public relations and media communications. It signals perhaps a greater confidence in the abilities of local police representatives and the social media platforms they use.

However, this new found confidence did not appear overnight. Professional media training was supplied to LAC users by public relations specialists. Thus the faith was in the media training system that delivers such expertise to operational police. Once the system of delivery could be tested and 'tamed', operational police could take on both the responsibility and the risk of managing their part of the Eyewatch network.

Social media policy

As police forays into social media have evolved and expanded, so too have policy responses to these developments. Symptomatic of the impact social media platforms are having on organizations, institutions and companies, police organizations have recognized the need for robust policies and procedural guidelines for this social media. Such policies and guidelines do not necessarily cover the terms of just organizational use, but also include individual use. The aforementioned examples of police misuse of social media in the UK and concerns over how social media may impact on community relations more generally have provided the impetus for police organizations to develop and implement clear and direct policies for social media engagement. For some police, this has led to the delineation of very clear boundaries over what social network sites can and cannot do. As one of our interviewees explained to us with regard to their Facebook page:

> ... we have to really try our SOP (standard operating procedures) around what we do and don't allow. We only allow fans, we don't allow friends; we don't allow anyone to post randomly on our wall, we only allow people to respond to the posts that we put up there. We've also disabled our

discussion wall. Now I'm not saying that is a perfect formula on how to proceed because obviously it is about having a two-way conversation and listening to what people want from us, but it comes down to being realistic about what you need to achieve from a legal perspective [and] the staff numbers you have to be able to sit there and moderate a Facebook site. But it still allows people to give us feedback and to leave comments in relation to the posts that we're leaving up there. We also run event pages and things like that around road campaigns, which have been quite effective. So ideally it would be great to obviously be able to have enough staff to moderate 24 hours a day and allow people to leave comments on anything that they would like and start a discussion, but we think this is a really, really good strong step into the social media space.

(SA Police PR Respondent 1)

It is clear that a lack of clarity around media policies or existing restrictions creates risks for both organizations and individuals who use social media platforms. Indeed, the social nature of the platforms themselves create challenges to existing guidelines:

We haven't gone down the road of social networking like Facebook yet. That's problematic because Facebook's got a whole lot of other issues for police and our policy about use of Facebook has been fairly restrictive.

(WA Police PR Respondent 1)

The NSW Police Force has no fewer than three separate policy documents that relate to social media engagement by the Force: the *Media Policy* (2013), the *Official Use of Social Media Policy and Guidelines* (2011) and the *Personal Use of Social Media Policy and Guidelines* (2011). Each of the three policies provides guidelines to officers on how media engagement, including that of social media, can be used to help the Force achieve their goals, as well as outlining the responsibilities and expectations of individuals with regard to media and social media activities. One primary consideration here is that social media misuse, whether by the police or members of the public, has the potential to embarrass the police and may even lead to the disintegration of courtroom proceedings and a defendant's right to a fair trial (Janoski-Haehlen 2012).

Beyond this, police also share a number of practical concerns about moving into social media platforms, which generally require more regular surveillance and maintenance than traditional media activities. In larger police organizations, this is not necessarily problematic, as around the clock staffing and extra resourcing can often support such activities. For smaller organizations, however, the decision to engage in social media communications is one not taken lightly. As one interviewee stated: 'The other downside about new media is that it's very hard to get additional resources to do these things so we're very hesitant about starting up new means of communication that are going to be a resource drain' (WA Police PR Respondent 1).

The decision-making process often involves the development of cost-benefit analyses, with police media staff having to 'sell' the concept to less technologically aware senior executive staff. As one interviewee related:

> I put up a proposal to the Commissioner that we can't get into the new spaces, an online environment, without supporting social media because we need to actually use that social media to drive our traffic to our news website ... the Commissioner wasn't au fait with some of the more modern communication methods such as Facebook and Twitter and all of those sorts of things, he might not know how to use it but he actually had a great understanding of why we actually need to be in the space, but he approves our go ahead to get onto Facebook and Twitter and YouTube, so we ploughed ahead with that.
>
> *(SA Police PR Respondent 1)*

They went on to say:

> What will stall us I suppose or become an issue for us will be I think we've pretty much reached a point now where we can't

do too much more until there are more resources. SAPOL was broken into 14 local service areas called LSAs and obviously right across the state, from metro through to rural and regional areas, and it would be really great if each of those either had their own Facebook page or actually had a sub-page within ours. But then how do you – pardon the pun – 'police' that as such? Who is going to be responsible in each of those LSAs for putting up that very local information, which is really what social media is all about, is creating obviously those communities at a local level.

(SA Police PR Respondent 1)

Police forays into social media platforms and growing recognition of their utility have now led to the development of a number of collegial networks and forums across the globe where the police can share their experiences of the use of social networking with their international colleagues. For example, the Social Media, the Internet and Law Enforcement conference (SMILE) has been set up to facilitate the discussion of the application of social media to law enforcement and the investigation of crime, community engagement, reputation management, recruitment and crime prevention (SMILE 2012, 2013). Social media is even bringing the police together as divergent approaches to the new technology are gradually unified and perhaps ultimately tamed.

Conclusion

Police organizations appear to be leading the criminal justice world when it comes to embracing social media technologies and platforms. What this chapter demonstrates is that, while often cautious and aware of the limitations and issues social media bring, failing to move into the space would deny police organizations key opportunities to communicate directly to the public. It is for this reason that social media platforms enable police to further broaden their audiences. Many of these audiences may not engage with the police message in their more traditional formats. The sheer pace of developments in this field and the willingness of police agencies to engage with social media demonstrates that police are more than aware of the great potential social media creates for the meeting KPIs focused on public perceptions of policing. Our data collected from Australian state police agencies and evidence from the overseas experience demonstrates that the police see digital and social media strategies as now on a par with their more traditional media activities. In part, this may highlight the important and influential role that public relations and communications specialists now play in policing, but what it also tells us is that the police are now acutely aware of the increased public scrutiny of their organizations and the measures available to them through social media that may enable them to engender public confidence.

If policing is becoming increasingly mediatized, and indeed hyperreal, social media is perhaps the most obvious example of this. Providing not just a space for discussion, social media platforms are providing the capacity for police organizations to disseminate key messages. Importantly, it is a space in which simulated policing takes place, including the gathering of evidence, the reporting of crime, the identification of suspects and the prevention of crime. Further, going by the popularity of these sites, the public are consuming this police information greedily. Social media provides a portal where both the panoptic and synoptic elements of 'the viewer's society' intersect and overlap. The public is just as keen to observe the police as the police are the public.

Notes

1. See, for example, recent cuts at News Ltd and Fairfax in the Australian context (Media Watch 2011).
2. The impact of declining print sales, reduced advertising revenues and the move to online content is explored in Jonathan Holmes, 'Paying for News', Episode 10, 9 April 2012, online at: http://www.abc.net.au/mediawatch/transcripts/s3472295.htm; and Jonathan Holmes, 'Media Watch Special: Interview with Greg Hywood', Episode 11, 25 April 2011, online at: http://www.abc.net.au/mediawatch/transcripts/s3199897.htm (accessed 21 April 2013).
3. Compare this with the NSW Police Force, the largest in Australia with over 16,000 officers for over 7,000,000 people (NSW Police 2013).

4. A newspaper located in the Australian state of Queensland.
5. A daily newspaper located in Victoria, Australia.
6. Australian Broadcasting Corporation, Australia's national state owned broadcaster.
7. Or more formally, at the local area command (LAC) level.

6

POLICING REALITY TELEVISION

Introduction

This chapter explores police involvement in the production of law enforcement 'reality television', also known in policing circles as 'observational documentaries' or 'ob-docs'. The chapter will situate 'ob-docs' as illustrative examples of *simulated policing* – the emerging practice of achieving, or attempting to achieve, operational policing outcomes through cyber-, media- or image-related modes of policing. We begin by outlining the emergence of these 'ob-docs' and discuss why they have become a popular form of police public relations work. Following this we outline the benefits such programmes bring to policing organizations and media production companies. Finally, using qualitative data from our interviews, quantitative data from an online survey and a content analysis of police 'ob-docs', we argue that this programming meets many of the desired outcomes, or logics, of police public relations in the twenty-first century.

Fact, fiction and faction: a blurring of boundaries or hyperreal policing?

As we have already argued in the preceding chapters, one of the key ways in which police engage the media – and by extension the public – is as a component of the investigative process. Such engagement might entail appeals for public help in solving cases, warnings to the public to 'be on the look out' for or 'beware' of particular individuals, identification of suspects, requests for information about particular events and so on. These interactions with the media often result in the soundbites we receive on nightly news broadcasts or radio news stories. This engagement has practical and operational utility aimed at tangible policing outcomes. However, beyond serving to assist with an investigation, these forms of media engagement also serve to communicate symbolically to the public about police and policing activities more generally, both dramatizing policing and reaffirming its moral functions of uncovering truth, delivering justice and fulfilling public duty. As Manning (1988: 33–4) puts it:

> Policing organizations are drama absorbing, drama processing, and drama producing ... They collect and transform messages received from the public ... The primary products of police organizations are thus symbolic – messages conveying statements to social groups about their moral well being [...].

The symbolic drama of policing, however, extends well beyond that delivered through the instrumental dissemination of information or appeals to the public for help. Policing constitutes drama and this drama has been strategically deployed in recent decades in both fictional and factual terms. Indeed, we have also witnessed a general increase in the amount of factual and fictional representations of policing and crime in the media more generally.

In a content analysis of fictional and factual media representations of crime, Reiner and Livingston (1997) were able to plot changes to the dramatization of crime across the mid to late twentieth century. Their research indicated close to a threefold increase in crime reportage in newspapers and a significant increase in the popularity of crime-based fictional drama on television.[1] There were also significant shifts in the themes of this fictional television programming, with more emphasis being placed on the suffering of victims and graphic depictions of violence, less emphasis on the social background of the offender and a significant rise in the representation of ancillary crimes not central to a story. Overall, such programming presents a picture of a society much more under threat by all-pervasive and violent crime than programming of the past.

Like factual representations of crime, fictional depictions of crime and law enforcement drama have long had a place not just in contemporary mainstream television programming, but in storytelling that can be traced back to the bible and Greek mythology (Reiner 2010). However, the development of a specific detective fiction has been traced to the birth and development of modern policing itself, and the same kinds of social anxieties about threats to social order by the 'dangerous classes' that symbolized that birth. In England, eighteenth-century accounts of 'true' crime, such as those depicted in the publication *The Newgate Calendar*, evolved from stories about murderers and other criminals being subject to the vengeance of god, to nineteenth-century accounts of the detective, a device through which truth (rather than vengeance) was to be attained (Knight 2004).

This new character of the detective represented the solution to conspiracy and subversion. Detectives were the 'unfailingly resourceful individual symbolizing a superior ideal of self-disciplined rationality, who is symbolically related to a well-ordered bureaucratic organization' (Reiner 2010: 186). Yet it was not until the mid-twentieth century that the routine 'beat' police officer began to appear as a leading character in police procedurals in the US and the UK (Reiner 2010). Indeed, the professionalization of policing was a vital component in the development of the police officer as a credible character (Manning 1997) that could populate mainstream depictions of law enforcement.

From the outset such depictions were subject to the influence of policing organizations. When the hit 1950s LA police drama *Dragnet* was filmed, William Parker, the Chief of the LAPD and leader of the professionalization movement, gave creator Jack Webb access to LAPD facilities (Reiner 2010). The programme's tag-line introduction voice-over of 'ladies and gentlemen, the story you are about to see is true', announced a new, more 'realistic' type of dramatization, and police involvement added to the pretence of accuracy. The symbolism accompanying police procedurals such as *Dragnet* emphasized professionalism: skill, dedication, adherence to the law, pride, and the following of well-established procedures.

Depictions of police in law enforcement and general crime television drama would go through a range of manifestations over the following half a century, many being less than flattering in their depictions of police, others showing police ready to break the rules to get a result. While some authors (Leishman and Mason 2003; Reiner 2010) have focused on these depictions and genres in some detail, we instead want to highlight the relationships between the police and the producers and creators of television fiction; the behind-the-scenes activities that impact these and other police-focused programming.

Like the *Dragnet* example, the making of fictional law enforcement programmes often sees police organizations acting as 'collaborators' or 'consultants' to writers, producers and directors. Such practices have been in place in Australia for many years, with police dramas such as *Wildside* (1977–99), *Blue Heelers* (1994–2006) and *Water Rats* (1996–2001)[2] all employing local police representatives to assist in developing storylines that 'accurately' reproduce and depict police practices and procedures. Internationally, the US produced *The Wire* (2002–8) was created by former police reporter David Simon and his co-creator was former Baltimore policeman Ed Burns, while the long running UK-produced *The Bill* (1984–2010) involved liaison with the Metropolitan Police Force.[3]

Such arrangements might seem 'cosy', however, problems can and do arise when disagreements between police and producers cause tensions. The Australian gritty procedural crime drama series *Wildside*, for example, makes for an interesting case that highlights the sensitivities of these relationships. The series, which focused on policing in inner-city Sydney, often portrayed corrupt and improper activity, with the line between law enforcement and law breaking often blurred or breached. While initially the NSW Police Force had consulted on the programme, the increasingly 'negative' storylines began to conflict with the preferred image of the Force. The depictions were interpreted as inaccurate representations of police activities that could bring the Force into disrepute (NSW Police Public Affairs Branch 1997). As a result NSW Police withdrew from the consultancy role, arguing that the creators continued to depict the police in a 'negative' light. While the programme's producers may have argued that indeed there were 'accuracies' in such portrayals and storylines, for the police 'accurate' portrayals in such dramas usually also means positive portrayals (Mawby 2007; Reiner 2000b).

When these arrangements go as planned, however, the opportunities for the police to disseminate positive public images are evident. Programmes such as *Blue Heelers* in Australia and *The Bill* in the UK are perfect examples of the capacity for fictional police dramas to resonate with the public. Characters such as Maggie Doyle (*Blue Heelers*) and Reg Hollis (*The Bill*) were well received by the public, and although fictional, the good publicity such 'policing representatives' foster no doubt benefits the policing organizations they depict. Furthermore, as we were told by a number of public relations respondents, such programmes often produce more interest in members of the public in joining the police service; that is, they are a positive recruitment tool.

'Factional' programming

While dramatic representations of policing continue to prevail, a newer form of representation now fills television programming schedules. Aside from continual changes to the representative image of the police officer him or herself,[4] Mason (2002) has argued that representations of policing and the criminal justice system have also taken on a 'factional' dimension, a hybridization of the fictional and factual mediatized image of policing. This form of presentation often manifests through particular styles of televisual programming, such as 'reality television', infotainment programmes that see the police engage in 'documentary-style' productions with media networks. The 'reality TV', or the infotainment genre more generally, originated in the US in the 1980s (Cavender and Fishman 1998). In the Australian context, programmes such as *The Force*,[5] *The Code*,[6] *Missing Persons Unit*,[7] *Crime Investigation Australia*,[8] *Crash Investigation Unit*,[9] *Forensic Investigators*, *The Recruits* and *Australia's Most Wanted* have all been promoted as behind-the-scenes accounts of 'true' policing activities. The phenomenon is of course not unique to Australian police television. Mawby (2002b: 38) has highlighted the growth of police reality television in the UK, where programmes like *Crimewatch UK*, *Cops with Cameras*, *Police Interceptors* and *Night Cops* are broadcast. Similarly, Cavender and Fishman (1998) have noted that such programmes are broadcast in France, the Netherlands, Germany, Mexico and Brazil, among others. The most successful example of the genre is no doubt the US syndicated programme *COPS*, which has run for over 23 seasons. *COPS* attests to the now long-lasting popularity of the genre with viewers.

As Jiggins (2007: 203) has noted, police departments worldwide dedicate 'considerable resources to managing their relationship with the media in order to generate positive publicity, and thus the part-nering of police in these observational documentaries is just another way in which police are expanding their repertoire of proactive, positive media activities.' The consultancy-style arrangements between programme producers and the police differs from the earlier dis-cussed fictional programmes in a number of ways. For example, police organizations generally enjoy a greater amount of influence over the final product, and there are also potentially lucrative finan-cial benefits received by police organizations for their cooperation. Similarly, these representations, while claiming to offer accurate insights into the job of policing, do so in ways that diverge from factual news depictions and draw on the dramatic elements of fic-tional, scripted programming. 'Real-life' operational police are the stars, but this is not the news as we know it.

According to Leishman and Mason (2003), there are three broad categories of reality television genres that can be identified:

1. the 'docu-soap', which follows the exploits of particular groups;
2. the 'bio-vision' game shows, which place volunteers in artificial living environments; and
3. the reality television programmes that follow emergency and rescue services, which we will call the 'ride-along'.

While Leishman and Mason see police and law enforcement observational documentaries or 'ob-docs' as largely being part of the third category, we would also suggest that such programmes increasingly cross over into the first category, drawing on the back stories and dramas of individuals that pure 'ride-alongs' often overlook.

For example, a series such as *The Recruits*, which traces the progress of a group of young police recruits, is certainly more docu-soap in style than ride-along – although it also includes elements of the later.

Technology has clearly played a large part in the expansion of law enforcement 'ob-docs'. The development of lightweight digital cameras and sound recording equipment has been vital in capturing the 'real' experience of policing that many of these programmes claim to portray. Such equipment has made it possible to follow, pursue and record events that take place in real time and at high speed. Production crews can trail and record the movements of the police, in and out of the patrol car, in 'media ride-along' fashion. The bumpy and chaotic hand-held camera footage, as is a common aesthetic in the genre, is seen as enhancing the gritty realism of the experience rather than detracting from the production values of the programmes as we might expect. Kammerer (2004) suggests that engagement with faux CCTV and surveilling techniques creates a 'rhetoric of surveillance' (Kammerer, 2004: 468). Likewise, grainy CCTV surveillance footage places the viewer in the position of the forensic officer. Evidence becomes entertainment, and the viewer is situated as the police officer, if only for the half hour television timeslot.

However, the popularity of this programming is not just about technical innovation. Viewing such programmes has also entailed a process of enculturation. The reality television medium, as a more general aesthetic form and phenomenon, has constructed law enforcement 'ob-docs' as acceptable viewing – and visa versa, where the CCTV aesthetic has become the style of reality television. As Ferrell et al. (2008: 131) put it: 'For a while now we have been treated to the spectacle of […] squad car camera footage, a window on crime that turns police officers into performers …'

Law enforcement 'ob-docs' are of a particular aesthetic that we have come to recognize and respond to as 'real' – 'real' police, 'real' villains, 'real' chases, 'real' time. And as the synoptic gaze draws its 'reality' from these programmes, it likewise reconstructs the cultural lives and expectations of the viewers. This ongoing 'spiral of culture and crime' (Ferrell et al. 2008: 132–3) changes public meaning, perceptions and reactions to crime and law enforcement. This truly simulated policing thus has concrete cultural effects that produce and reproduce meaning. This kind of spiralling hyperreality has produced what has been termed the CSI effect (Huey 2010), where the public expects police investigations and forensic procedures to mirror those observed in fictional or factional broadcasting.

Likewise, while policing organizations might have traditionally been averse to media activities, the shift into reality-style programming has mirrored shifts in police attitudes to media relations more generally – and indeed helped form these attitudes in a spiralling feedback loop. Police organizations are now desirous of involvement in such programming. The introduction of proactive media strategies has meant that police observational documentaries – once something that caused much fear and trepidation within police organizations – are now seen as an opportunity. Yet the 'ob-doc' model now also forms the basis of police multimedia work, where the 'ride-along' is staged from within as an internal media opportunity. The aesthetic of police-shot news footage is beginning to resemble the 'ob-doc'.

The perfect symbiosis?

Some 20-odd years ago Manning (1992: 249) noted that '[t]he American urban police have long hoped that technology would enhance their status as professionals ...', and while he concluded that in fact 'technology is a ploy in games of power and control within organizations' (Manning 1992: 391), on another level technology is indeed enhancing the status of the police – just in more diffuse ways than he had perhaps anticipated.

Central to the genre of policing reality programming is the relationship between the police and media production companies (Mason 2002; Mawby 2007). The benefits for both parties are many. For producers of such programmes and the television networks that air them, police 'ob-docs' can attract a broad range of viewers, leading to high ratings that naturally translate into valuable advertising revenue for broadcasters. In Australia, programmes such as *The Force* and *The Recruits* have performed consistently well in measures of ratings,[10] and have held these strong rating positions over a number of series. These programmes also have the added benefit of being relatively easy and cheap to produce, once clearance has been granted and resources supplied or made available by policing organizations.

For policing organizations, the potential benefits are also significant. In the first instance, these programmes offer the opportunity for the police to present the images of police and police work that they want seen by the public. Police organizations, along with other government agencies,[11] have realized that actively opting to be involved with these programmes is a potentially image-boosting investment (Mawby 2007; Reiner 2000b). For example, recent NSW Police Force Annual Reports, under the banner of 'Public Trust and Confidence', have acknowledged film and television opportunities as offering 'a platform to promote our business' and core objectives (NSW Police Force 2008: 41; NSW Police Force 2009: 25).

Police involvement in these programmes differs from the usual consultancy-type roles that have traditionally typified police television work. In these scenarios, production companies, who present their particular programme idea for review, approach police organizations. Taking into account their organizational media objective and priorities, if the police are satisfied with the brief presented to them, they will enter into a contractual arrangement with these production companies, allowing them to film the requisite footage and have access to serving and other police representatives. Such arrangements will also typically involve the provision of liaison officers, who help mediate relations between production staff, filming crew and the police and public with whom they are interacting. Similarly, legal measures are also implemented to enable crews to film with minimal legal impediments, which could slow up the filming and airing process. Contractual arrangements are drawn up between the police and these production companies, enabling police assurance that the programmes meet their intended aims. Moreover, the police hold veto rights over what goes to air and the angles promoted in these programmes (Burton 2007; Lawrence and Bissett 2009; Daily Telegraph 2008). They can also be good income earners for police agencies, helping to offset public relations budgets, for which police (and governments alike) have often been criticized (for example, O'Brien 2008).

The partnering of police organizations with production companies and television networks represents a significant shift from some earlier forms of documentary making that delivered offerings such *as Cop It Sweet* in the 1990s in Australia, and *The Secret Policeman* in the 2000s in the UK. *Cop It Sweet* had a devastating effect on NSW Police when screened on ABC in the early 1990s. In this ground-breaking example of a police 'ride-along', examples of differential and racist policing targeting Aboriginal people in Redfern, an inner-city suburb of Sydney, were uncovered. The fallout was disastrous for NSW Police, resulting in immeasurable damage to the Force's reputation and public and institutional confidence. Whether or not present and future officers have learned the lessons about differential policing, the lessons about media management and engagement were certainly learned. While the 'new' approach to the filming of police 'ride-alongs' is not without its problems,[12] the potential for negative fallout is certainly at the forefront of media department minds when the police are weighing up the pros and cons of police reality programmes. As Commissioner Hogan-Howe commented during the Leveson Inquiry (2012: 789):

> ... usually great care is taken to make sure that, first of all, the press who are at the event are chaperoned. They have no right of entry into the properties so they should not go into the properties. Number two is that the individuals who are the suspects and are the subject of arrest when you get there, or were being sought when you arrived, are not identified, and there should be nothing, the written nor the visual accounts, that allow that to happen. It is really to get the story that the police are taking action in an area about a particular type of crime, be it drugs or whatever, not that this individual was a subject of the investigation.

This is important in terms of individual rights in any jurisdiction, but there is an added dimension in jurisdictions like the UK, where the Human Rights Act 1998 has been implemented.

As policy documents reveal, however, the police are also developing clear guidelines and rationales for their involvement in observational documentaries. The *London MPS Media Policy* document (MPS 2005), for example, gives some insight into the decision-making process:

> The MPS receives numerous approaches and requests from television production companies for co-operation with the making of television documentaries and dramas. While many of these provide opportunities to project the work and achievements of the MPS and possibly generate income, they can be time-consuming and require considerable resources to enable them to proceed. There can also be occasions when the proposals may be in conflict with one another. All approaches from television documentary or drama programmes should be filtered through the DPA[13] who will consult with the relevant units and officers to decide whether to pursue the proposal.

So while these arrangements proffer far greater power to police organizations in the control of image, both parties in the relationship engage in constructing representations of the police when they collaborate on such infotainment projects. As Mason (2002: 4) argues, '[t]he reality cop show is another constructed representation of the police', managed by the police through their media relations offices. Not only does this raise questions about the ability of media outlets to critically present such representations (and negative portrayals of the police often lead the police to cut cooperation with media organizations as in the case of *Wildside*), but it also creates concerns about the sort of information being imparted to the public who rely so heavily on media representations to form their opinions on matters of crime and policing. However, if these programmes are, as we have suggested, used as a device to build the status of policing and confidence and legitimacy in the organization, it is important to know the precise content of the programmes and how such content might be deployed. We discuss the content of a range of these programmes in the following section.

Content of observational documentaries: a NSW case study

With the aim of better understanding the trends and themes evident in police observational documentaries we conducted a content and narrative analysis on three police observational documentaries with the support of student research assistants.[14] A predetermined coding matrix was used to systematically explore the portrayals of the NSW Police, policing, crime and justice in these programmes (Mawby 2011). Season two of *RBT* (18 episodes), season 1 and 2 of *The Recruits* (21 episodes in total) and season 5 of *The Force* (12 episodes) were analysed. Both quantitative and qualitative data on depictions in these law enforcement 'ob-docs' was collected (Mason 1992; GAO 1996; Monk-Turner et al. 2007). The decision to analyse these particular programmes was threefold: firstly, these particular programmes were readily available in DVD form; secondly, each of the programmes focused on different elements of policing and accordingly were shot in varying styles and formats; finally, each programme had different objectives.[15]

The content analysis component of the research aimed to obtain quantitative data on the operational procedures presented in the programmes, the types of offences portrayed, the consequences imposed on offenders, and the demographics of police officers, victims and offenders in these programmes. The narrative analysis component collated qualitative data in the form of quotes, themes and storylines, focusing on the way in which themes of legitimacy (non-operational procedures) including evidence of goodwill, discretion and fairness were displayed, as well as considering any direct statements made about the police in these programmes. This narrative analysis in particular was designed to explore in greater depth the general understanding that viewers of these programmes might hold of the NSW Police, their role in the community, and the nature of their interactions with the public, both at a programme-specific level and more generally.

Operational procedures

When results for the three programmes were combined, the most common operational procedures depicted in these programmes were arrests (83 occurrences out of 459), questioning (79 occurrences), searches (62 occurrences) and breath checks (52 occurrences). These programmes also frequently depicted evidence of police effectiveness including demonstrating the detection of crime (41 occurrences), the solving of crime (38 occurrences) and the prevention of crime (22 occurrences). Additional activities depicted included crowd control, patrol, investigation and drug testing. The breakdown of these operational procedures is indicated in Table 6.1.

Non-operational procedures

Our narrative analysis also depicted numerous occasions where the police engaged in non-operational, or goodwill, procedures, demonstrating discretion and fairness exercised by members of the NSW Police Force. Direct statements made to the camera, either by the narrators of these programmes or officers themselves, valorized the police by highlighting the courage, dedication and positivity of police officers towards the work that they do. For example:

NARRATOR: 'It is their [the police force's] job to get there and do the best they can.'

(*The Force*)

OFFICER: 'We brought her home because it is our duty, a duty of care.'

(*The Recruits*)

TABLE 6.1 Police operational procedures on observational documentaries

Operational procedures	Percentage
Arrests	15.9
Searches	11.9
Questioning	15.1
Breath checks	10.0
Detection of crime	8.9
Solving crime	8.2
Prevention of crime	4.8
Additional activities	25.2

These programmes were also shown to depict the emotional or 'human' side of police officers, particularly *The Recruits*, which followed the struggles, stresses and triumphs of training and probationary constables, depicting the kindness and thoughtfulness of members of the police to the community. Other notable representations of non-operational procedures included showing the personal background of police officers, (solely in *The Recruits*) including their family and relationships (75 occurrences), demonstrating the police engaging in confidence-building, including explaining to the public the options available to them in given situations and the duty of care police feel they owe to the public (50 occurrences), and the police explaining their actions, showing police officers to be reasonable (43 occurrences).

Narrative analysis indicated that each individual programme had its own particular focus, revealing similar but slightly different representations of the police and the nature of their work. When combined, however, the key non-operational themes to emerge were that of statements about the job of policing (25 per cent), engagement in confidence-building activities (20 per cent), and the display of emotions by officers (20 per cent), officer's personal backgrounds (16 per cent), warnings to public/offenders (7 per cent), discretion (7 per cent) and policing as a social service (5 per cent).

That these programmes present these narratives and this content is not of course evidence that the public viewers necessarily consume these messages in the way intended. However, as we will see below, there is evidence these messages do hit the target in terms of organizational expectations. In the following section we look at how this content meets the media objectives of our case study police organization, the NSW Police Force.

Media objectives

What both the content and narrative analyses of the programmes demonstrate is that a close alignment exists between the key messages and themes in these programmes and the stated objectives of the NSW Police Force as set out in Table 6.2. As stated in the NSW Police Media Policy, the key objectives when engaging with the media are to:

1. maximize assistance and information from the public to help solve crime;
2. correct or clarify information in the community;
3. warn people of dangers or threats;
4. create discussion in the community and/or among criminals during investigations;
5. deter criminal activity by increasing the perception of detection;
6. highlight good police work;
7. increase police visibility;
8. reassure the community and reduce the fear of crime;
9. provide transparency and maintain community faith in policing and our system of justice.

(NSW Police Public Affairs Branch 2011: 4)

TABLE 6.2 Police media objectives as reflected in observational documentary themes

NSW Police Force Public Affairs Branch media objectives	Programmes directly demonstrating media objectives
1. Maximize assistance and information from the public to help solve crime	X
2. Correct or clarify information in the community	RBT
3. Warn people of dangers or threats	RBT The Force
4. Create discussion in the community and/or among criminals during investigations	X
5. Deter criminal activity by increasing the perception of detection	RBT The Force The Recruits
6. Highlight good police work	RBT The Force The Recruits
7. Increase police visibility	RBT
8. Reassure the community and reduce the fear of crime	The Force The Recruits
9. Provide transparency and maintain community faith in policing and our system of justice	The Force The Recruits RBT

For example, the programme RBT directly matched objectives 2, 3, 5, 6, 7 and 9 through its depictions of, among other things, police explaining the operational procedures to the audience and offenders, warning about the dangers of driving under the influence and highlighting good police work and transparency by showing the detection of offenders and adherence to standard operational procedures.

Likewise, *The Force* was seen to illustrate objectives 3, 5, 6, 8 and 9 through its use of warnings of the threat of victimization, demonstrating the consequences imposed on each offender for their crimes, highlighting police effectiveness, reassuring the community and providing transparency in police work by illustrating the operational procedures involved. This programme was also seen as emphasizing the role of NSW Police in providing social services to the community including incidences of the police assisting homeless persons, rescuing members of the public from houses, taking people to hospital, assisting victims of house fires and preventing danger to other members of the community.

Furthermore, *The Recruits* demonstrated objectives 5, 6, 8 and 9 by encouraging the perception that the police are everywhere, showing police engagement in confidence-building activities in the community, promoting the image that the police are approachable and providing transparency by explaining procedures and informing the public of the reasons behind their actions. *The Recruits* was also seen to focus on 'humanizing' the NSW Police by depicting the personal journey of trainee police officers – their personal and family background and the emotions they experience going through the training programme – and emphasizing that the NSW Police are important members of the community.

Even though objectives 1 and 4 were not so clearly depicted in the programmes analysed, one could argue that these programmes also indirectly resulted in the achievement of these objectives, especially when viewed in conjunction with our survey results.

Policing (reality) television

Interviews undertaken with Australian directors of police public relations attest to the relative importance placed on police organizations being involved in 'ob-doc' production. Clearly, this involvement is about much more than just image management. In NSW at the time of our research interviews, the NSW Police Force was contracted to be involved in no less than six separate observational documentaries (NSW Police PR Respondent 1), with a number of other offers from production companies under consideration. Western Australian Police were also engaged in a number of 'ob-docs' and had been for some time. Indeed, all Australian state police organizations have had some involvement in 'ob-doc' production. However, as we have suggested above, involvement of policing organizations in television production goes beyond observational documentaries. As this Victoria police respondent reveals:

> We just don't deal with the observational type programmes. We deal with true crime programmes such as things that would go to air on *Crime Investigation Australia* or the Crime Channel on Foxtel. People who are writing true crime books – we provide that research facility for them as well. You know, a whole bunch of different things as well as our operational requirements, which you know, to escort specialist filming vehicles when they're out filming on the road so they can do that safely.
>
> *(Vic. Police PR Respondent 1)*

In NSW, the media unit deals with a range of media communications including what they call 'special projects'. And as our respondent notes:

> Yeah. The Media Unit deals with reactive inquiries from the media and managing that information flow and also dealing with identifying and dealing with proactive media opportunities. Now that includes both news, feature and special projects. Special projects entails a whole range of things but our focus at the moment is predominantly film and television.
>
> *(NSW Police PR Respondent 3)*

That film and television opportunities are given so much emphasis and afforded so much importance demonstrates the potential positive outcomes police organizations feel they can realize: 'We've got four film and television projects currently on the go in Western Australia and you'll find other states, particularly in New South Wales, are far more inclined to use that' (WA Police PR Respondent 1).

The involvement in observational documentaries is, as we have suggested, about image. However, image work is also linked to the range of other logics that we have outlined in this book – the management of risk, the responsibilization of the public and the building of trust and legitimacy. As the head of WA Police Media told us in regard to their involvement in the programme *The Force*:

> We were the first state to sign up to *The Force*. It was a wholly a West Australia Police programme when it commenced, I think four-and-a-half years ago. It now involves New South Wales, Northern Territory and Tasmania. We see that as a highly valuable way of, high impact way of – you know what the greatest benefit is? It's been able to portray the realism of policing and also our professionalism. I'm not so interested as the media boss is in showing us catching a crook as how courteous or helpful the police officers are. It's difficult to measure the value of that. We've done one set of external research that came back that said people's views had significantly changed about policing as a result of seeing that. So we're doing that. We're doing a spin-off series with the Seven Network on dogs. We've just commenced a series with Foxtel called *Kalgoorlie Cops*, which focuses on the gold fields and we're also doing a project for the BBC which will involve one of our officers going to the UK …
>
> *(WA Police PR Respondent 1)*

While, as we have discussed, commercial arrangements with television production companies can provide lucrative income streams for police organizations, the WA Police were quick to point out they received no such benefit in their original engagement with *The Force*. However, whatever the outcome this income appears not to be the key justification for police involvement in such productions. Rather, these provide another outlet for the extension of simulated policing, not only showing the police 'doing something' as our NSW Police respondents put it, but also providing narratives of deterrence and attempting to build trust in police and legitimacy in the police organization. As Tyler (2006) and Hough et al. (2010) have noted, legitimacy in the organization can also have the effect of increasing public compliance with the law and cooperation with the police. Thus the governing rationality here suggests this simulated policing is perceived by its advocates to have very real effects. As the head of the NSW multimedia unit put it:

> Deterrent, it's the word … Actually the catchword of an awful lot of these programmes is that at the end of the day it's deterrent that will stop them. It's to stop them drink driving, it's to stop someone who watches *The Force* – and *The Force* is another one, an observational documentary, just tracking cops in their various roles from general duties right through to specialist squads and literally sticking behind them like glue and following their moments.
>
> *(NSW Police PR Respondent 2)*

While humanizing policing was another justification for police engagement in these programmes, it was clear that there was a broader strategy that saw particular programmes partnered for specific purposes as the NSW Director of Public Affairs notes:

> … there's three sides to that, humanizing the job is good, there'd be those who are saying … some elements of the organization rely on a fear factor simply to stop something happening so if the riot squad turn up at a party that's out of control they want people to stop what they're doing the moment their presence is there so they actually don't have to do anything human … that's why they cruise around in [black] vehicles and wear … scary looking clothes because people go 'OK I get the picture'… . [E]ach show will have a different corporate objective like you know *Crash Investigation Unit* clearly has road safety messages in it so that's why we make that show and because when you're confronted with those

investigations you get people thinking about those sorts of issues.

(NSW Police PR Respondent 1)

Clearly then this simulated policing is targeted to clear objectives; a range of operational messages are being disseminated in an attempt to foster behavioural changes in members of the public, or at the very least get them to reflect on their behaviour. Moreover, these messages are controlled by police organizations when necessary. However, production companies self-regulate what they put to air to in any event, given the mutually beneficial status of the programmes to the producers, the networks and the police. A NSW Police Force respondent put it thus:

We get to vet it. We get to vet it. We make sure that we're not going to portray ourselves in a way that is wrong and we're not going to let something that is clearly wrong go to air. But we've allowed things going through, it's run with the legal side as well and some people mightn't like some of the stuff. As we said with *Drug Lords*, I mean there's material there that some of the police don't like seeing but in some ways other officers see that as a … great education process, so that's there. So yeah, we oversight it … I can't think of many programmes where we'd even make dramatic changes on anything.

(NSW Police PR Respondent 2)

WA Police saw the objectives of 'ob-docs' similarly:

[The objectives of these programmes are to] [d]emonstrate the professionalism of the police; raise public confidence in policing in our jurisdiction; allow the community to better understand the challenges that the police face; allow the community to understand the types of decision-making that the police have to make. For example, there's been recent controversy about the use of Tasers and the roll out of those to general police. Through shows like *The Force*, we're able to show that the training that occurs with things like Tasers and how people don't just immediately whip it out and Taser somebody but often, how a situation in a street might evolve. So if initially there's an argument, the police try to talk, to use verbal judo to talk the person around and then ultimately, if it escalates and they have to use their force option.

(WA Police PR Respondent 3)

Interestingly, the West Australian Corruption and Crime Commission released a critical report in October 2010, shortly after this interview, demonstrating that Tasers were now a 'compliance tool' and 'were increasingly being used against people resisting arrest, up from 20 per cent of Taser deployments in 2007 to 43 per cent in 2009' (Watson, cited in Guest 2010). The report followed the public release of video footage of a man in police custody being Tasered 13 times by WA Police.[16] This episode demonstrates the blurred line between agenda setting, preferred messages and image work.

As one WA Police PR Respondent put it when discussing the value of police observational documentaries:

Well the most important thing is to maintain public confidence. That really is the central tenet of the whole business. We want to communicate to the public through the media and I often say to my staff, when you are dealing with journalists you have to take the view that you are communicating to the public and they're just a conduit to that.

(WA Police PR Respondent 3)

So these programmes provide another outlet for the extension of simulated policing: not only showing police 'doing something' as our NSW Police respondents put it, but also providing narratives of deterrence and attempting to build trust in the police and legitimacy in the police organization showing positive images of policing. In order to explore these themes further, we surveyed viewers of these programmes in order to gain a better understanding of the ways in which viewers perceived these representations. We will now discuss these findings.

Survey results

An Internet-based survey instrument was deployed in order to test the relationships between public perceptions of policing and viewers and non-viewers of police observational documentaries. That is, we aimed to establish whether those who watched police reality television were likely to have more positive perceptions of policing than those who did not. The survey collected both qualitative and quantitative data by providing capacity for both closed and open-ended questions.[17]

The survey was distributed to the public via the NSW Police Facebook site, Twitter account and website. Concurrently it was promoted electronically through Sydney and regional social media networks. Due to the nature of social networking, existing respondents shared and recruited future respondents from among their own networks, further broadening the respondent base (Castillo 2009). By placing the survey in the formats discussed it captured a sample in which a majority were likely to have viewed at least one of the programmes under study (expressly the police Facebook/Twitter cohort). However, we were also able to capture a cohort less likely to have regularly viewed the programmes (the broader snowball sample). In total we obtained 583 useable questionnaires (out of over 850 surveys that were either fully or partially completed).

Quantitative results

To test the relationship relationships between public perceptions of policing and viewers and non-viewers of police observational documentaries, two survey scales were developed. Firstly, a seven item scale was created to measure public perceptions of the police. The first three items of this scale incorporated judgments about police professionalism, honesty, trust, community presence, and fairness, factors previously found to be important measures of procedural justice and to influence opinions of police legitimacy (Gaeta 2010; Hinds and Murphy 2007; Jackson and Sunshine 2007; Lee 2011; Murphy et al. 2008; Tyler 1997; Tyler and Huo 2002). The next three items incorporated judgments of effectiveness. The final item constituted a judgment of police presence in the community. These items constituted questions 4 to 10 inclusive in the survey as indicated below.

- The NSW Police Force perform their job professionally.
- The NSW Police Force treat all people fairly and equally.
- Most NSW Police are honest.
- NSW Police are effective in solving crime.
- NSW Police are effective in preventing crime.
- NSW Police are effective in preventing crime.
- Do you believe NSW Police have a strong community presence?

We called this construct Perceptions of the Police Index (PoPI). A Cronbach's alpha test conducted on the PoPI indicated a high level of reliability (a 0.916) across the seven items, suggesting the items related closely as a measure of the underlying concept (PoPI). The perceptions of police scale was transformed into an ordinal level measure using four categories as follows based on responses to the 10 questions: "strongly disagree" (1), "disagree" (2), "agree" (3), and "strongly agree" (4), with strongly disagreeing equating to negative perceptions of police and strongly agreeing equating to very positive perceptions of police.

The scores recorded on the PoPI also reflected some of the key measures used by the Australian Productivity Commission (Steering Committee for the Review of Government Service Provision 2011), allowing us to assess our Internet-based non-representative sample cohort next to a random population sample. Although some of the other items differed in character, the strong relationship between our data and those of the Productivity Commission review cited above provide some evidence as to the validity of our non-representative sample. For example, Table 6.3 indicates the percentage of each sample group who either agreed or strongly agreed with three key items measuring procedural fairness and justice in both surveys.

Table 6.4 represents the television episode viewing index (TV index) which summarizes the observational documentary viewing

TABLE 6.3 Measures of procedural fairness and justice

	Current study	*SCRGSP Report NSW Police*
Perform job professionally	81%	80%
Treat people fairly and equally	66%	68%
Police are honest	79%	78%

habits of the sample (n 583). This TV index categorized viewing habits from those that rarely (n 104) viewed any episodes of the three programs to those that watched some (n 100), many (n 203), or most (n 139).

We then conducted a one-way analysis of variance test (ANOVA) using our PoPI as the dependent variable and the TV viewing index as the independent variable to test whether there was any effect of the level of viewing of police documentaries on perceptions of the police.

This analysis indicated that there is a statistically significant effect of the degree of TV viewership on perceptions of the police (F = 19.336, p = < 0.001). Being an omnibus test, however, ANOVA cannot tell us which mean variations are statistically significant.

Subsequently we then conducted a post-hoc Scheffe test. This revealed that there was a statistically significant increase in perceptions of police between those that rarely watched the programs and those that watched many of the programs that we had assessed (pB 0.001). Further, and as might be expected, there was a statistically significant difference between those that rarely watched the programs and those

TABLE 6.4 Television Observational Documentary Viewing Index

		Frequency	*Percent*	*Valid %*	*Cumulative %*
	Rarely	123	21.1	21.1	21.1
	Some	108	18.5	18.5	39.6
Valid	**Many**	210	36.0	6.0	75.6
	Most	142	24.4	24.4	100.0
	Total	583	100.0	100.0	

that watched most of the programs (p = < 0.001). There was also a statistically significant difference between those that watched some of the programs and those that watched most of the programs (p = < 0.0001), although not between those that watched some and those that watched many (p = 0.138). Neither was there statistically significant difference between those that watched many and those that watched most of the programs (p = 0.055) or between those that rarely watched the programs and those that watched some (p = 0.105). These findings are represented in Figure 6.1. Thus, we are able to say that there is a significant positive relationship between the number of these programs viewed and positive perceptions of police.

It should also be noted that these police observational documentaries were also considered to be quite accurate in their depictions of the police. Seventy six per cent of respondents considered these programs to be somewhat or very accurate in response to the question "How accurate do you think these programs are in representing the everyday activities of the NSW Police?" This consideration of the programs to be relatively accurate can be seen as reinforcing the relationship between the volume of episodes viewed and the perceptions of police index.

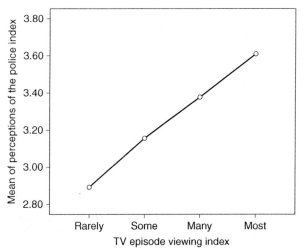

FIGURE 6.1 Mean perceptions of police verus TV viewing index.

Qualitative results

The qualitative data obtained from our online survey confirmed that the police are generally depicted and assessed by viewers quite positively in these programmes through an emphasis on the 'human' aspect of police officers, the non-violent nature of most of the depictions, their adherence to standard operating procedures and the social service that they provide to the community. As one respondent stated in relation to the general professionalism depicted in the programmes:

> The level of admiration I have for the NSW Police has been increased because of this show, I think the officers featured do a remarkable job of keeping their cool and remaining respectful in the face of appalling behaviour.
>
> *(Respondent 143)*

Another noted that the programmes humanize the police and make them more familiar to the general public. This is important as this, according to the research on trust and legitimacy, is also likely to build trust with the notion that police and public share the same values and beliefs. As the respondent suggested, the programmes make it '… easier to see police officers as humans the same as everyone else instead of authorities in uniform' (Respondent 203).

Those respondents who were of the opinion that these programmes were not accurate representations of the NSW Police, although in a minority in our survey, mostly made mention of their emphasis on dramatic crimes, the edited nature of these programmes and their view that these programmes were more for promotional, amusement and commercial purposes. As one suggested:

> I'm increasingly concerned by the broader rationale for having such television shows. I wonder if they emphasize the more dramatic crimes unnecessarily and give both an unrealistic public depiction of the prevalence of such crime and lend credence to law and order policy which calls for greater police powers without reasonable justification.
>
> *(Respondent 16)*

Another suggested strongly that:

> I see these shows as promotimg [*sic*] largely uncontoversial [*sic*] aspects of thier [*sic*] work, making it effective propaganda and not a basis on which to decide how effectibe [*sic*] or honest police are.
>
> *(Respondent 1)*[18]

It is clear from the data presented in this chapter that police 'ob-docs' present a generally positive representation of policing. The programmes are vetted by respective police organizations and usually represent a commercial arrangement between the respective police organization and the television production company. Our content analysis indicates that significant air-time in these programmes is given over to explaining police procedure, humanizing policing and generally attempting to reassure the viewing public that the police are honest, hardworking and trustworthy. Indeed, as our discussion of NSW Police Media Objectives and the content analysis of the 'ob-docs' indicate, these productions clearly meet almost all the key media objectives.

Our survey data reveals that a large proportion of our sample believes the representations of police in 'ob-docs' are accurate. Moreover, it indicates that there is a significant relationship between the hours spent watching these programmes and the likelihood of making positive judgements about the effectiveness, fairness and professionalism of the police. This analysis does not tell us whether those who have positive perceptions of the police simply watch more 'ob-docs', or those who watch more 'ob-docs' develop more positive perceptions of the police, that is it does not inform us of the direction of causality. However, it certainly seems to indicate that watching the kinds of 'ob-docs' supported by the NSW Police does no damage to the public perception of policing.

Clearly a key message from the 'ob-docs' analysed here is that they attempt to present a police service (or police services) that is organized, transparent, procedurally and ethically fair and human. That is, the image being portrayed is one of an effective and trustworthy hardworking police who do a tough job. They also present a police service capable of detecting and preventing crime aimed at anyone who might feel inclined to offend – a message of deterrence.

Conclusion

Observational documentaries are just one example of what we see as the increasing deployment of forms of simulated policing in the relationship between the police, the media and the public. The factional documentaries screened in Australia tend to be much less dramatic than, for example, their North American counterparts and there may be a good operational and empirical basis for this. That is, observational documentaries in the form televised in Australia tend to meet the expectations of police media policy, they tend to contain strong images of procedural justice and other activities aimed at confidence-building and deterrence, they tend to be regarded as reasonably accurate by viewers, and indeed, if our survey sample is somewhat accurate, viewers of these 'ob-docs' tend to have positive perceptions of policing.

The synoptic seductions of the viewer society – the insatiable desire of the public gaze to consume images of policing – is being turned into a strategic advantage for police organizations. While this has involved some level of transparency, allowing the public to see the 'real' and 'human' sides of policing, this has also been carefully managed as police organizations are coming to terms with the dynamics of mediatized television engagement. And while contractual arrangements with producers mean the police have a veto over what is televised, the use of this veto is infrequent. This is not simply that the police are now comfortable with higher levels of transparency. Rather, the images contained in 'ob-docs' are mutually produced, managed and acted out – production companies self-police and a veto is rarely required. Production companies that attempt to diverge from preferred images may well find themselves locked out of future arrangements to their own detriment.

The hyperreality of the observational documentary simulates policing. These images in fact come to stand for policing to the extent that the public expect to be policed in the manner represented – they are a hyperreal simulation of policing. Indeed, this symbolic policing does take place. Deterrence messages are circulated, trust and confidence are built, images are enhanced and policing is seen to be occurring. And if policing has always been about image and representation, perhaps that is enough.

Notes

1. During 1955–63 only 8 per cent of top ten programmes were crime programmes, rising to 12 per cent in the final period. This rise was mainly attributable to an increase in crime programmes, compared with cop shows which declined from 6 per cent to 4 per cent of all top ten programmes between 1955 and 1991 (Reiner and Livingston 1997: 15).

2. *Wildside*, *Blue Heelers* and *Water Rats* were all long-running Australian television dramas focusing on various aspects of policing. *Wildside*, which ran for two years, focused on detective activities in inner-city Sydney. *Blue Heelers*, which was broadcast on Channel 7 for 13 seasons, focused on the police station in fictional Mount Thomas, a small country Victorian town, and *Water Rats*, which ran for six seasons on Channel 9, was based around the activities of the NSW Water Police and the crimes they encountered.

3. http://www.independent.co.uk/news/media/tv-radio/the-bill-britains-most-famous-television-police-drama-is-almost-an-industry-in-its-own-right-914410.html (accessed 21 April 2013).

4. For example, see Reiner (2010) on policing typologies.

5. *The Force* promotes itself as a 'real-life cop series', highlighting 'the raw reality of life as a police officer' (The Force Channel 7 TV Show Website 2008). The show, broadcast on Channel 7, focuses on situations involving both NSW and Western Australia Police Forces.

6. Similar to *The Force*, but broadcast on Channel 9.

7. *Missing Persons Unit*, broadcast on Channel 9, describes itself as the 'real-life Without a Trace', where viewers can assist police in finding missing 'loved ones' (Channel 9 – Missing Persons Unit Website 2008). The show follows staff from the NSW Police Missing Persons Unit as they investigate missing persons cases.

8. *Crime Investigation Australia* is broadcast on Foxtel's pay television Crime Investigation channel. The series examines 'Australia's most infamous murder cases', speaking with police investigators, witnesses and victims' families, and re-enacting events in many of the cases (Channel 9 – CIA 2008). The programme was also screened by Channel 9 (a free-to-air station).

9. *Crash Investigation Unit* follows the NSW Police Crash Investigation Unit as they investigate the causes of fatal car accidents around the state.

10. http://www.7perth.com.au/view/releases/20060823172946

11. This scenario is not unique to the police. Programmes such as *Border Security* depict the 'good work' of Australian Customs, Quarantine and Immigration departments.

12. For example, a chief constable of the South Wales Police noted during the Leveson Inquiry that the organization's decision to be involved in the programme *Traffic Cops* was regretful because some of the behaviour depicted was not 'the organisation that I want to reflect as being representative of South Wales Police' (Vaughan, in Leveson 2012: 788). Similarly, the NSW Police were also caught out when they allowed sensitive operational practices to go to air, threatening current and future organised crime investigations (http://topdocumentaryfilms.com/australian-druglords/).

13. Director of Public Affairs.

14. Following the work of Monk-Turner et al. (2007) and Mason (1992).

15. See the appendix for a more detailed explanation of the methods employed.

16. http://video.theaustralian.com.au/1606567920/WA-Police-Taser-man-13-times

17. Surveying occurred over four weeks during August and September 2011 using a web-based convenience sample and also snowballing sampling techniques.

18. The last comment is from the 'overall satisfaction after viewing these programmes' comment section of the questionnaire.

SECTION III
Policing the police

In the previous section we explored the ways new technologies and social media have changed the ways in which the police engage with the media and subsequently the public. Such changes have provided the environment for a variety of new forms of simulated policing as well as assisting police organizations in deploying key logics. Despite this, the changing structure of police–media relationships is not without discontent. This final section of the book explores the ways in which structured relationships between the police and the media, and indeed between the police and the public, are resisted or challenged.

Chapter 7 discusses the ways in which the very technologies that make simulated policing possible are also often used as tools in tactics of resistance. Here we draw on the work of Michel de Certeau (1984), among others, in mapping the way in which the power relationships operating between the police and the media and the police and the public can be subverted.

Chapter 8 explores more traditional forms of resistance that operate in the police-media relationship. Here we discuss resistances by journalists to the centralization of police media contact through professional police media units. In particular we explore the tactics of journalists in sourcing stories outside of the prescribed information channels. We also tie these resistances to some of the findings and recommendations of the recent Leveson Inquiry (2012) in the UK and a range of other recent investigations into the independence of the media.

7

NEW TECHNOLOGIES AND STRUGGLES OF REPRESENTATION

Introduction

While police organizations have developed an enhanced capacity to frame and produce stories about crime and law and order, they do so in an increasingly multimediated world. New and online technologies have led to a greater capacity to monitor police work and disseminate images of policing that resist police-preferred narratives. The growth of blogging, police or 'Copwatch' websites and the capacity for sousveillance more generally are offering increasingly complex and diverse avenues of resistance. Indeed, technologies such as CCTV — traditionally the tools of police work — are increasingly being used against the police, echoing what de Certeau (1984) would suggest are tactical strategies of citizen consumers to reinvent technologies for innovative and/or unintended purposes. Moreover, some components of the traditional press remain steadfastly opposed to the capacities of the police to control image dissemination, engaging in their own tactics of resistance to such control. This chapter explores these resistances and some of the novel approaches taken when 'watching the watchers'.

As the preceding chapters have explored, over the last thirty years we have witnessed the ways in which policing organizations have developed increasingly sophisticated modes of communication with the public. In the past few years alone, the use of emergent forms of social media such as Facebook, YouTube and Twitter have changed the (inter)face between the police and the public, providing police organizations with the capacity to bypass the traditional or 'old' forms of media. In many respects, these new modes of communications between the police and the public have enabled contact to become more direct. We have also witnessed new opportunities for the surveillance of the public presented by social media; criminal cases are being won and lost on evidence collected from social media platforms.[1] When combined with the enhanced technologies of surveillance through recording and monitoring devices, what we have now are police organizations that have significantly enhanced capacities (operational and non-operational) through their technological engagement. However, at the other end of the scale, these technologies are also challenging police capacities. The very same technologies and forums police are employing have also provided the public with more sophisticated ways in which to monitor the police and publicly disseminate and circulate images and narratives that potentially counter those coming from police.

Technologies integrated into smartphones, for example, not only provide individuals with the ability to record police activities, good and bad, but they also enable users to upload content almost instantaneously to YouTube and other virtual sites. These technologies are being used to capture episodes of malpractice, corruption, abuse and differential policing. The public dissemination of such images can directly counter the preferred image of policing that police themselves produce through the very same platforms. So, while the police are 'arming' themselves with the technology to help them fight crime, citizens are also embracing the capacities such technologies provide them to produce counter-images. Such practices have seen the establishment of organized counter-surveillance groups and the development of online and technological platforms to enhance such practices. Websites such as copwatch.org now proliferate, facilitating the work of citizen journalists, film-makers and bloggers who resist dominant police-preferred narratives. Before we explore such developments in more detail though, let us look at the contexts that have made such conditions possible.

Policing and technological ambiguities

Some 25 years ago Peter Manning (1988) noted the deep ambiguities of technologies for policing and police communications. While contemporary crime problems are framed by way of technology – today we could think of cyber-crime, money laundering, bio-security, terror networks and the like – this 'technological conceit' means that solutions to these problems are also, somewhat uncritically, to be found in technology. However, the recourse to such technology produces not just solutions but many associated problems as well. As Manning (1988: 7) explains:

> Police communications technologies have been adopted also
> as a means of organizational surveillance, guidance and con-
> trol: nominal control of police officers, especially those at the
> bottom of the discretionary pyramid, and ostensible control of
> the external environment. […] They are assumed to enhance
> the image and prestige of the police.

Manning goes on to suggest that these are empirically untested assumptions, questioning whether the technology really does achieve the ends that police assume. What is clear, however, is that technologies have changed the ways in which the police view themselves and they way in which others view the police. That is not to suggest that technologies 'organize' police or policing, or that they are responsible for the shape of the police organization or bureaucracy. Rather, technologies, deployed in the context of policing and its complex political and organizational structures, have produced a set of recursive feedback loops that in turn unsettle, disassemble and reassemble policing and its attendant practices and images. Such processes, particularly when coupled with broader social restructuring, have rendered policing itself more 'precarious' (Waddington 1999b: 62). This precariousness is evidenced in the continual rebadging or rebranding of policing in contemporary times. Whether to 'serve and protect', or to 'protect the community with your support', or to 'prevent, detect and investigate', the policing *raison d'état* is fluid and contingent.

Along the same lines, policing is dramaturgical. The capacity of police organizations to direct the theatre of policing does have its limits though. Like any theatre critics, the audience and the producers all have a part to play in the form of the narrative that unfolds, and all may hold different readings of this narrative. As Manning (2003: 3) argues: 'Police are a rich, almost natural material for drama, yet they are vulnerable, like all occupations that maintain a front and backstage version of their work, to intrusions and the unexpected. Police order life and are ordered by it.'

Indeed, policing is a performance. It occurs before an audience and is always staged in one form or another (Manning 2003). Policing is visual. It must been 'seen' to be happening. That does not mean that citizens always have to see police officers doing police work, but they do require some sort of visual representation or symbolism that signifies the presence and order of the police, as we have demonstrated in our discussions of image work. Yet these images are rarely fixed in meaning. Ferrell et al. (2008) note the capacity of image leaks from one medium to another – cross-postings, downloads, the cutting of images loose from their origins, their circulation from street, to cell phone, to YouTube. In this way, images produced in the name of state-sanctioned social control can also become images of resistance – cut adrift and in different hands, in a different context. It is little wonder then that police organizations have taken to attempting to control images in the face of these potential resistances. Yet such control is increasingly fanciful in a multimediated world. As the capacities for image production and reproduction multiply and proliferate, the control of image slips ever further away. Control and resistance thus blur together, both reinforcing the other yet ever seeking to contain the other.

We have argued in the previous chapters that police organizations, largely as a result of their growing public relations and media arms, are potentially increasing their capacity to frame news about crime and social order. So, while their relationship with the media is synergistic, and the traditional media at least have less of a capacity to mediate preferred police messages, there are still a plethora of avenues through which counter-narratives and counter-images can emerge. As the old media withers new platforms take its place.

Strategies, tactics and resistance

While little has been written about contemporary police media work, even less research has explored the ways in which resistances or challenges to this work operate. As outlined in Chapter 3, Michel de Certeau's strategies and tactics of resistance are important analytical frames through which we can both examine strategies of surveillance and social control, as employed by the police, and tactics of resistance to such strategies, as deployed by those vulnerable or opposed to such control attempts. We might assume that the new technologies and platforms the police are proactively engaging with give them greater powers of control over image – and indeed they do. However, by extending and broadening these strategies they are also creating opportunities for counter-strategies or 'tactics' of resistance. So while the few watch the many, the many are now also watching the few, and much more closely than ever before. Moreover, they are using technologies with the capacities to produce solid evidence of police malpractice should they observe it.

Sousveillance, or inverse surveillance, is a term coined by Steve Mann (Mann et al. 2003) to explain the countering of 'organizational surveillance'. Positioning itself against or alongside surveillance practices, sousveillance describes the use of surveillance technologies and tactics that invert the traditional panoptic model; that is, technology is used 'to mirror and confront bureaucratic organizations' (Mann et al. 2003: 333). While such activity is typically deployed by the disenfranchised and lower classes to increase equity through revealing the usually hidden power of key state institutions such as the police (Huey et al. 2006), anyone with the technological capacity has the ability to conduct sousveillance, and not simply for the reasons stated. Similarly, counterveillance is where surveillance technology used by the watcher is turned upon them – for example, when CCTV footage in a prison is used to reveal abuse by prison officers (Welch 2011) or when police Taser cameras reveal their overuse.

Counterveillance, sousveillance and other forms of resistance can be understood in de Certeau's terms as *tactics* of the weak (1984: 36). A tactic must play within the terrain imposed upon it and 'organised by the law of a foreign power' (1984: 37). 'It does not have the means to keep to itself ... it is a manoeuvre ... within the ... enemy's field of vision ... and within enemy territory' (1984: 37). Most of the tactics of resistance we explore below very precisely play out in the enemy's field of vision. They are wrapped up in what Mathiesen (1997) has called the 'viewer society' – where the panoptic and synoptic gaze intersect, overlap and fold in on themselves: not just a 'mass media', as Mathiesen foresaw, but an assemblage of synoptic networks – some of which provide entertainment and infotainment, some of which provide information and some of which provide counter-surveillance possibilities. What constitutes media today extends way beyond newspapers and television. There are the Internet extensions of this traditional media, as well as professional and amateur blogs and new Internet news pages (Toch 2012). And of course there is the proliferating social media led, currently, by Twitter, Facebook and YouTube.

Technologies integrated into smartphones not only enhance the ability of citizens to record police malpractice, but also provide the capacity for users to upload content almost instantaneously to YouTube, Facebook and other virtual platforms. These developments should come as little surprise when you consider that some of the biggest opportunities to witness police misconduct occur out on the beat, with the rank-and-file officers who are carrying out the day-to-day work of operational policing. Their high visibility, coupled with their high levels of discretion, leave them vulnerable to such counterveillance.

As Toch (2012:86) notes in a discussion of police–citizen confrontations:

> ... [T]oday's bystanders tend to appear at the scene heavily armed with recording equipment. This means that if a gadget-armed spectator decides to share his or her experience, he or she can email at warp speed a segment of the action to anyone who has another cell phone or available computer.

No longer is it necessary to have the traditional media uncover examples of police misbehaviour, brutality or corruption; such information comes increasingly from a technologically savvy and equipped public. Indeed, some citizens exert their right just to capture the moment. They wait, digital camera at the ready, for a moment to occur. This willingness to film everything and anything has become synonymous with the generation who have grown up with the technology to do so.

The beating of African American construction worker Rodney King on 3 March 1991 by officers of the Los Angeles police department constituted a watershed moment in the capacity for citizen counterveillance or sousveillance – albeit an almost accidental one (Manning 2003). King, with two passengers, had been involved in a high-speed pursuit with police officers and had initially resisted police directives. He was subsequently arrested, Tasered and subjected to 56 baton blows and six kicks before he was 'swarmed' by police and dragged on his abdomen to the side of the road. George Holliday, a resident bystander, began filming the beating from the balcony of his nearby apartment. Holliday's first inclination was to hand the footage over to the LAPD. Unbelievably, by today's standards at least, the LAPD dismissed the video as inconsequential, leading Holiday to pass in on to the media. The rest is, as they say, history. The public outcry over the police brutality depicted in the footage resulted in four police being charged and tried, with their subsequent acquittal triggering the 1992 LA Riots. As the *Report of the Independent Commission on the Los Angeles Police Department* put it:

> Our commission owes its existence to the George Holliday videotape of the Rodney King incident. Whether there even would have been a Los Angeles police department investigation without the video is doubtful, since the efforts of King's brother, Paul, to file a complaint were frustrated, and the report of the officers involved was falsified. Even if there had been an investigation, our case-by-case review of over 700 complaints indicates that without the Holliday videotape the complaint might have been adjudged to be 'not sustained,' because the officers' version conflicted with the account by

> King and his two passengers, who typically would have been
> viewed as 'not independent.' (1991: ii)

Here the citizen bystander, operating within the very strategies of power and indeed within its rules, not only provides a moment of resistance, but also has the effect of changing future strategies and tactics.

More recently similar tactics revealed suspect police actions that took place resulting in the death of Ian Tomlinson, a London newspaper vendor caught up in London G20 protests and the subsequent security crackdown. Video footage captured by an American businessman depicted Tomlinson being struck on the leg from behind by a police officer wielding a baton, then pushed to the ground by the same officer. The images indicated no provocation on the part of Tomlinson – and he was not a protester. Indeed, he was struck while walking along the street with his hands in his pockets (Lewis 2009). While he managed to walk away after the incident, Tomlinson collapsed and died only minutes later. In May 2011 an inquest found that Tomlinson had been unlawfully killed by a police officer – although the officer charged with his manslaughter was subsequently found not guilty of the offence. However, without the video of this incident, taken by a bystander and published first in the *Guardian* and *Guardian On-line*, then in media outlets worldwide, our understanding of the sequence of events on that day may have been very different. As Nick Davies (2009) asked at the time: 'Why did it take six days and citizen journalism to shed light on Ian Tomlinson's death?' At the heart of Davies' question was concern over the way in which the police, and perhaps the media too, had attempted to mislead the public over the events of that day and downplay the role of the police in Tomlinson's death. This incident highlights both how the increasingly proactive role of police media activities in disseminating preferred images and narratives of policing can frame events, and the role of citizen journalism and sousveillance can resist such images and narratives.

However, such tactics rarely go unchallenged. Indeed, the threat of sousveillance by the public has already provoked change in police practices: 'When the police act as though cameras were the equivalent of guns pointed at them, there is a sense in which they are correct. Cameras have become the most effective weapon that ordinary people have to protect against and to expose police abuse' (McElroy 2010: para. 18).

As Keane (2011: 1) notes:

> A lot of American police departments do not like their officers being filmed. Right from the time recording devices were invented, authorities had a monopoly on surveillance of citizens. The spread of hand-held, mobile recording devices has ended that monopoly: now police, security forces and armies must operate with the knowledge they may well be filmed during the course of responding to unrest. While citizens may face an ever closer panopticon-like state of permanent surveillance by CCTV, facial recognition software and mobile phone and internet monitoring (and, for that matter, being filmed by other members of the public themselves), authorities themselves are now under far more surveillance than ever before.

There is also some legal ambiguity in the US about the right of citizens to film the police. While a Philadelphia Police Commissioner specifically reminded staff via a memo that citizens had the right to film police doing their jobs (Keane 2011: 1), in Illinois, 'an obscure state eavesdropping law' was invoked in an attempt to prosecute people filming the police. A number of other US states have attempted to use similar laws for this purpose.

Perhaps the most well publicized example of sousveillance is the organization Copwatch. Originating in Berkeley in 1990, 'Copwatch' is 'an all-volunteer organization dedicated to monitoring police actions and non-violently asserting our rights' (Berkeley Copwatch 2012: para. 1).[2] It is worth noting that the goals of Berkeley Copwatch are somewhat demonstrative of sousveillance movements more generally. The group aims to:

1. Reduce police violence by directly observing the police on the street, documenting incidents and keeping police accountable. We maintain principles of non-violence while asserting the rights of the detained person. We provide support to victims whenever possible. We also seek to educate the public about

their rights, police conduct in the community and issues related to the role of police in our society.

2. Empower and unite the community to resist police abuse. We will do this by sharing information with the community, conducting 'Know Your Rights' trainings, sponsoring rallies, supporting victims and other community-based efforts to deal with the problem.

3. Encourage people to solve problems WITHOUT police intervention. We want to explore alternatives to calling the police.

4. Most importantly, we encourage people to exercise their right to observe the police and to advocate for one another.

(Berkeley Copwatch 2012: paras 2–5)

Another well-publicized example of counterveillance was the drone used by Internet journalist Tim Pool to cover the US Occupy protests. The *Parrot AR* drone, creatively christened the 'occucopter', was a lightweight four-rotor helicopter used 'to help them expose potentially dubious actions of the New York police department' (Sharkey and Knuckey 2011). The item can be purchased cheaply on Amazon and controlled by an iPhone. The device's onboard cameras can feed live images to the iPhone and also stream live images to the Internet (Sharkey and Knuckey 2011). In Pool's case the occucopter was used to capture and stream images of police activity during the Occupy protests. The cheap availability of such drones creates the opportunity for intensified surveillance and counterveillance capabilities. Indeed, in February 2012 the US Congress directed aviation regulators in the US to move towards establishing guidelines for the wider use of drones by both the state and private individuals (Schulz 2012). For example, local law enforcement agencies intend to use the drones for surveillance purposes.[3] Indeed, 18 police departments, universities and other government agencies have clearance from the US federal government to send up a range of drones (Sengupta 2012).

These activities and counter-activities alert us to some of the criticisms made of forms of sousveillance. Gary Marx (2003: 371) notes that while sousveillance pertains to be, and indeed can be, a democratizing intervention, it is not without its discontents. He cautions that it may lead to an intensification in suspicion and, as a consequence, a spiral in surveillance in general.

The democratization of surveillance as a result of low cost and ease of use can introduce a healthy pluralism and balance (as well as reciprocal inhibitions in use for fear of retaliation). On the other hand this may also help create a more defensive and suspicious society with an overall increase in anxiety-generating and resource-consuming surveillance and counter-surveillance.

Huey et al. (2006) also note that while one social group may be ideologically aligned to groups like Copwatch that practise sousveillance techniques, others sometimes feel that such groups do not at all represent their interests. Moreover, they cite critics who highlight the fact that Copwatch has no oversight mechanism for its own activities, nor do its leaders generally seek broader community input into their policies and practices.

Cop on cop: policing and the image in self-regulation

As Manning (2003: 85) observes, the 'filming of police work serves to monitor the police as well as citizens'. Charge offices, holding cells, station lobbies and the like are saturated with CCTV cameras providing a potential web of police self-regulation. Patrol car mounted cameras, capturing images of traffic stops, are also 'used as deterrents and controls upon officer's behaviour' (2003: 85). And while we normally conceive of public and semi-public CCTV as a social control measure – which it is – it can also serve the purpose of monitoring and regulating police behaviours. As Manning (2003: 103) puts it: 'Citizen "feedback" is stimulated by the omnipresence of images. [...] Self-produced visual media also penetrate private officer–citizen relations and are reframed as prefigurative or as a warning of mistakes at work ... analogous to war stories.'

Policing organisations have embraced other new technologies aimed at complementing operational policing. The use of mobile digital terminals (MDTs) allows the police multiple information feeds and system linkage in the patrol car. Officers can now search information systems and records in transit. Such systems also take police communications, and calls away from a closed radio frequency, making it only accessible on the sender's, the backup's and the recipient's screens. Yet this new processing of information leaves an indelible digital trace of police activity, allowing for the increased oversight surveillance and panoptic self-government of police activity.

Managing social media strategies

While most discussions of counterveillance envisage interactions between the police and citizens (or 'audience and performer'), the technology and context underlying such performances is becoming increasingly important (Manning 1996: 273). The collapse of time and space (Giddens 1991a) and the displacement of location have made cyber-realities increasingly important sites of analysis. Our research into the movement of police image work, and subsequently operational policing, into the realm of social media tells us much about the technological challenges of contemporary policing and the ways in which the strategies used to deploy such technologies also open up temporal space for resistance.

Indeed, it is clear that police public relations professionals recognise the difficulty in 'policing' the very social media forums they have created. The proper mediation of these forums requires a constant online oversight, a resourcing issue few police organizations currently have the capacity to manage. Indeed, in Tasmania resourcing was the reason the state police had not yet engaged Facebook:

> ... there are budget cuts across all state government agencies at the moment, so yeah, that's the issue I've got to face at the moment because it's the kind of environment you can't get into without monitoring it properly and participating fully and obviously populating the site and getting that two-way conversation going with the community. So I can't set it up to fail and so it's really a resourcing issue at the moment, because obviously especially with a policing site it would attract interesting characters too I'd imagine and interesting postings that obviously you need to keep an eye on it pretty strictly.

> *(Tasmania Police PR Respondent 1)*

It is quite clear both from our monitoring of police social media sites and from the information passed on by our police respondents that malicious and/or unwelcome posts do appear on their sites, particularly the Facebook platform. As this South Australian respondent notes:

> The comments that are left on Facebook are overwhelmingly positive and it's great for police officers to be able to see that instant sort of feedback in relation to the jobs that they're covering. Of course you're always going to get some detractors.
>
> *(SA Police PR Respondent 1)*

Some unwelcome posts will have nothing to do with ideology or resistance per se but constitute personal slights or revenge on a particular officer. Such instances also highlight that the sites are moderated and the offending material will generally be removed quickly when detected. This is demonstrated in the following response:

> I mean you'll get someone who you noticed a few weeks ago had slagged an officer that she presumably met on a dating site and they'd obviously dated and then she … He obviously dumped her and she got up and named in, you know, 'Watch out for Officer Briggs of …' wherever. Now, I don't know if it's right or wrong but we took that down, we did remove the content and we do, we will monitor and modify.
>
> *(NSW Police PR Respondent 2)*

The respondent further backed up these comments and highlighted the capacity for negative information in comments to spread quickly through the community of users on the police Facebook platform:

> That was one of the concerns going into Facebook land, that it's there, all those … users we've got at the moment, they're seeing all that. Every time someone puts something up it's potentially ending up in a lot of people's desktops, so you do have to monitor it and ensure that it's there. So there are little things like that.
>
> *(NSW Police PR Respondent 2)*

Indeed, concern about the negative impact of having and maintaining a social media presence meant that policing organizations, even when resourcing was not such an issue, were sometime slow to engage. As a NSW respondent noted: '… to be honest, we probably took quite a bit of concern about that in the first place. I mean it took longer to get the Facebook page up than anything else, and I've got to say, I probably held back as much as anybody, concerned that it would be very, very negative, a lot of negative comment about police' (NSW Police PR Respondent 2).

On the whole, however, the police respondent noted that, while they did mediate and remove unwanted posting, usually other Facebook users come to the defence of the police and reprimand or indeed lampoon the errant poster. Again, as one of our NSW respondents explains: 'Yeah, well Facebook, the community actually talks more as advocates for you a lot of the times' (NSW Police PR Respondent 2).

Another NSW respondent elaborates:

> The reality is it hasn't been that much, it's been a lot more informative and a lot of the negative stuff gets knocked down by the advocates very quickly. If someone has something they don't like, people jump out. You know, you'll get the FTP fuck the police sort of comment that will come up there and someone will write 'Well that's rude, you don't have to say that sort of stuff, there's hardworking men.' They may be cops, they might be friends of cops, I don't know. You try to put intelligence on a person, you can't tell but it's amazing the number of advocates who will come out jump over somebody who wants to be negative.
>
> *(NSW Police PR Respondent 2)*

The challenge for policing public relations professionals and media teams then is to have their message heard above those that seek to circulate a counter-narrative and those that actively engage the police information platforms. As one Victoria Police respondent noted, this is often a complicated and difficult task:

One of the things with social media and we've seen it come out of the Occupy Melbourne and the Protest activity – there's a lot of white noise in that space and there's a lot of competing social media. So we can be putting in the tweets and putting the information up on our Facebook and using our social media, but then you know, so's everybody. There's a lot of competition out there and I guess a lot of contradictory information, which is why it's important that we communicate in a way that people actually get.

(Vic. Police PR Respondent 2)

One challenge then with social media is, well, that it is social – anyone can do it. Police are competing in an environment of information saturation and overload. A second challenge is that in this social environment, the platform itself suggests there will be interaction. This then becomes not just a resourcing issue, but an issue of policy, consistency and accuracy. If policing agencies really want to capitalise on social media there has to be a two-way discussion. As one of our Victoria Police respondents put it:

I mean it is our site and we should, if people are discussing things, posing questions or they have certain beliefs that we actually should be giving our views as an organization and, we should be setting the record straight. Or if they're talking about particular things, we should be using that as an opportunity to actually tell people what we do and how we do it and linking I suppose to further information where there's areas of interest.

(Vic. Police PR Respondent 2)

There is then the challenge and the fine line between mediating the forum, shutting down and deleting dissent, and actually having a discussion. One of our South Australian Respondents clarified this further:

Now I'm not saying that is a perfect formula on how to proceed because obviously it is about having a two-way conversation

> and listening to what people want from us, but it comes down to being realistic about what you need to achieve from a legal perspective, the staff numbers you have to be able to sit there and moderate a Facebook site.
>
> *(SA Police PR Respondent 1)*

While police engagement with the community via social media sites has generally been regarded as a success by police public relations professionals, others have expressed concerns about police vulnerability on these sites, the 'dark side' of social media that 'may be used against you' (Wren 2011). For example, as a response to the creation of the Victoria Police Force Facebook page, some members of the public created a 'fan page' named 'I hate Victoria Police', which attracted a large number of 'likes' (Flower 2010). Similarly, official police Facebook pages themselves have come under attack from their 'fans'. Alongside public comments such as 'cops are tops' it is not uncommon to also see comments that criticize the police for breaking their own rules or reacting poorly to individual criminal matters. For example, one poster on the NSW Police Force Facebook page wrote: 'I had my house vandalized and needed the police. I couldn't even get them on the phone.' Similarly, another poster dissatisfied with the police wrote: 'I'm still waiting since 12am this morning. I've been told you get a pizza delivered quicker!'

When chastised by Queensland Police and warned to 'keep your comments civil' and that 'users who continue to post speculative comments will be banned', one poster questioned why the police have posted certain news reports 'if you don't want speculation and stupid comments?' Another wrote: 'you are seriously telling us off over that?' In the face of criticism, the police often defend their actions. For example, when one poster criticized police officers using their mobile phones while driving, the police responded by telling them 'police are exempt from certain road rules under legislation, including the use of mobile phones.'

The continual monitoring of these sites by the police means such comments often do not last long before being deleted, further antagonizing some of those who interact on the page. In response to content being deleted, one poster commented, 'people have the right to have their say here and to debate. So why are the police deleting posts? Are you now the thought police?'

Conclusion

Policing organizations are increasingly using new and social media and related technologies in strategies that seek to extend the reach of policing. In doing so they are not just producing new governable spaces, they are also responding to the desires of the viewer society where policing becomes entertainment and the police key actors in this entertainment. This expansion also opens up a variety of moments for tactics of resistance where the preferred images of policing can be challenged or subverted.

Within the broader policing remit the examples of the death of Ian Tomlinson and the beating of Rodney King, and the role citizen-initiated technologies played in their aftermath, indicate the ways in which the technologies and platforms of the surveillance society can be subverted – albeit after the fact. They also indicate how alternative narratives of policing can increasingly be made visual and disseminated.

While high-profile cases such as the Tomlinson case occasionally seep into the public's imagination, eroding the dominance of preferred images of policing, social networking and citizen journalism are also providing more mundane points of resistance, such as those seen in the posting of negative commentaries on police Facebook pages.

To fully understand surveillance we need to further explore the tactics of resistance and practices of everyday life that follow. Not to do so would be, in de Certeau's words, to ignore networks of 'antidiscipline' that are in fact central to the practice of everyday life. New forms of 'simulated policing' (O'Malley 2012) – reality television as deterrence policing, Facebook as Neighbourhood Watch, YouTube as a crimestoppers identification tool – are becoming common strategies. However, as the Ian Tomlinson example indicates, such 'simulated policing' is not without its discontents.

Notes

1. As the recent conviction of two juveniles in the US Steubenville case attests: http://ideas.time.com/2013/03/17/steubenville-rape-guilty-verdict-the-case-that-social-media-won/.
2. 'Berkeley Copwatch is based on the idea that WATCHING the police is a crucial first step in the process of organizing. We do not attempt to interfere in police activity or to resist police misconduct physically. It is our hope that, one day, mass outrage at police and government violence will increase to a point where fundamental change in the nature of policing becomes inevitable' (Berkeley Copwatch 2012: para. 1).
3. Fox News (2012) 'Lawmakers erect challenges to drones in US airspace', 14 June. Available: http://www.foxnews.com/politics/2012/06/14/lawmakers-erect-challenges-to-drones-in-us-airspace/ (accessed 6 September 2012).

8

RESISTANCES AND OLD MEDIA

Introduction

In the previous chapter we discussed broad forms of resistance to preferred police narratives and images, whereby new technologies and/or social media are being used as platforms of resistance. In this chapter we explore what could be referred to as more traditional forms of media – print and television – and resistances to police control of information in that context. Here we focus on the ways in which journalists attempt to circumvent both the often limiting structured access (Chibnall 1977) they have to information and the content of the information being released to them. As investigative journalists see it, having informal links to the police is paramount in the search for a news scoop or an update on a breaking story, and most certainly for information about police corruption, malpractice, abuse of power or police internal politics. However, it is not just journalists who seek to circumvent these official channels. Indeed, the police themselves will, for their own range of reasons, sometimes wish to reveal information through informal means, enacting their own form of resistance.

In this chapter we examine the ways in which journalists resist the straightforward consumption of preferred police narratives and stories disseminated by police media departments and their officers – the likes of which we explored in Chapter 4. This is then followed by an exploration of how the police themselves will sometimes circumvent the official channels and policies of information release developed by professionalized media departments for those within the organization. To start, however, we will outline the context of the research discussed in the chapter.

Research context

It is important that we provide the context for the research data that appears in this chapter. The chapter is more specific in focus than most in the book and draws on a research case study of journalists in NSW and their perceptions and accounts of dealing with the NSW PMU at a particular point in time and in a particular political context. That is, the research interviews with journalists and media officers it draws on were conducted in 2006 and 2007. We make this specific clarification because, as we have identified throughout this book, the relationships between the police, the media and the public are fluid and shift with technological innovations and changing bureaucratic and organizational structures.

As we outlined in the introduction and appendix, while we have researched police public relations professionals across five Australian jurisdictions, we have only researched staff-level media unit officers and journalists in the NSW jurisdiction. Moreover, this specific piece of research was undertaken before significant restructuring and expansion of the NSW Police Public Affairs Department in the late 2000s and early 2010s. Despite this, we believe that the themes that emerged from this study still have resonance and may remain reflective of, and have implications for, understandings of police–media–public relations today across a range of jurisdictions. It should be noted, however, that we are not suggesting that these same relationships and dynamics still exist in the NSW Police Force today. In fact, many recent changes in the NSW context came about as a response to some of the issues that are discussed here and have been pushed by progressive assistant commissioners and upper-level professional staff. However, such concerns have been highlighted as problems in other jurisdictions, as many of the recent media inquiries, both in Australia and the UK, attested to.

Indeed, the themes that emerge from our interviews take on increased significance in light of the Leveson (2012) inquiry in the UK and the Finkelstein (2012) inquiry into the independence of the media in Australia. Similarly, Elizabeth Filkin's (2012: 7) report, commissioned by the London Metropolitan Police Service into *Ethical Issues Arising from the Relationship Between Police and Media*, made a number of key recommendations that are worth noting here:

1. It is critical for policing legitimacy that the MPS are as open and transparent as they can be and the media plays an important part in this. On occasions the MPS has not been open enough in providing the right information to the public.
2. The media is vitally important in holding the MPS to account on behalf of the public.
3. The media is essential in informing the public about the work of the police service and the role of the criminal justice system.
4. It is impossible for the organization to control every contact with the media. Any proposed solution will rely on police officers and police staff 'living' a set of core principles and making judgments about their application.
5. In the past it has not been sufficiently clear to police officers and staff what principles should underpin contact with the media. This has resulted in practices which have been damaging.
6. Where relationships with the media appear partial or selective, this creates a serious problem which is damaging to public confidence and to the MPS.
7. Police officers and staff are the best ambassadors for the organization in providing information to the public. They are part of the public they serve.
8. The problems that I have been told about and the changes that I suggest are to do with broad organizational issues including leadership and management throughout the MPS. A narrow view focused only on the specific task of handling the media will not be productive.

Taken in the context of these key recommendations, our research interviews provide evidence of the importance of these recommendations to policing organizations in their engagement with the media and the public. The culture of control that may be fostered by police organizations can build resentment between the police and journalists. This is to the detriment of the perceived legitimacy of the organization, which can only be maintained when there is a level of transparency and a dialogical approach to communications (Mawby 2002a). Police organizations need not only be granted legitimacy by the citizens they police. They also require that legitimacy be granted by the media with which they engage and by members of police organization itself.

Journalists resisting

As we saw in Chapter 4, journalists are often very compliant, knowingly or otherwise, in parroting police media releases in ways that simply reproduce the official police line or frame of reference. Yet, at the same time, the more experienced and innovative journalists who interact with the police are, on the whole, well aware of when the police attempt to control and structure both their access to information and the information itself. The considerable restructuring we have outlined in this book as to how journalists and the police communicate, with police media units increasingly acting as filters or conduits for the flow of information between police and media representatives, has clearly altered the dynamics between the media and the police. Some journalists are not easily deterred by some of the access problems such a restructuring might bring.

Unofficial sources

One of the ways in which journalists try to circumvent the gatekeeping role of police public relations departments is by establishing their own police contacts and sources. These unofficial sources, usually emanating from within police organizations, allow journalists to actively resist the controlled release of information by the police. This fostering of sources is not a recent phenomenon. Chappell and

Wilson (1969) addressed the issue of reliance upon unofficial sources by journalists as far back as the 1960s. For journalists today, the use of contacts is still seen as practically essential to being able to carry out their investigative roles impartially (see also Grabosky and Wilson 1989; Wilson 1992). For example, Filkin (2012: 13) reported that *The Sun* journalist Mike Sullivan had three or four hundred police contacts on his phone, with around one hundred to one hundred and fifty of them being generally 'happy to talk' to him about ongoing cases or investigations. She goes on to suggest that 'there is contact – which is neither recorded or permitted – between the media and police officer and staff, at all levels' (Filkin 2012: 13).

It follows then that journalists and reporters do not always so easily succumb to police attempts to control their access to and release of information. In fact, as our interviews with journalists reveal, many actively resist engaging with official media officers and units when they feel their access to important information is being obstructed:

> When they start to say 'look, let's get in the way of this exercise' then, that's when I get cross and that's when I don't want to deal with them. Because that's not their job, their job is simply to protect their reputation and tell the truth. Their job is not to obstruct someone else trying to tell the truth.
>
> *(Journalist 3)*

Corresponding with the findings of both the Leveson Inquiry (2012) and Filkin's inquiry (2012), journalists emphasized to us that 'you do have to develop independent sources'. That is, police contacts who can provide journalists with information beyond the official information release. This contact with unofficial sources constitutes not just one-off instances of information exchange in reaction to particular events or stories, although such unofficial contacts are often reignited by such events. Rather, these unofficial contacts are more likely to operate as structured allegiances that can be seen as competing and/or operating in tandem with official channels of information dissemination and communications. This was supported by a number of other journalists:

Almost exclusively my contact with police is with people who are not working in the media area of the force or the marketing area of the force. They're people that are actually doing front line jobs. And they are a range of people from detectives, to Superintendents that run Local Area Commands in the suburbs, to coppers on the beat. People that I've gotten to know one on one over the last roughly ten years, and know that I can be trusted and for them to talk fairly frankly off the record to me about things, that's how I get my stories.

(Journalist 5)

Indeed, the fostering of unofficial contacts has been seen as vital to journalists attempting to carry out their investigative roles effectively. Great importance is placed on the building of such relationships, and it is easy to understand how journalists might build up a significant phone contact list over the length of a career. As one journalist we spoke with noted:

It's really important that you have your own police contacts as a journalist, especially sources that you don't have to talk to on the record … If you want to sort of move to the next level of journalism, if you want to break stories for instance – because [media units] disseminate […] these stories to everyone – so, if you want to actually break a story or have a new angle on a story, it's good to know a police officer that's working on the job.

(Journalist 1)

Again, this resonates with the evidence presented by Filkin. As UK-based journalist Mike Sullivan (cited in Filkin 2012: 13) put it: '… if there is an investigation, I can be talking to a contact from the police service three days out of five, but then may not speak to them for another year or two'. Another experienced journalist noted that he understood the defensiveness of the police to his overtures given his work. It was, as he suggested, very unlikely that he would be involved in the production of a 'good news' story about policing.

Beyond this, however, some journalists have felt that policies restricting or structuring journalistic contact with police can be unproductive:

Just because these are the rules the government sets up in terms of dealing with police, it doesn't mean you have to play by them. You rely on your own contacts. And that's what I do, I work the edges. Information comes from a variety of sources.

(Journalist 2)

As another journalist commented during the Leveson Inquiry:

… there is increasingly limited access to the actual police officers on the ground, and it tends to be that the press office is there to provide standard information and if we want to go further than that and find out more, we will try to go to the individual officers, but sometimes we are referred back to the press office.

(Faber, cited in Leveson 2012: 766)

So for the more serious of journalists, attempts to manage the ways in which they conduct their business have meant that they have had to adapt their investigative and research techniques over time. In resisting cultures of control that can develop over the release of information, their tactic of resistance is to 'work the edges'. As well as this though, they attempt to exploit the very weaknesses that strategies of control can facilitate, for these strategies of control also have the capacity to disenfranchise those within the organization itself, officers who feel restrained by the official rules of police public relations work.

Perversely then, attempts at 'taming of the system' produce new resistances as journalists seek new avenues for the dissemination and receipt of information. The strategies of control produce capacities for resistance that contribute towards the success (or failure) and progression of systems of control (Foucault 1982). Power relationships will often be unstable, ambiguous and reversible, as our examples demonstrate (Hindess 1996). In line with Hunt and Wickham's (1994) Foucauldian analysis of 'attempts' at governing, in many ways the use of police media departments as tools for governing information flow can only ever be partial, incomplete and fluctuating. Resistances from journalists to the centralization of power and the dissemination of preferred messages to produce 'truth' are constant and often successful and built into systems of control. As Foucault (1981: 52) commented, 'discourse is not simply that which translates struggles or systems of domination, but it is a thing for which and by which there is struggle.' Thus attempts at information control on the part of police media units or press officers can often lead journalists to source their information from unofficial police contacts they have fostered, cementing these informal and unofficial lines of communication. In this sense, Filkin's (2012: 49) recommendation that 'communication be based on more extensive, open and impartial provision of information to the public …' is important for the future legitimation of policing.

It is also important not to overstate the role of social and new media in tactics of resistance and subsequently to downplay the way in which traditional journalists navigate the new policing–media environment. While the press release and the police media officer or unit has created new challenges for journalists, experienced investigative journalists still have their means of getting key information. As one experienced journalist, who noted 'a lot of my career has been involved in exposure of police corruption', told us:

> I've always tried to maintain good relations with PR people because they can still be informants. They can let their guard down too and drop something to you by way of a genuine insight quite apart from the line or the corporate spin they might be pushing, particularly if you ask them questions. And umm, there are other journalist techniques to get around the corporate armour that is put up and that is also off the record, off the record means without attribution as to the source, and you can have conversations to assist your understanding of something and with public relations practitioners, particularly the ones who have been around for a while, who have had a bit of experience, who just don't go into mindless defensive techniques, particularly with somebody like me.
>
> *(Journalist 12)*

Here the tactic was very much to work within the prescribed environment, but to use trust and journalistic experience to draw out the information required for a story.

Another experienced journalist who had also been involved in the exposure of serious police corruption among other stories that would largely be seen as negative to the police, told a similar tale:

> [When I'm obstructed] then I go through the backdoor, 'cause I can. I will give them the benefit of the doubt and go through the front door until I feel they're starting to play games with me and then I'll simply go round the backdoor and I will say to someone 'what's really going on mate?', 'cause I've got my own contacts, and they are much, much, more reliable than the media unit. Because apart from anything else, the media unit don't really know that much.
>
> *(Journalist 3)*

This journalist also noted that he understood the defensiveness of the police to his overtures as, given his work, it was very unlikely that he would be involved in the production of a 'good news' story about policing.

Another investigative journalist confirmed that for some information you just have to have your sources beyond the regular police media officers: 'You actually just find people outside [the media unit], you have to otherwise you just get the official line' (Journalist 11).

The relationship between journalists and the police is thus complex and multifaceted. Journalists deploy a range of tactics in resisting the preferred police narrative on important stories. Indeed, it is still the 'old media' that break many of the negative stories concerning policing. However, it remains unclear just how well the contemporary media strategies actually work in suppressing negative stories precisely because these will be stories that don't break.

Internal resistances

Journalists, however, are not the only ones in these relationships who actively resist attempts to govern their activities. The police themselves can also resist the efforts of police hierarchies and/or governments to closely manage and monitor their role in communications with the media and the public. Evidence across the globe suggests that the police are often instrumental in leaking information to the media. There are numerous reasons for this but, as the Leveson Inquiry (2012: 987) concluded, 'sometimes the motive is little other than personal disgruntlement or the desire to wound colleagues'.

Rank-and-file police resisting

Guidelines directing police interactions with the media impact the police operating at all levels but in particular rank-and-file police officers, those working in the operational areas of policing. Most police media policies these days dictate who is authorized to speak to media representatives, what they are sanctioned to discuss and the ways in which officers are expected to negotiate their contact with the media. For some officers, these increasing levels of administrative regulations create an environment where they feel their level of autonomy is being undermined. The formalization of media protocols and the increasing importance of public affairs and media officers removes yet more of their discretionary power as information dissemination becomes more centralized and sanitized. As the Leveson Inquiry found (2012: 765):

> It is crucial for police forces to have a press office. The key role is to ensure a steady flow of information to reporters without unnecessarily hampering operational officers with inquiries and to ensure journalists working on an in-depth story speak to the most appropriate officer at the most appropriate time.

Some two decades ago Wilson (1992: 172) argued that the centralization of police media activities can result in police officers being reluctant to pass on potential news to media units and media officers. One police media officer articulated the internal relationship with serving police officers in the following manner:

> Some police officers are skeptical of our role in the Police Media Unit because we are obviously dealing with the media all the time ... They don't quite see us or accept us as part of

the actual Police Service … I don't know that they don't trust us: I think it's more that they see us as another body who are on their back wanting information … they just see us as part of the media and not part of them.

(PMU Staffer 5)

Journalists too have suggested there can be animosity between some serving officers and professional media officers: 'I think you'll find that there are any number of coppers out there in the field that have absolutely no regard for the Head Office media people … But you know, they [media professionals] are able to throw their weight around because they've got the Commissioner's backing' (Journalist 5).

The concerns many street-level police have with the police media professionals manifests in a variety of ways and for a number of reasons. As discussed above, some police may distrust them purely because they associate police media professionals with the media, whom they may also distrust; both are after all seeking information from operational police that they may not necessarily wish to circulate or may see no value in circulating. As one media representative in the Leveson Inquiry commented:

Press officers are (usually) available whereas police officers are frequently too bogged down with all their other duties to talk. When a query emerges on a daily newspaper, speed of response is critical. Good press officers, who understand how newspapers work and journalists' requirements, concerns and pressures, can actually help explain to reluctant officers on your behalf why it may be mutually beneficial to release certain pieces of information.

(Lawton, cited in Leveson 2012: 765)

Others feel that they would rather bypass PMUs and deal with journalists directly when trying to get across a message about a particular crime or offence. As one of our interviewees put it: 'Police leak stuff to the media all the time and, sometimes it can be for malevolent reasons, but sometimes it can't be' (Journalist 3).

Journalists suggested that they had little difficulty in finding police whom they could talk to 'off the record' about various policing matters: 'The police hierarchy have got to accept the fact they are never going to stop detectives and other coppers from talking to journalists off the record' (Journalist 5).

One likened the police organization to a sieve:

> The police service, let's be frank, it leaks like a sieve, and it's so political, not just from the top end, it's political at the bottom end. There's so many frustrated government workers that are always ringing up the papers saying you know, 'I'm not giving my name, but this, this and that' and then [we] check it out and it's fair dinkum.
>
> *(Journalist 1)*

And, as has been discussed, having contacts outside the media offices was seen as important for journalists being able to do their job and get the real stories the police want told:

> If you want to actually break a story or have a new angle on a story, it's good to know a police officer that's working on the job. And he will say 'well you know what, with this job there was a huge stuff up, they didn't give us this, this and that, and they didn't give us enough resources or whatever, and, we had major problems with it'. Now the Media Unit would probably leave that piece of information out of course, and then that's when you've gotta kind of put it to them ... Like with the Redfern Riots,[1] there was talk about them not being provided with proper equipment and things like that. We only got that from the police on the ground, we didn't get that from the Media Unit. So basically all the critical stories you will see are from our own contacts.
>
> *(Journalist 1)*

An increasingly concerning trend is the attempts by the police and government watchdogs to trace information leaks to journalists (Putnis 1996). This manifests in the seizure of journalists' telephone records and raids of news offices. In 2008 in Queensland accusations were made by the Police Union that Police Internal Affairs were monitoring phone records to see if officers had been speaking with journalists, as well as checking police bank accounts to see if they were being paid for supplying journalists with information (Bita and Fraser 2008). With the move to digital encryption of radios among many police forces now, the problem of leaks and threats to sanction 'leakers' could easily escalate (Morri 2008; Penberthy 2008; Spicer 2008). This again speaks to the need for clear guidelines, transparency and ethics of media engagement within police organizations.

But the leaking of information to journalists is not necessarily confined to the rank-and-file level. As Filkin (2012) again made clear, this has occurred at all levels of the MPS. In NSW senior police have also been accused of leaking information to the media, so much so that former NSW Police Commissioners Ken Moroney and Peter Ryan issued a number of warnings to senior colleagues against speaking with the media lest they face criminal charges (Mercer 2006; Williams 2002).

In our own research, one journalist stated that what he called the 'unofficial' leaking of information from the media office itself was a problem. In particular this respondent believed it could have negative effects on the operational work of policing:

> The Media Unit wasn't independent, not at all, not at all, and it's still not, and in that form there's a hell of a lot of corruption … but the corruption comes in the form of leaked information. In fact it's the information leaked from that Unit that police didn't want made public.
>
> *(Journalist 9)*

More recent structural changes may have ameliorated these claims. Nonetheless, this does demonstrate the more general point that journalists feel that even the formal channels of police media engagement can be leaky. As a result, off the record contact between PMU staff and journalists was also said to be common: '… you're getting a lot of off record contact between journalists and people who work in those positions [police media officers], and that is a strong source for a lot of journalists' (Journalist 5).

Some journalists also believed, along the same lines, that information was given to 'favourites' of the media office or their staff:

> The leaks now come from the Media Unit you see, they go to their favourite journo, so now instead of journalists or crime reporters having to develop a relationship with police and get to understand them and how they operate, it all goes through this monolith of a Media Unit they have there.
>
> *(Journalist 9)*

This naturally upset some journalists who felt they were disadvantaged by these sorts of arrangements: 'Maintaining the integrity of your investigation is absolutely important, and you shouldn't have leaks to the media, to media favourites, for all sorts of power [reasons]' (Journalist 12).

For this reason one journalist accused the media of being out of touch with the culture and spirit of the police–media interface:

> You need to have somebody who understands police culture and media culture, understands what the true needs and purpose of that Media Unit is, and you know and is fair minded, you can't favour one against another even if you've copped a pasting off the *Herald*, even so that does tend to make you want to favour one over the other.
>
> *(Journalist 9)*

One journalist even said they avoided informing the PMU about stories they were about to file because in the past the PMU had given the story to rival outlets to try and get an advantage over the journalist:

> One of their ways of dealing with me is to leak what I give to them … I don't tell them what I've got until the absolute last minute, and the reason for that is that if I tell them what I've got it will be in *The Daily Telegraph* tomorrow. So their way of

neutralizing me is to say 'oh shit, [Journalist 3] found out about this, oh shit, give it to the *Tele*'. So the *Tele* run a little piece on page thirty and it neutralizes what I have to do.

(Journalist 3)

Along a similar vein to the PMU playing 'favourites', other journalists believed that they contravened their own 'non-exclusive' policy by giving specific stories to one journalist or outlet rather than all media outlets.

These reflections speak to Putnis' (1996: 208–9) claim that police sometimes obstruct journalists by revealing their exclusives to other journalists or chosen media outlets. It also resonates with Filkin's (2012: 14) claim that 'influence and favour have played a part and have affected what should be an unbiased relationship between the MPS and the media'.

Conclusion

As we noted at the beginning of this chapter, the landscape within which police–media interactions now take place has changed significantly, bringing with it resistances to those changes. Taking the NSW Police Force and their public relations department as an example, we have highlighted the significant challenges faced in centralizing media operations while bringing journalists and rank-and-file officers along with them through these changes. Despite this, the current media policy of NSW Police is perhaps the most open and transparent we have been able to source in the writing of this book, which raises questions over the actual policy details of other police organizations and how they impact on the journalists they interact with? What we are seeing, however, across the larger and more resourced police organizations is more than just the implementation or change of policy when it comes to dealing with the media; rather, we have, in less than a decade, witnessed a more holistic approach to media activities and interactions within police forces. This has involved extensive media training for officers, increased capacity for individual officers to speak to the media depending on the seriousness of the investigation, new methods of disseminating information as we discussed in Chapter 4, and the roll out of new and social media activities that, if used correctly, create a more dialogical relationship between the police, media and public.

Nonetheless, the interviews discussed here, and the examples from recent inquiries, illustrate the fine line that police media offices and public relations departments tread between feeding the synoptic hunger of the public, providing information in a timely and transparent way to journalists and the media, and conducting the kind of image work required of public relations – and indeed required for the legitimation of police organizations more generally. Journalists who may feel hard done by in this new 'professionalized' world of police–media relations are watching this tightrope balancing act carefully. Sourcing information is now much more difficult than just buying a local copper a beer in a pub, and the risks for attempting to do so are much greater in a world where communications between police and reporters are increasingly heavily monitored.

While it is well and good to be critical of policing organizations in their relationships with journalists – and we need to be – this criticism should also accompanied with a similar note of critical engagement with the media. That is, while police organizations may at times experience crises in public confidence and legitimacy, the media are generally held in much lower esteem by the public. Indeed, it could be argued that media organizations have been far less amenable to change and external oversight and regulation than policing organizations (Finkelstein 2012). A recent survey of consumer confidence in professions (Roy Morgan Research 2011) found that journalists rated fourth from last in a list of 30 occupations, ahead only of real estate agents, advertising people and car salesmen. The same survey, on the other hand, saw police rated more highly than at any other time in the past 35 years of surveying, with 69 per cent of respondents suggesting police behaved ethically and honestly – interestingly, even outflanking university lecturers at 61 per cent. The journalists ranking at 11 per cent could leave one wondering just whose legitimacy needs improving?

While we have seen a withering of print media in recent years, investigative journalism is still far from dead. Good investigative journalists have their own tactics at getting to the story behind the story. It is unlikely that increasing attempts at controlling information by media departments can 'tame' this system. Perversely they may actually have the opposite effects as tactics of resistance continually subvert and undermine strategies of control.

Note

1. The Redfern Riots in February 2004 were triggered by the death of a 17-year-old Indigenous boy by the name of T. J. Hickey (Weatherburn 2006). Hickey, who had an outstanding warrant for his arrest, was riding his bike through the streets of Redfern when he spotted the police. Aware of the warrant, and presumably under the impression the police were after him, Hickey fled the police. While trying to avoid the police, Hickey lost control of his bike and crashed, becoming impaled on the spike of a metal fence, causing his death (Kennedy 2004). Residents of Redfern, blaming police for the incident, gathered to mourn Hickey, a gathering that turned violent, escalating to a full-scale riot. Police, in their attempts to quell the riot were found to be significantly under-resourced, with 40 officers sustaining injuries. A subsequent inquiry into the death of T. J. Hickey cleared the police of any involvement. Further investigations were critical of the police's preparedness for the riot.

CONCLUSION

During the week we were completing this book two brothers, raised in the USA but born in Chechnya and of Muslim heritage, detonated two improvised explosive devices near the finishing line of the Boston Marathon. The blast killed three people almost instantly and was reported to have seriously maimed or injured over 160 others. The explosions were captured by numerous hand-held digital recording devices, largely in the hands of civilians lining the street waiting for the marathon runners to reach the finish. Within minutes the 'Twittersphere' was alive with images and accounts from the scene of the bombing, 24-hour news channels televised live coverage of the bomb site and subsequent manhunt, and Boston Police hit the social media.

Up until the moment of the bombing the Boston Police Department had only released a slow flow of tweets on their official Twitter account[1] – around six per day, the final of which read: 'This must look so nice for the athletes!!! Great Job!!' Then, just before 3 p.m., Boston time, the police made the following tweet: 'Boston Police confirming explosion at marathon finish line with injuries' (#tweetfromthebeat).[2] After this, further tweets were published by Boston Police, giving updates on the injury toll: 'Boston Police looking for video of the finish line' (#tweetfromthebeat) and calling for information from the public:'Members of the community wanting 2 assist this investigation anonymously can call BPD's Crime Stoppers Tip Line …' (#tweetfromthebeat). Then a clear indication of the direction of the investigation was given:'FBI has taken over the investigation' (#tweetfromthebeat).

The BPD twitter feed continued to provide information about street closures, where the media should position their televised live-feed trucks and the scheduling of press conferences. The feed also quashed rumours of an arrest and mobile phone networks were shut down so that no further bombs could be remotely detonated.

During this period, the public looked on. Cyberspace buzzed with conjecture, motive, fact and fiction. By the time the news channels updated us, social media had already broken new news. Platforms such as Twitter and Reddit were often hours ahead of televised reports. Somewhat anachronistically, Lee's Sydney morning newspaper arrived at his front door – no mention of the Boston bombings of course. Meanwhile in New York, McGovern logged onto Facebook to be alerted to events in Boston. Following events in real time, she witnessed the USA move onto a higher level of alert, putting in place increased security and restrictions on public movement.

As competition grew between media outlets to break news on the story, numerous examples of mistaken claims and misinformation emerged. CNN, quoting 'unofficial' but 'credible' sources, incorrectly reported the arrest of a suspect, claims which some broadcasters repeated but many others, such as NBC and CBS, strongly refuted. Numerous times Boston Police and the FBI came out on social media and in television broadcasts to 'set the story straight': not only had they not made an arrest, but they had no one in custody, admissions that forced CNN and others to backtrack on their earlier claims. For a while it seemed there were no suspects and few clues.

Despite the confusion, however, over a thousand investigators trawled through hours of CCTV footage and digital images and video (CBC News 2013) provided by the public, with potential suspects soon emerging. Evidentiary video and still photos were then circulated on social media and televised on news channels. We (the public) looked on, searching social media, scouring television coverage, sharing information, recalling anecdotes told by survivors, pop wisdom and theories. We floated on a wave of information – we were not just viewing, we were involved in this hyperreal assemblage of news, views and clues; time and space had collapsed. And in fact, for many, they were involved, putting the pieces of the puzzle together in their own online 'police' investigation (Associated Press 2013). Meanwhile, in Iraq at least 33 people were killed and more than 160 were injured in a series of bombings across the city (Mosbergen 2013) – we (the public) didn't notice.

Following their identification the two suspects went on a rampage in which vehicles were carjacked, a university police officer was shot dead, shops were held up and explosives were thrown from a car during a pursuit and shootout. Boston was shut down, residents were told to lock themselves inside, and television networks were forced by the police to delay their coverage in case the suspects were themselves tipped off by the immediate coverage.

One suspect was killed in a gun-battle with police. The other escaped the police net. After a tip-off from a local resident he was located holed up in a small boat in a suburban house. Police swooped and images of the prostrate suspect circulated, along with those of celebrating residents and jubilant police, like big game hunters with their quarry, had their photo opportunity, a PR 'money shot'.

The entire episode had been played out live, in real time, on social media. Twitter, Facebook and Reddit allowed witnesses and residents in Boston to share events that television crews were restrained from broadcasting. Via first-hand accounts and the relaying of Boston Police radio content, social media broke the news, mobile phones provided the clues and we all engaged in a collective hunt for the bombers as we sifted through an overload of information. Transmission was briefly halted, reality delayed, as police closed in. The operation over, transmission was restored and we in the viewer society turned our attention to the next event or spectacle – in fact, we will it. There is something strangely seductive in witnessing human disaster from afar. The synoptic gaze seeks out both information and entertainment and crime news has become a part of this voyeuristic amusement. This is not 'faction' (Leishman and

Mason 2003) but something way beyond it. The medium is not just the message (compare McLuhan 1964), the medium is the entertainment but it is plugged into an infinite information assemblage.

As this book has argued, new communications technologies and social media are reshaping the relationships between the police, the media and the public – the Boston Bombing example reinforces this. We have demonstrated this by comprehensively mapping the new and emerging media activities of police organizations and the technologies through which these activities take place. Of special interest in our discussions have been the ways in which police organizations are increasingly proactively deploying new technologies and platforms as a way of promoting preferred police messages. Police organizations were already becoming more proactive in their image work by the 1990s, and the following decades have seen this proactivity multiply, enhanced by new technologies and social media.

Beyond this, we have also explored police attempts to influence and control media messages. By nature the development of professionalized media offices have facilitated the development of this 'culture of control'. Yes, as we have also demonstrated, these attempts at control are imperfect; that is, in the project of proactive police communications work, new and emerging media technologies and platforms are also being deployed to also promote and produce counter-discourses and resistances to preferred police messages. In some instances these resistances occur externally to police organizations – by the public or the media – while in other cases, the resistances occur from within policing organizations themselves. While there has been some work internationally that investigates sousveillance, citizen journalism and the proliferation of 'copwatch'-style websites as another form of synopticism (for example Huey et al. 2006), we have offered one of the few analyses of how such resistances operate in relation to new media policing environments.

Beyond detailing the current conditions of the police–media–public communications networks, we have also offered new frames of analysis for understanding these relationships. Drawing on three theoretical frameworks – 'synopticism', 'simulated policing' and the 'strategies and tactics of everyday life' – we have conceptually analysed original empirical research.

Drawing on the work of O'Malley (2010), we have argued that 'simulated policing' has allowed us to explore and explain how forms of policing, once thought of as being simply about the manufacture of images, are actually performing operational policing functions. For example, traditional policing is being reframed through new technologies such as Facebook as a platform for Neighbourhood Watch and YouTube as a platform for Crimestoppers.

The second conceptual framework, Mathiesen's (1997) concept of 'the viewer society', has allowed us to explore how the few watch the many, and how the many also watch the few (Welch 2011). In this way, Mathiesen's thesis provides a fertile conceptual base from which to research not just police use of new media, but also technologies aimed at disciplining and normalizing (panopticism), and the public fascination and desire to view police activity (synopticism).

And finally, our third theoretical frame, de Certeau's (1984) notion of the tactics of the weak, has allowed us to explore 'counterveillance', 'sousveillance' and resistances to police-preferred messages through the reimagining of new technologies and media platforms, enabling citizens and others not only to counter police attempts at image management and control, but also to take up policing roles, all of which reduces the asymmetry and undermines or circumvents police power (see also Marx 2003).

The world of police media and public relations is ever changing, expanding and highly volatile. In five years time it may not resemble the conditions we have explored in this book. By then, this analysis, like the newspaper still rolled up on the coffee table, may also be old news.

Notes

1. https://twitter.com/Boston_Police
2. #tweetfromthebeat being their hash tag for street-level policing news.

APPENDIX
RESEARCH METHODS

As we have explained in the Introduction, this book is the culmination of over a decade's worth of empirical research into the ways in which police, media and public relationships operate. In order to paint a clearer picture of the fieldwork we have undertaken, this Appendix will detail the research methods employed in each of the separate research projects that make up the empirical data on which this book is based. We will present these explanations chronologically, beginning with our earliest studies in this field and ending with our most recent project. Whilst the details we provide will not provide sufficient detail for exact replications of our studies, they will provide the context for much of the data that appears in the book, and explain the underlying research questions and methods that drove each of the projects.

Qualitative data relating to police media practices was drawn from interviews and documentary analysis from two sample periods. The first period, between 2006 and 2007, involved face to face semi-structured interviews with a range of key stakeholders in the police-media relationship in NSW, in particular current and former NSW Police Force Media Unit personnel (both sworn and unsworn staff) and media representatives (police and crime reporters and newsroom managers from television, radio and print media).

Journalists

The journalists who participated in the research were from a range of reporting fields and included General Reporters, Police Reporters, Senior Crime Reporters, Newsroom Managers, Political Commentators and Investigative Reporters as indicated in Table A1.

Ex NSW PMU Staff and Political Persons

This group of interviewees was made up of largely of former employees of the NSW Police Media Unit. One interviewee had since entered the political realm and another was of this cohort was a member of parliament (see Table A2).

TABLE A.1 Journalist code names

Analysis code	Field
Journalist 1	Newspaper/Other print
Journalist 2	Television/Other print
Journalist 3	Television/Other print
Journalist 4	Newspaper
Journalist 5	Newspaper
Journalist 6	Radio
Journalist 7	Newspaper
Journalist 8	Newspaper
Journalist 9	Other print/Television
Journalist 10	Newspaper
Journalist 11	Newspaper
Journalist 12	Television/Other print
Journalist 13	Television
Journalist 14	Newspaper
Journalist 15	Newspaper/Other print
Journalist 16	Television/Other print

TABLE A.2 Ex-police media unit/other code names

Analysis code	Field
Ex-PMU/Other 1	Politics
Ex-PMU/Other 2	Politics
Ex-PMU/Other 3	Police
Ex-PMU/Other 4	Police/Politics
Ex-PMU/Other 5	Police
Ex-PMU/Other 6	Police
NSW Shadow Police Minister	Politics

NSW PMU Staff

This cohort was made up of current NSW Police Media Staff. In Table A4 we note either their civilian or colicing background.

Interviews examined the social world of the respondents, relationships and situations (Denzin and Lincoln 2000: 8), drawing out common themes and relating them to broader macro level theoretical understandings of police media relations and the role of PMUs. During the interviews a range of major themes were explored, including:

* Experience as a journalist/Media Unit staffer;
* Importance of positive police-media relations;
* Changes in the police-media relationship over time;
* Understanding of the function/role of the NSW PMU;
* Level and nature of contact between stakeholders in the relationship;
* Quality of the relationship, and;
* Power balance of the relationship.

Of interest too were the historical changes police-media relations had undergone in the state. As such, interviews were supplemented with documentary analysis, in an attempt to build a picture of the history of police-media relations generally, and the NSW PMU specifically. Analysis was carried out on public documents, such as media articles and reports of inquiries; personal documents, such as autobiographies; administrative documents, such as official reports, annual reports, policy guides, and progress reports; and formal studies and reports related to the topic. As such, the analysis was primarily

TABLE A.3 Police Media Unit staff code names

Analysis code	Field
PMU Staffer 1	Civilian
PMU Staffer 2	Police
PMU Staffer 3	Police
PMU Staffer 4	Police
PMU Staffer 5	Civilian
PMU Staffer 6	Civilian

'descriptive-comparative research', whereby a variety of documents were examined in an attempt to explore and explain the event in question. The primary question being asked of the documents was about the condition of emergence of the NSW PMU, and the social, political and cultural context from which it emerged (Saratankos 1993: 275).

The second interview period was conducted in 2010 and 2011 with 13 key media communications decision makers across five separate Australian police jurisdictions; namely, directors and managers from public affairs, media and communications branches of police forces in five Australian states (NSW, Victoria, Tasmania, Western Australia and South Australia) as noted in Table A4.

Interviewees were purposively sampled on the basis that they could provide the researchers with an understanding of the ways in which the police engage proactively with the media, specifically social media, and the policies and practices being employed within these strategies. These interviews were supplemented with documentary analysis of official police policy and other documents, in particular NSW Police Force documents, together with supplementary historical data from various periods in time relating to these police documents.

In addition to our qualitative research interviews and documentary analysis, we also undertook an analysis of police observational documentaries and a survey of public perceptions of these observational documentaries, with a particular focus on the NSW Police Force. The aim of this student-assisted project was two-fold:

TABLE A.4 Public relations professionals/directors of public affairs

Analysis code	Field
NSW Police PR Respondent 1	Director, Public Affairs Branch, NSW Police Force
NSW Police PR Respondent 2	Manager, Corporate Communications Department, NSW Police Force
NSW Police PR Respondent 3	Manager, Police Media Unit, NSW Police Force
NSW Police PR Respondent 4	Assistant Commissioner, Corporate Services, NSW Police Force
WA Police PR Respondent 1	Special Projects Officer, Police Media Office, WA Police Force
WA Police PR Respondent 2	Manager, Police Media Office, WA Police
WA Police PR Respondent 3	Director, Media and Public Affairs, WA Police
Vic Police PR Respondent 1	Manager, Operational External Police Media Unit, Media and Corporate Communications, Victoria Police
Vic Police PR Respondent 2	Acting Assistant Director, Media and Corporate Communications, Victoria Police
Vic Police PR Respondent 3	Senior Sergeant, Film and Television Office, Media and Corporate Communications, Victoria Police
SA Police PR Respondent 1	Media Director, South Australian Police
SA Police PR Respondent 2	Operations Inspector of Media, South Australian Police
TAS Police PR Respondent 1	Manager, Media Unit, Tasmanian Police

1. To explore the relationship between levels of consumption (viewing) of observational documentary (reality TV) depictions of police work and the expression of confidence, trust, and legitimacy in the NSW Police Force.
2. To explore depictions of police and policing in observational documentaries, and whether stated police objectives are being met through the broadcasting of observational documentaries.

The survey component of the research took the form of an online survey using the KeySurvey program, and was advertised on the NSW Police Force Facebook and Twitter pages, as well as a number of other online sites. The survey consisted of a combination of closed (Likert scale – attitudinal fixed alternative) and open-ended questions aimed at producing data that would offer a level of comparison to that produced in the Productivity Commission Report Into Government Services. As such, the survey explored the following hypotheses:

1. That viewers of Police Observational Documentary programs have a high satisfaction and confidence in Police and the Criminal Justice System.
2. That Police objectives in giving access to television program makers are met.

Furthermore, the survey collated data on individuals' viewing experience of police observational documentaries, paying particular attention to the programs The Recruits, RBT and The Force. Respondents were asked about the frequency of their viewing and confidence/satisfaction in the police both as depicted in observational documentaries, and in general. The survey also included a number of open-ended questions in order to elicit responses beyond the cloased questions.

The police observational documentary analysis component of the project was qualitative and quantitative in nature; that is, content and narrative analyses of the most recently aired series of the programs *RBT* (Season 2, 18 episodes), *The Force* (Season 5, 12 episodes) and *The Recruits* (Seasons 1 and 2, 21 episodes) were chosen. Content analysis involved the recording of common themes depicted in the programs, in particular, the 'operational' and 'non-operational' procedures undertaken by police. Operational procedures include activities such as police patrols and investigations, typical on-duty tasks. Non-operational activities included the depiction of actions outside of those typically expected during the job of policing, such as police discussing/showing emotions on screen or perform social services that not necessarily part of the duty of a police officer.

In addition to this, quantitative content analysis was undertaken of the same programs. In this analysis, records were maintained of the outcomes of cases shown in the programs, including the consequences for offences/offenders, the demographic representation of characters in the programs, and the types of offences focused on. This data acquired from content analysis was quantitative in nature.

BIBLIOGRAPHY

Altheide, D. and Snow, E. (1979) *Media Logic*. Beverly Hills, CA: Sage.

Armistead, J. (2012) 'Facebook catches crim', *Townsville Bulletin*, 15 August. Available online at: http://www.townsvillebulletin.com.au/article/2012/08/15/353351_news.html (accessed 21 April 2013).

Associated Press (2013) 'Reconsidering the Internet detectives in Boston manhunt on Reddit and 4Chan: the benefits and pitfalls', *NY Daily News*. Available online at: http://www.nydailynews.com/news/national/online-sleuths-boston-manhunt-reddit-4chan-article-1.1322658 (accessed 20 April 2013).

Australian Federal Police (n.d.) *Media Service Charter*. Available online at: http://www.police.act.gov.au/~/media/act/pdf/act-policing-media-service-charter.ashx (accessed 12 April 2013).

Avery, J. (1981) *Police – Force or Service?* Sydney: Butterworths.

Barker (2001) *Legitimating Identities: The Self-Presentations of Rulers and Subjects*: Cambridge: Cambridge University Press.

Baudrillard, J. (1983) *Simulations*. New York: Semiotext(s).

Baudrillard, J. (1994) *Simulacra and Simulation*. Ann Arbor, MI: University of Michigan Press.

BBC News Online (2009) *Police Open Up to Social Media*, 20 November. Available online at: http://news.bbc.co.uk/2/hi/technology/8363064.stm (accessed 26 April 2013).

Beck, U. (1992) *Risk Society: Towards a New Modernity*. London: Sage.

Beetham, D. (1991) *The Legitimation of Power*. Basingstoke: Palgrave Macmillan.

Berkeley Copwatch (2012) Berkeley Copwatch website. Available online at: http://www.berkeleycopwatch.org/.

Bita, N. and Fraser, A. (2008) 'Police hunt media leaks', *The Australian*, 29 September. Available online at: http://www.theaustralia.news.com. au/story/0,25197,24416718-2702,00.html (accessed 29 September 2008).

Bloustien, G. and Israel, M. (2006) 'Crime and the media', in A. Goldsmith, M. Israel and K. Daly (eds), *Crime and Justice: A Guide to Criminology*. Sydney: Lawbook Co.

Boda, Z. and Szabó, G. (2011) 'The media and attitudes towards crime and the justice system: a qualitative approach', *European Journal of Criminology*, 8 (4): 329–42.

Bottoms, A. and Tankebe, J. (2012) 'Beyond procedural justice: a dialogic approach to legitimacy in criminology', *Journal of Criminal Law and Criminology*, 102: 119–70.

Bradford, B. and Jackson, J. (2010) 'Trust and confidence in the police: a conceptual review', Social Science Research Network. Available online at: http://papers.ssrn.com/sol3/papers.cfm?abstract_id=1684508 (accessed 25 October 2010).

Bradford, B., Jackson, J. and Stanko, E. (2009) 'Contact and confidence: revisiting the impact of public encounters with the police', *Policing and Society*, 19 (1): 20–46.

Bradley, D. and Cioccarelli, P. (1989) 'Chasing Vollmer's fancy: current developments in police education', in D. Chappell and P. Wilson (eds), *Australian Policing: Contemporary Issues*. North Ryde: Butterworths.

Brogden, M. (1987) 'The emergence of the police – the colonial dimension', *British Journal of Criminology*, 27 (1): 4–14.

Burn, C. (2010) 'The New South Wales Police Force customer service programme', *Policing*, 4 (3): 249–57.

Burton, B. (2007) 'Need to curb a PR industry spinning out of control', *Sydney Morning Herald*, 7 August. Available online at: http://www.smh. com.au/news/opinion/need-to-curb-a-pr-industry-spinning-out-of-control/2007/08/06/1186252624551.html (accessed 7 August 2007).

Castillo, J. J. (2009) 'Snowball sampling, experiment resources', *Explorable*. Available online at: http://www.experiment-resources.com/snowball-sampling.html (accessed 26 April 2013).

Cavender, G. (2004) 'Media and crime policy: a reconsideration of David Garland's *The Culture of Control*', *Punishment and Society*, 6 (3): 335–48.

Cavender, G. and Fishman, M (1998) 'Television reality crime programs: context and history', in M. Fishman and G. Cavender (eds), *Entertaining Crime*. New York: Aldine De Gruyter, pp. 1–18.

CBC News (2013) 'Vancouver riot probe techniques may help Boston Police', *CBC News*. Available online at: http://www.cbc.ca/news/

canada/british-columbia/story/2013/04/16/bc-boston-video-evidence. html?cmp=rss (accessed 20 April 2013).

Chan, J. B. L. (1997) *Changing Police Culture: Policing in a Multicultural Society*. Cambridge: Cambridge University Press.

Chan, J. B. L. (1999) 'Governing police practice: limits of the new account-ability', *British Journal of Sociology*, 50 (2): 251–70.

Chan, J., Goggins, G. and Bruce, J. (2010) 'Internet technologies and crim-inal justice', in Y. Jewkes and M. Yar (eds), *Handbook of Internet Crime*. Cullompton: Willan.

Chappell, D. and Wilson, P. (1969) *The Police and the Public in Australia and New Zealand*. St Lucia, Qld: University of Queensland Press.

Chermak, S. and Weiss, A. (2005). 'Maintaining legitimacy using external communication strategies: an analysis of police–media relations', *Journal of Criminal Justice*, 33 (5): 501–12.

Chibnall, S. (1977) *Law-and-Order News: An Analysis of Crime Reporting in the British Press*. London: Tavistock.

Cohen, S. (1972) *Folk Devils and Moral Panics: The Creation of the Mods and Rockers*. London: MacGibbon & Kee.

Coleman, R. and McCahill, M. (2011) *Surveillance and Crime*. London: Sage.

Colquhoun, P. (1796) *A Treatise of the Police of the Metropolis*, 2nd edn. London: H. Fry.

Cooke, L. and Sturges, P. (2009) 'Police and media relations in an era of freedom of information', *Policing and Society*, 19 (4): 406–24.

Cottle, S. (2003) *News, Public Relations and Power*. London: Sage.

Cutlip, S. M. (1994) *The Unseen Power: Public Relations, a History*. Hillsdale, NJ: Lawrence Erlbaum Associates.

Daily Mail (2011) 'Twit and Twitter: 'looter' posts photo of himself and his booty online as police say tweets were used to co-ordinate riots'. Available online at: http://www.dailymail.co.uk/news/article-2023667/ London-riots-Looter-posts-photo-booty-Facebook.html#ixzz 2R9YEpyXL (accessed 12 April 2013).

Daily Telegraph (2008) 'Corruption reporting for Pacific Island Jo', *Daily Telegraph*, 28 December. Available online at: http://www.news.com.au/ entertainment/story/0,28383,24850251-5016681,00.html (accessed 29 December 2008).

Davies, N. (2008) *Flat Earth News: An Award-Winning Reporter Exposes Falsehood, Distortion and Propaganda in the Global Media*. London: Chatto & Windus.

Davies, N. (2009) 'Can the police and the media trust each other?', *The Guardian*, 27 April. Available online: http://www.guardian.co.uk media/2009/ apr/27/ipcc-police-g20-death-media (accessed 18 February 2012).

Davis, A. (2000) 'Public relations, news production and changing patterns of source access in the British national media', *Media Culture and Society*, 22 (1): 39–59.

Davis, A. (2003) 'Public relations and news sources', in S. Cottle (ed.), *News, Public Relations and Power*. London: Sage.

De Certeau, M. (1984) *The Practice of Everyday Life*. Berkeley, CA: University of California Press.

Deacon, D. and Golding, P. (1994) *Taxation and Representation: The Media, Political Communication and the Poll Tax*. London: John Libbey.

Deleuze, G. (1995) 'Postscript on control societies', in G. Deleuze (ed.), *Netotiations 1972–1990*. New York: Columbia University Press.

Denef, N., Kaptein, P., Bayerl, S. and Ramirez, L. (2012) *Best Practice in Police Social Media Adaptation*, COMPOSITE, European Commission FP7 Contract No. 241918.

Denzin, N. and Lincoln, Y. (2000) *Strategies of Qualitative Enquiry*. Thousand Oaks, CA: Sage.

Douglas, M. (1992) *Risk and Blame: Essays in Cultural Theory*. London: Routledge.

Doyle, A. (2003) *Arresting Images: Crime and Policing in Front of the Television Camera*. Toronto: University of Toronto Press.

Doyle, A. (2006) 'An alternative current in surveillance and control: broadcasting surveillance footage of crimes', in K. Haggerty and R. Ericson (eds), *The New Politics of Surveillance and Visibility*. Toronto: University of Toronto Press.

Doyle, A. (2011) 'Revisiting the synopticon: reconsidering Mathiesen's "The Viewer Society" in the age of Web 2.0', *Theoretical Criminology*, 15: 283–99.

Drew, J. and Mazerolle, L. (2009) 'Eras of policing', in R. Broadhurst and S. Davies (eds), *Policing in Context*. Melbourne: Oxford University Press.

Eco, U (1972) *Towards a Semiotic Inquiry into the Television Message*, Working Papers in Cultural Studies. University of Birmingham.

Edwards, C. (2005) *Changing Policing Theories for 21st Century Societies*. Sydney: Federation Press.

Emsley, C. (1983) *Policing and Its Context*. London: Macmillan.

Emsley, C. (1996) *The English Police: A Political and Social History*. Harlow: Pearson Education.

Emsley, C. (2002) 'The history of crime and crime control institutions', in M. Maguire, R. Morgan and R. Reiner (eds), *The Oxford Handbook of Criminology*. Oxford: Oxford University Press.

Ericson, R. V. and Haggerty, K. D. (1997) *Policing the Risk Society*. Oxford: Oxford University Press.

Ericson, R.V. and Haggerty, K. D. (eds) (2006) *The New Politics of Surveillance and Visibility*. Toronto: University of Toronto Press.

Ericson, R.V., Baranek, P. M. and Chan, J. B. L. (1989) *Negotiating Control: A Study of News Sources*. Milton Keynes: Open University Press.

Ericson, R.V., Baranek, P. M. and Chan, J. B. L. (1991) *Representing Order: Crime, Law and Justice in the News Media*. Toronto: University of Toronto Press.

Feeley, M. and Simon, J. (1992) 'The new penology: notes on the emerging strategy of corrections and its implications', *Criminology*, 30 (4): 449–74.

Ferrell, J., Hayward, K. and Young, J. (2008) *Cultural Criminology*. London: Sage.

Filkin, E. (2012) *The Ethical Issues Arising From the Relationship Between Police and Media: Advice to the Commission of the Police of the Metropolis and His Management Board*. MPS. Available online at: http://content.met.police. uk/News/Elizabeth-Filkin-report-published/1400005701012/ 1257246741786 (accessed 12 April 2013).

Finkelstein, R. (2012) *Report of the Independent Inquiry into the Media and Media Regulation*. Commonwealth of Australia, Canberra.

Finnane, M. (1987) 'Introduction: writing about police in Australia', in M. Finnane (ed.), *Policing in Australia: Historical Perspectives*. Kensington, NSW: New South Wales University Press.

Finnane, M. (1990) 'Police and politics in Australia – the case for historical revision', *Australian and New Zealand Journal of Criminology*, 23 (4): 218–28.

Finnane, M. (1994) *Police and Government: Histories of Policing in Australia*. Melbourne: Oxford University Press.

Finnane, M. (1999a) 'From police force to police service? Aspects of the recent history of the New South Wales Police', in D. Dixon (ed.), *A Culture of Corruption: Changing an Australian Police Service*. Sydney: Hawkins Press.

Finnane, M. (1999b) 'Police unions in Australia: a history of the present', *History of Crime, Policing and Punishment Conference*. Canberra: Australian Institute of Criminology in conjunction with Charles Sturt University.

Finnane, M. (2000) 'Police unions in Australia: a history of the present', *Current Issues in Criminal Justice*, 12 (1): 5–19.

Finnane, M. (2002) *When Police Unionise: The Politics of Law and Order in Australia*. Sydney: Institute of Criminology.

Fishman, M. (1981) 'Police news: constructing an image of crime', *Urban Life*, 9 (4): 371–94.

Fitzgerald, T. (1989) *Commission of Inquiry into Possible Illegal Activities and Associated Police Misconduct*. Brisbane: Government Printer.

Fleming, J. and McLaughlin, E. (2010) '"The public gets what the public wants?" Interrogating the confidence agenda', *Policing*, 4 (3): 199–202.

Flower, W. (2010) 'Facebook police page is faked', *Herald Sun*, 10 March. Available online at: http://www.heraldsun.com.au/news/victoria/face-book-police-page-is-faked/story-e6frf7kx-1225838903646 (accessed 27 August 2011).

Foucault, M. (1977) *Discipline and Punish: The Birth of the Prison*. New York: Pantheon Books.

Foucault, M. (1981) 'The order of discourse' in Young, R. (ed.), *Untying the Text*. Boston: Routledge & Kegan Paul.

Foucault, M. (1982) 'The subject and power', *Critical Inquiry*, 8 (4): 777–95.

Fox News (2012) 'Lawmakers erect challenges to drones in US airspace', 14 June. Available online at: http://www.foxnews.com/politics/2012/06/14/lawmakers-erect-challenges-to-drones-in-us-airspace/ (accessed 6 September 2012).

Freckelton, I. (1988) 'Sensation and symbiosis', in I. Freckelton and H. Selby (eds), *Police in Our Society*. Sydney: Butterworths.

Gaeta, T. (2010) 'Catch and release: procedural unfairness on primetime television and the perceived legitimacy of the law', *Journal of Criminal Law and Criminology*, 100 (2): 523–53.

GAO (1996) *Content Analysis: A Methodology for Structuring and Analysing Written Material*. United States General Accounting Office, Program Evaluation and Methodology Division. Available online at: http://archive.gao.gov/d48t13/138426.pdf (accessed 26 April 2013).

Garland, D. (1996) 'The limits of the sovereign state: strategies of crime control in contemporary society', *British Journal of Criminology*, 36 (4): 445–71.

Garland, D. (2001) *The Culture of Control: Crime and Social Order in Contemporary Society*. Oxford: Oxford University Press.

Gibson, J. and Jacobsen, G. (2010) 'The hazards of police-speak', *Sydney Morning Herald*. Available online at: http://www.smh.com.au/nsw/the-hazards-of-policespeak-20100730-10zsl.html (accessed 26 April 2013).

Giddens, A. (1991a) *Modernity and Self Identity*. Stanford, CA: Stanford University Press.

Giddens, A. (1991b) *The Consequences of Modernity*. Cambridge: Polity Press.

Gilling, D. (1997) *Crime Prevention. Theory, Police and Politics*. London: UCL Press.

Godfrey, G. F. (1957) 'Police and the press', *Australian Police Journal*, 11 (4): 301–13.

Goldsmith, A. (2010) 'Policing's new visibility', *British Journal of Criminology*, 50 (5): 914–34.

Grabosky, P. N. and Wilson, P. (1989) *Journalism and Justice: How Crime Is Reported*. Leichhardt, NSW: Pluto Press.

Gradeless, R. (2009) 'Police and lawyers develop social networking pages', *Social Media Law Student*. Available online at: http://socialmedialaws tudent.com/featured/police-and-lawyers-develop-social-networking-pages/ (accessed 26 April 2013).

Grattan, M. (1998) 'The politics of spin', *Australian Studies in Journalism*, 7: 32–45.

Greer, C. and McLaughlin, E. (2010) 'We predict a riot? Public order policing, new media environments and the rise of the citizen journalist', *British Journal of Criminology*, 50 (6): 1041–59.

Greer, C. and McLaughlin, E. (2011) 'The Ian Tomlinson inquest was justice seen to be done', *The Guardian*, 3 May. Available online at: http://www.guardian.co.uk/commentisfree/2011/may/03/ian-tomlinson-inquest-live-blogging (accessed 3 May 2011).

Guest, D. (2010) 'Man tasered 13 times by WA police was subject to excessive force, says report', *The Australian*, 4 October. Available online at: http://www.theaustralian.com.au/news/nation/man-tasered-13-times-by-wa-police-was-subject-to-excessive-force-says-report/story-e6frg6nf-1225933953993 (accessed 19 July 2011).

Hall, S., Critcher, C., Jefferson, T., Clarke, J. and Roberts, B. (1978) *Policing the Crisis: Mugging, the State and Law and Order*. New York: Holmes & Meier/Macmillan.

Halliday, J. (2013) 'Met police investigated 75 officers over Facebook and social networks misuse', *The Guardian*, 12 April. Available online at: http://www.guardian.co.uk/media/2013/apr/12/met-police-investigate-75-officers-facebook (accessed 12 April 2013).

Hartley, S. (2011) 'Manchester riots: social media, live blogs and justice', *The Guardian*, 1 September. Available online at: http://www.guardian.co.uk/uk/the-northerner/2011/sep/01/manchester-riots-social-media-smc-mcr> (accessed 26 April 2013).

Hindess, B. (1996) 'Discipline and cherish: Foucault on power, domination and government', *Discourses of Power: From Hobbes to Foucault*. Oxford: Blackwell.

Hinds, L. (2009) 'Public satisfaction with the police: the influence of general attitudes and police–citizen encounters', *International Journal of Police Science and Management*, 11 (1): 54–66.

Hinds, L. and Murphy, K. (2007) 'Public satisfaction with police: using procedural justice to improve police legitimacy', *Australian and New Zealand Journal of Criminology*, 40 (1): 27–42.

Hogg, R. and Brown, D. (1998) *Rethinking Law and Order*. Annandale, NSW: Pluto Press.

Hohl, K., Bradford, B. and Stanko, E. (2010) 'Influencing trust and confidence in the London Metropolitan Police: results from an experiment testing the effect of leaflet drops on public opinion', *British Journal of Criminology*, 50 (3): 491–513.

Hollins, N. and Bacon, W. (2010) 'Spinning the media: when PR really means police relations', *Crikey*. Available online at: http://www.crikey.com.au/2010/03/29/spinning-the-media-when-pr-really-means-police-relations/ (accessed 26 April 2013).

Home Office (2004) *Building Communities, Beating Crime: A Better Police Service for the 21st Century*. Norwich: HMSO.

Hough, M., Jackson, J., Bradford, B., Myhill, A. and Quinton, P. (2010) 'Procedural justice, trust and institutional legitimacy', *Policing: A Journal of Policy and Practice*, 4 (3): 203–10.

Hudson, B. (2003) *Justice in the Risk Society: Challenging and Re-Affirming Justice in Late Modernity*. London: Sage.

Huey, L. (2010) '"I've seen this on CSI": criminal investigators' perceptions about the management of public expectations in the field', *Crime Media Culture*, 6 (1): 49–68.

Huey, L. Walby, K. and Doyle, A. (2006) 'Watching the downtown east-side: exploring the use of (counter) surveillance as a tool of resistance', in T. Monahan (ed.), *Surveillance and Security: Technological Politics and Power in Everyday Life*. New York: Routledge.

Hunt, A. and Wickham, G. (1994) *Foucault and the Law: Towards a Sociology of Law and Governance*. Boulder, CO: Pluto Press.

Independent Commission on the Los Angeles Police Department (1991) *Report of the Independent Commission on the Los Angeles Police Department*. Available online at: http://www.parc.info/client_files/Special%20Reports/1%20-%20Chistopher%20Commision.pdf.

Indermaur, D. and Roberts, L. (2009) *Confidence in the Criminal Justice System*. Canberra: Australian Institute of Criminology.

Innes, M. (1999) 'The media as an investigative resource in murder inquiries', *British Journal of Criminology*, 39 (2): 269–86.

Innes, M. (2004) 'Crime as a signal, crime as a memory', *Journal for Crime, Conflict and the Media*, 1 (2): 15–22.

Institute of Customer Service (2011) *UK Customer Satisfaction Index Results July 2011*. Available online at: http://www.instituteofcustomerservice.com/1711-7669/UK-Customer-Satisfaction-Index-Results-July-2011.html (accessed 30 October 2011).

Jackson, J. and Sunshine, J. (2007) 'Public confidence in policing: a neo-Durkheimian perspective', *British Journal of Criminology*, 47 (2): 214–33.

Jackson, J., Bradford, B., Hough, M., Kuha, J., Stares, S., Widdop, S., Fitzgerald, R., Yordanova, M. and Galev, T. (2011) 'Developing European indicators of trust in justice', *European Journal of Criminology*, 8 (4): 268–85.

Janoski-Haehlen, E. (2012) 'The implications of social media use in the courts', *Valparaiso University Law Review*, 46 (1): 43–68.

Jewkes, Y. (2004) *Media and Crime*. London: Sage.

Jewkes, Y. (2011) *Media and Crime*, 2nd edn. London: Sage.

Jiggins, S. (2004) 'An Examination of the Nature and Impact of Print Media News Reporting on Selected Police Organisations in Australia'. Unpublished thesis, University of Canberra.

Jiggins, S. (2007) 'The news media', in M. Mitchell and J. Casey (eds), *Police Leadership and Management*. Sydney: Federation Press.

Kammerer, D. (2004) 'Video surveillance in Hollywood movies', *Surveillance and Society*, 2 (2/3): 464–73.

Keane, B. (2011) 'Reversing the panopticon: police officially relaxed about being filmed', *Crikey*. Available online at: http://www.crikey.com. au/2011/11/01/reversing-the-panopticon-police-officially-relaxed-about-being-filmed/ (accessed 15 September 2012).

Keelty, M. (2006) *Between the Lines: New Powers and Accountability for Police and the Media*, Australian Press Council Annual Address, 23 March. Available online at: http://www.afp.gov.au/afp/page/Publications/Speec hes/230306PressCouncilPowers.htm (accessed 20 March 2007).

Kelling, G. L. and Moore, M. H. (1989) *The Evolving Strategy of Policing*. Washington, DC: US Department of Justice, Office of Justice Programs, National Institute of Justice.

Kelly, P. A. (1987) *Police and the Media: Bridging Troubled Waters*. Springfield, IL: Thomas.

Kennedy, L. (2004) 'New witness claims police chased teenager who died', *Sydney Morning Herald*, 19 February. Available online at: http://www.smh. com.au/articles/2004/02/18/1077072713275.html (accessed 3 March 2008).

Kiel, H. (1989) 'Partners in crime', *Legal Service Bulletin*, 14 (6): 254–7.

Knight, S. (2004) *Crime Fiction 1800–2000*. London: Macmillan.

Larkin, T. (2011) 'Social media earns its stripes in disaster communications', *Police Bulletin*, 357: 36–7. Available online at: http://www.police.qld. gov.au/services/reportsPublications/bulletin/2011/april2011.htm (accessed 26 April 2013).

Lawrence, K. and Bissett, K. (2009) '$1m paid to police for TV ratings', *Daily Telegraph*, 2 February. Available online at: http://www.news.com. au/dailytelegraph/story/0,22049,24992707-5001021,00.html (accessed 2 February 2009).

Lee, J. A. (1990) *Report of the Royal Commission of Inquiry into the Arrest, Charging and Withdrawal of Charges Against Harold James Blackburn and Matters Associated Therewith*. Sydney: Parliament of New South Wales.

Lee, M. (2007) *Inventing Fear of Crime: Criminology and the Politics of Anxiety*. Cullompton: Willan.

Lee, M. (2011) 'Force selling: policing and the manufacture of public confidence?', in M. Lee, G. Mason and S. Milivojevic (eds), *The Australian and New Zealand Critical Criminology Conference 2010, Proceedings*. Sydney: Sydney Institute of Criminology, University of Sydney, 1–2 July 2010.

Lee, M. and McGovern, A. (2012) 'Image work(s): "simulated policing" and the new police (popularity) culture', in K. Carrington, M. Ball, E. O'Brien and J. Tauri (eds), *Crime, Justice and Social Democracy*. Basingstoke: Palgrave Macmillan, pp. 120–32.

Lee, M. and McGovern, A. (2013) 'Force to sell: policing the image and manufacturing public confidence', *Policing and Society*, 23 (2): 103–24.

Leishman, F. and Mason, P. (2003) *Policing and the Media: Facts, Fictions and Factions*. Cullompton: Willan.

Leveson, Lord Justice (2012) *An Inquiry Into the Culture, Practices and Ethics of the Press: Executive Summary*. London: TSO.

Lewis, J., Cushion, S. and Thomas, J. (2005) 'Immediacy, convenience or engagement? An analysis of 24-hour news channels in the UK', *Journalism Studies*, 6 (4): 461–77.

Lewis, P. (2009) 'Ian Tomlinson death: Guardian video reveals police attack on man who died at G20 protest', *The Guardian*, 7 April. Available online at: http://www.guardian.co.uk/uk/2009/apr/07/ian-tomlinson-g20-death-video (accessed 8 June 2012).

Loader, I. and Mulcahy, A. (2003) *Policing and the Condition of England*. Oxford: Oxford University Press.

Lovell, J. S. (2002) *Media Power and Information Control: A Study of Police Organizations and Media Relations*. Washington, DC: US Department of Justice.

Lovell, J. S. (2003) *Good Cop/Bad Cop: Mass Media and the Cycle of Police Reform*. New York: Willow Tree Press.

Lusher, J. E. A. (1981) *Report by Mr. Justice Lusher of the Commission to Inquire into New South Wales Police Administration*. Sydney: Parliament of New South Wales.

McElroy, W. (2010) 'Are cameras the new guns?', *Gizmodo*. Available online at: http://www.gizmodo.com.au/2010/06/are-cameras-the-new-guns/ (accessed 12 October 2012).

McGovern, A. (2009) 'The best police force money can buy: the rise of police PR', *Proceedings of the Critical Criminology Conference*. Melbourne: Australian and New Zealand Crime and Justice Research Network, Monash University.

McGovern, A. (2011) 'Tweeting the news: criminal justice agencies and their use of social networking sites', in M. Lee, G. Masonand and S. Milivojevic (eds), *Critical Criminology Conference*. Sydney: University of

Western Sydney and Sydney University, Australian and New Zealand Crime and Justice Research Network.

McGovern, A. and Lee, M. (2010) 'Cop[ying] it sweet: police media units and the making of news', *Australian and New Zealand Journal of Criminology*, 43 (3): 444–64.

McGovern, A. and Lee, M. (2012) 'Police communications in the social media age', in P. Keyzer, J. Johnston and M. Pearson (eds), *The Courts and the Media in the Digital Era*. Ultimo, NSW: Halstead Press.

McLaughlin, E. and Murji, K. (1998) 'Resistance through representation: "storylines", advertising and Police Federation campaigns', *Policing and Society*, 8 (4): 367–99.

McLuhan, M. (1964) *Understanding Media: The Extensions of Man*. New York: McGraw-Hill.

Mann, S., Nolan, J. and Wellman, B. (2003) 'Sousveillance: inventing and using wearable computing devices for data collection in surveillance environments', *Surveillance and Society*, 1 (3): 331–55.

Manning, P. (1978) *Policing: A View from the Street*. Santa Monica, CA: Goodyear.

Manning, P. K. (1988) *Symbolic Communication: Signifying Calls and the Police Response*. Cambridge, MA: MIT Press.

Manning, P. K. (1992) *Organizational Communication*. Hawthorne, NY: Aldine de Gruyter.

Manning, P. K. (1996) 'Dramaturgy, politics and the axial media event', *Sociological Quarterly*, 37 (2): 261–78.

Manning, P. K. (1997) 'Media loops', in F. Baily and D. Hale (eds), *Popular Culture, Crime and Justice*. Belmont, CA: Wadsworth.

Manning, P. (1999) 'Reflections: the visual as a mode of social control', in J. Ferrell and N. Websdale (eds), *Making Trouble*. New York: Aldine de Gruyter.

Manning, P. K. (2003) *Policing Contingencies* Chicago: Chicago University Press.

Marenin, O. (2003) 'Media, policing and accountability: the American experience', *The Role of the Media in Public Scrutiny and Democratic Oversight of the Security Sector*. Budapest: Working Group on Civil Society of the of the Geneva Centre for the Democratic Control of Armed Forces.

Marsh, I. and Meville, G. (2009) *Crime, Justice and the Media*. London: Routledge.

Marx, G. (2003) 'A tack in the shoe: neutralizing and resisting the new surveillance', *Journal of Social Issues*, 59 (2): 369–90.

Mason, P. (1992) 'Reading *The Bill*: An Analysis of the Thames Television Police Drama'. Unpublished thesis, Bristol and Bath Centre for Criminal Justice.

Mason, P. (2002) *The Thin Blurred Line: Reality TV and Policing*, British Criminology Conference Selected Proceedings, Vol. 5. Available online at: http://www.britsoccrim.org/volume5/003.pdf (accessed 15 June 2009).

Mason, P. (2003) 'Visions of crime and justice', in P. Mason (ed.), *Criminal Visions: Media Representation of Crime and Justice*. Cullompton: Willan.

Mason, P. (2009) 'Crime, media and the state', in J. Sim, D. Tombs and D. Whyte (eds), *State, Power, Crime: Critical Readings in Criminology*. London: Sage, pp. 343–70.

Mathiesen, T. (1997) 'The viewer society: Michel Foucault's "panopticon" revisited', *Theoretical Criminology*, 1 (2): 215–34.

Mawby, R. C. (1998) 'Policing the image', *Criminal Justice Matters*, 32 (1): 26–7.

Mawby, R. C. (2002a) *Policing Images: Policing, Communication and Legitimacy*. Cullompton: Willan.

Mawby, R. C. (2002b) 'Continuity and change, convergence and divergence: the policy and practice of police-media relations', *Criminal Justice*, 2 (3): 303–24.

Mawby, R. C. (2003) 'Completing the "half-formed picture"? Media images of policing', in P. Mason (ed.), *Criminal Visions: Media Representations of Crime and Justice*. Cullompton: Willan.

Mawby, R. C. (2007) 'Criminal investigation and the media', in T. Newburn, T. Williamson and A. Wright (eds), *Handbook of Criminal Investigation*. Cullompton: Willan.

Mawby, R. C. (2010a) 'Police corporate communications, crime reporting and the shaping of policing news', *Policing and Society*, 20 (1): 124–39.

Mawby, R. C. (2010b) 'Chibnall revisited: crime reporters, the police and "law-and-order news"', *British Journal of Criminology*, 50 (6): 1060–76.

Mawby, R. C. (2011) 'Using images to understand crime and justice', in P. Davies, P. Francis and V. Jupp (eds), *Doing Criminological Research*, 2nd edn. London: Sage, pp. 223–44.

Media and Public Affairs Branch (2012) *Social Media Case Study*. Brisbane: Queensland Police Service. Available online at: http://www.police.qld.gov.au/services/reportsPublications/other/socialmedia.htm (accessed 1 May 2013).

Media Watch (2011) 'Media Watch Special: Interview with Greg Hywood', ABC Television, 25 April. Available online at: http://www.abc.net.au/mediawatch/transcripts/s3199897.htm (accessed 21 April 2013).

Mercer, N. (2006) 'Top cop orders: force be with me', *Sunday Telegraph*, 30 July, Sydney.

Metropolitan Police Service (2005) *Draft Media Policy*. London: MPS.

Metropolitan Police Service (2011) *Media Relations SOP*. Metropolitan Police Service.

Monk-Turner, E., Martinez, H., Holbrook, J. and Harvey, N. (2007) 'Reality TV: continuing to perpetuate crime myths?' *Internet Journal of Criminology*. Available online at: http://www.internetjournalofcriminology.com (accessed 26 April 2013).

Morri, M. (2008) 'Police radio blackout is a concern for civic safety', *Daily Telegraph*, 15 September, Sydney. Available online at: http://www.news.com.au/dailytelegraph/story/0,22049,24344146-5001031,00.html (accessed 15 September 2008).

Morri, M. (2010a) 'Unsafe streets – triple threat to women hidden by police', *Daily Telegraph*, 28 July. Available online at: http://www.dailytelegraph.com.au/news/nsw-act/unsafe-streets-triple-threat-to-women-hidden-by-police/story-e6freuzi-1225897745894 (accessed 28 July 2010).

Morri, M. (2010b) 'This is not anti cop but anti spin', *Daily Telegraph*, 28 July. Available online at: http://www.dailytelegraph.com.au/news/nsw-act/this-is-not-anti-cop-but-anti-spin/story-e6freuzi-1225897744962 (accessed 28 July 2010).

Morri, M. (2010c) 'NSW Police release more crime detail after victims voice campaign launched by the Daily Telegraph', *Daily Telegraph*, 8 July. Available online at: http://www.dailytelegraph.com.au/news/nsw-police-release-more-crime-detail-after-victims-voice-campaign-launched-by-the-daily-telegraph/story-e6freuy9-1225889155738 (accessed 27 April 2013).

Morri, M. and Jones, G. (2010) 'NSW Police hold state of secrecy on crimes including rape and murder', *Daily Telegraph*, 5 July. Available online at: http://www.dailytelegraph.com.au/news/nsw-police-hold-state-of-secrecy-on-crimes-inncluding-rape-and-murder/story-e6freuy9-1225887766556 (accessed 27 April 2013).

Mosbergen, D. (2013) 'Children In Iraq "mourn with Boston"', *Huffington Post*, 17 April. Available online at: http://www.huffingtonpost.com/2013/04/17/iraq-children-boston_n_3104058.html (accessed 20 April 2013).

Moses, A. (2009) 'Twitter con gives police tweet idea', *Sydney Morning Herald*, 26 May. Available online at: http://www.smh.com.au/news/technology/articles/2009/05/26/1243103526499.html (accessed 26 April 2013).

Murphy, K., Hinds, L. and Fleming, J. (2008) 'Encouraging public cooperation and support for police', *Policing and Society*, 18 (2): 136–55.

National Police Web Managers Group (2010) 'Twitter-followers September 2010', *National Police Web Managers Group Blog*. Available online at: http://npwmg.blogspot.com/2010/10/twitter-followers-september-2010.html (accessed 13 November 2010).

Netterfield, S. (1994) *Marketing Police Services*, Conference of Commissioners of Police of Australasia and the South West Pacific Region, Canberra, 14–19 March.

News.com.au (2010) 'Police recruit uses twitter to tweet on training'. Available online at: http://www.policecareer.vic.gov.au/police/life-at-the-academy/follow-our-recruit (accessed 21 April 2013).

NSW Police Force (1950) *Report of the Police Department of NSW for the Year 1949.* Sydney: Parliament of New South Wales.

NSW Police Force (1965) *Police Department of NSW Annual Report for 1964.* Sydney: NSW Police Department.

NSW Police Force (1972) 'New-look Public Relations Branch', *NSW Police News,* October, pp. 364–5.

NSW Police Force (1974) *Annual Report of the Police Department for 1973.* Sydney: NSW Police Department.

NSW Police Force (1976) *Police Department Annual Report 1975.* Sydney: NSW Police Department.

NSW Police Force (1979) *NSW Police Department Annual Report 1978.* Sydney: NSW Police Department.

NSW Police Force (1983) *Report of the NSW Police Department 1 January 1982–30 June 1983.* Sydney: NSW Police Department.

NSW Police Force (1986) *Report of the NSW Police Department 1985–1986.* Sydney: NSW Police Department.

NSW Police Force (2002) *Media Policy.* Sydney: NSW Police.

NSW Police Force (2004a) *Media Policy.* Sydney: NSW Police.

NSW Police Force (2004b) *NSW Police Website.* Sydney: NSW Police. Available online at: http://www.police.nsw.gov.au (accessed 10 December 2004).

NSW Police Force (2008) *NSW Police Annual Report 2006–07.* Sydney: NSW Police Force.

NSW Police Force (2009) *2007–08 NSW Police Force Annual Report.* Sydney: NSW Police Force Public Affairs Branch. Available online at: http://www.police.nsw.gov.au/about_us/publications/annual_report (accessed 20 May 2009).

NSW Police Force (2010a) *Annual Report 2008–2009.* Sydney: NSW Police Force.

NSW Police Force (2010b) *NSW Police Force Annual Report 2009–2010.* Available online at: http://www.police.nsw.gov.au/__data/assets/pdf_file/0011/184880/NSWPF_Annual_Report_2009-10.pdf (accessed 26 August 2011).

NSW Police Force (2011a) *NSW Police Force Website.* Sydney: NSW Police Force. Available online at: http://www.police.nsw.gov.au (accessed 20 October 2011).

NSW Police Force (2011b) *NSW Police Force Media Policy* Available online at: http://www.police.nsw.gov.au/about_us/policies__and__procedures/policies/media_policy (accessed 10 December 2011).

NSW Police Force (2013) *NSW Police Force Website*. Sydney: NSW Police Force. Available online at: http://www.police.nsw.gov.au (accessed 20 March 2013).

NSW Police Force Public Affairs Branch (2011) *Media Policy*. Sydney: NSW Police Force Public Affairs Branch.

NSW Police Force Public Affairs Branch (2013) *Media Policy*. Sydney: NSW Police Force Public Affairs Branch.

NSW Police Media Unit (1990) *Media Effectiveness Survey*. Sydney: NSW Police Service.

NSW Police Media Unit (2008a) 'Images released following attempted abduction – Tempe', in NSW Police Force (ed.), NSW Government.

NSW Police Media Unit (2008b) 'Tasers issued to all Local Area Commands', *Media Release Archives*, NSW Police Force Website, NSW Police Force.

NSW Police Public Affairs Branch (1997) 'Wildside contract cancelled', *Police Service Weekly*, 9 (50): 17.

NSW Police Public Affairs Branch (2010) *Media Policy*. Sydney: NSW Police Force.

O'Brien, N. (2008) 'PR for police spins to $10m', *The Australian*, 7 July, Sydney. Available online at: http://www.theaustralian.news.com.au/story/0,25197,23979270-2702,00.html (accessed 7 July 2008).

O'Malley, P. (1996) 'Risk and responsibility', in A. Barry, T. Osborne and N. Rose (eds), *Foucault and Political Reason: Liberalism, Neo-Liberalism and Rationalities of Government*. Chicago: University of Chicago Press.

O'Malley, P. (2010) 'Simulated justice: risk, money and telemetric policing', *British Journal of Criminology*, 50 (5): 795–807.

Pearson, G. (1983) *Hooligan: A History of Respectable Fears*. London: Macmillan.

Pearson, M. (2005) *Police Digital Communications and the Media*, Humanities and Social Sciences Papers, Faculty of Humanities and Social Sciences, Bond University.

Penberthy, D. (2008) 'Hamstrung by NSW Police's new communication system', *Daily Telegraph*, 15 September. Available online at: http://www.new.com.au/dailytelegraph/story/0,22049,24344038-5001031,00.html (accessed 15 September 2008).

Philo, G. (1990) 'Seeing is believing', *British Journalism Review*, 1 (4): 58–64.

Pope, J. (1954) *Police–Press Relations: A Handbook*. Fresno, CA: Academy Library Guild.

Puplick, C. (2001) '1965', in M. Hogan and D. Clune (eds), *The People's Choice: Electoral Politics in 20th Century New South Wales*. Sydney: Parliament of New South Wales and University of Sydney.

Putnis, P. (1996) 'Police–media relations: issues and trends', in D. Chappell and P. Wilson (eds), *Australian Policing: Contemporary Issues*. Sydney: Butterworths.

Queensland Police Service (2013) *A Farewell Note from Executive Director Kym Charlton*, Facebook, 31 January. Available online at: https://www.facebook.com/QueenslandPolice/posts/10151401207143254%3E (accessed 26 April 2013).

Rawlings, P. (2002) *Policing: A Short History*. Cullompton:Willan.

Reiner, R. (1978) *The Blue-Coated Worker*. Cambridge: Cambridge University Press.

Reiner, R. (2000) *The Politics of Police*. Oxford: Oxford University Press.

Reiner, R. (2002) 'Media made criminality: the representation of crime in the mass media', in R. Reiner, M. Maguire and R. Morgan (eds), *The Oxford Handbook of Criminology*. Oxford: Oxford University Press.

Reiner, R. (2003) 'Policing and the media', in T. Newburn (ed.), *Handbook of Policing*. Cullompton:Willan.

Reiner, R. (2008) 'Policing a postmodern society', in T. Newman (ed.), *Policing: Key Readings*. Cullompton:Willan.

Reiner, R. (2010) *The Politics of the Police*. Oxford: Oxford University Press.

Reiner, R. and Livingstone, S. (1997) 'Discipline or Desubordination? Changing Media Images of Crime, Economic and Social Research Council'. Unpublished.

Rose, N. (1999) *Powers of Freedom: Reframing Political Thought*. Cambridge: Cambridge University Press.

Rose, N. (2000) 'Government and control', *British Journal of Criminology*, 40 (2): 321–39.

Rowe, J. (2007) 'Heroin epidemic! Drugs and moral panic in the western suburbs of Melbourne 1995–1996', in S. Poynting and G. Morgan (eds), *Outrageous! Moral Panics in Australia*. Hobart,Tas.:ACYS Publishing.

Roy Morgan Research (2011) 'Image of Professions Survey 2011: Police Now at Highest Ever Rating for Ethics and Honesty', Roy Morgan Research. Available online at: http://www.roymorgan.com/news/polls/2011/4655/ (accessed 9 April 2013).

Saratankos, S. (1993a) *Social Research*. Melbourne: Macmillan Education Australia.

Saratankos, S. (1993b) *Interviewing in Social Research*. Melbourne: Macmillan Education Australia.

Savage, S. and Tiffen, R. (2007) 'Politicians, journalists and "spin": tangled relationships and shifting alliances', in S. Young (ed.), *Government Communication in Australia*. Port Melbourne: Cambridge University Press.

Schlesinger, P. and Tumber, H. (1993) 'Fighting the war against crime: television, police, and audience', *British Journal of Criminology*, 33 (1): 19–32.

Schlesinger, P. and Tumber, H. (1994) *Reporting Crime: The Media Politics of Criminal Justice*. Oxford: Clarendon Press.

Schulz, G. W. (2012) 'FAA documents raise questions about safety of drones in US airspace', *Wired*, 14 August. Available online at: http://www.wired.com/threatlevel/2012/08/faa-documents-raise-questions-about-safety-of-drones-in-u-s-airspace/ (accessed 6 September 2012).

Sengupta, S. (2012) 'Who is flying drones over America?', *New York Times*, 14 June. Available online at: http://bits.blogs.nytimes.com/2012/07/14/who-is-flying-drones-over-america/ (accessed 13 September 2012).

Sharkey, N. and Knuckey, S. (2011) 'Occupy Wall Street's "occucopter" – who's watching whom?', *The Guardian*, 21 December. Available online at: http://www.guardian.co.uk/commentisfree/cifamerica/2011/dec/21/occupy-wall-street-occucopter-tim-pool (accessed 15 February 2012).

Skogan, W. (2006) 'Asymmetry in the impact of encounters with the police', *Policing and Society*, 19 (1): 20–46.

Slovic, P. (1999) 'Trust, emotion, sex, politics, and science: surveying the risk-assessment battlefield', *Risk Analysis*, 19 (4): 689–701.

Social Media, the Internet, and Law Enforcement (2012 and 2013) *SMILE Conference*, Available online at: http://lawscommunications.com/smile/ (accessed 15 December 2012).

Sparks, R. (2000) 'The media and penal politics: review essay', *Punishment and Society*, 2 (1): 98–105.

Spicer, T. (2008) 'Eroding your right to know', *Daily Telegraph*, 15 September, Sydney. Available online at: http://www.news.com.au/dailytelegraph/story/0,22049,24346805-5001031,00.html (accessed 15 September 2008).

Steering Committee for the Review of Government Service Provision (2011) *Report on Government Services*. Melbourne: Australian Commonwealth Government.

Stevens, L. (2012) 'ConnectedCOPS win big with social media', *ConnectedCOPS*. Available online at: http://connectedcops.net/2012/09/12/connectedcops-win-big-social-media/ (accessed 1 May 2013).

Sunshine, J. and Tyler, T. R. (2003) 'The role of procedural justice and legitimacy in shaping public support for policing', *Law and Society Review*, 37 (3): 513–48.

Surette, R. (1998) *Media, Crime and Criminal Justice: Images, Realities, and Policies*. Belmont, CA: West/Wadsworth Publishing.

Surette, R. (2001) 'Public information officers: the civilianisation of a criminal justice profession', *Journal of Criminal Justice*, 29 (2): 107–17.

Surette, R. and Richard, A. (1995) 'Public information officers: a descriptive study of crime news gatekeepers', *Journal of Criminal Justice*, 23 (4): 325–36.

Tiffen, R. (2004) 'Tip of the iceberg or moral panic? Police corruption issues in contemporary New South Wales', *American Behavioral Scientist*, 47 (9): 1171–93.

Toch, H. (2012) *Cop Watch: Spectators, Social Media, and Police Reform*. Washington, DC: American Psychological Association.

Toronto Police (2013) 'Social media', *Toronto Police Website*. Available online at: http://www.torontopolice.on.ca/socialmedia/ (accessed 6 January 2013).

Tyler, T. (1997) 'The psychology of legitimacy: a relational perspective on voluntary deference to authorities', *Personality and Social Psychology Review*, 1 (4): 323–45.

Tyler, T. (2006) *Why People Obey the Law*. Princeton, NJ: Princeton University Press.

Tyler, T. R. and Huo, Y. J. (2002) *Trust in the Law: Encouraging Public Cooperation with the Police and Courts*. New York: Russell Sage.

Van Grove, J. (2011) 'Greater Manchester Police names and shames rioters on Twitter', *Mashable*. Available online at: http://mashable.com/2011/08/11/manchester-police-twitter/ (accessed 12 November 2011).

Victims Services (2011) *A Guide to the Media for Victims of Crime*. Sydney: NSW Department of Attorney General and Justice, NSW Government. Available online at: http://www.victimsclearinghouse.nsw.gov.au/agd-basev7wr/vocrc/documents/pdf/bk16_media-guide.pdf (accessed 23 April 2013).

Victoria Police (2013) 'Eyewatch', *Victoria Police Website*. Available online at: http://www.police.vic.gov.au/content.asp?Document_ID=35566 (accessed 20 March 2013).

Waddington, P. A. J. (1999a) 'Police (canteen) sub-culture: an appreciation', *British Journal of Criminology*, 39 (2): 286–309.

Waddington, P. A. J. (1999b) *Policing Citizens: Authority and Rights*. London: Routledge.

Weatherburn, D. (2004) *Law and Order in Australia: Rhetoric and Reality*. Annandale, NSW: Federation Press.

Weatherburn, D. (2006) 'Riots, policing and social disadvantage: learning from the riots in Macquarie Fields and Redfern', *Current Issues in Criminal Justice*, 18: 20.

Weber, M. (1964) *The Theory of Social and Economic Organization*. New York: Free Press.

Welch, M. (2011) 'Counterveillance: how Foucault and the Groupe d'Information sur les prisons reversed the optics', *Theoretical Criminology*, 15 (3): 301–13.

Williams, S. (2002) *Peter Ryan: The Inside Story*. Camberwell: Penguin.

Wilson, D. (2008) 'Histories of policing', in R. Broadhurst and S. Davies (eds), *Policing in Context*. South Melbourne: Oxford University Press.

Wilson, J. Q. and Kelling, G. L. (1982) 'Broken windows: the police and neighbourhood safety', *Atlantic Monthly*, March. Available online at: http://www.lantm.lth.se/fileadmin/fastighetsvetenskap/utbildning/Fastighetsvaerderingssystem/BrokenWindowTheory.pdf (accessed 10 March 2013).

Wilson, P. (1992) 'The police and the media', in P. Moir and H. Eijkman (eds), *Policing Australia: Old Issues, New Perspectives*. South Melbourne: Macmillan Education Australia.

Wood, H. (2007) 'The mediated conversational floor: an interactive approach to audience reception analysis', *Media Culture Society*, 29 (1): 75–103.

Wren, C. J. (2011) 'Police vulnerability on Facebook and Twitter', *Police Crunch*, 10 May. Available online at: http://policecrunch.com/2011/06/01/officials-warn-facebook-and-twitter-increase-police-vulnerability/ (accessed 4 August 2011).

Yim, Y. and Schafer, B. D. (2009) 'Police and their perceived image: how community influences officers' job satisfaction', *Police Practice and Research*, 10 (1): 17–29.

Young, J. (1971) *The Drugtakers: The Social Meaning of Drug Use*. London: Paladin.

INDEX